AN AMERICAN RABBINATE

A FESTSCHRIFT

FOR

WALTER JACOB

OTHER BOOKS IN THIS SERIES

Essays in Honor of Solomon B. Freehof, Walter Jacob, Frederick C. Schwartz, Vigdor W. Kavaler (eds.), 1964, x, 333 pp.

J. Leonard Levy, Prophetic Voice, Solomon B. Freehof, Vigdor W. Kavaler (eds.), 1970, xiv, 233 pp.

Spoken and Heard, Sermons and Addresses by Solomon B. Freehof, (with a bibliography), 1972, x, 264 pp.

World Problems and Personal Religion, Sermons, Addresses, and Selected Writings of Samuel H. Goldenson, M. L. Aaaron (ed.), 1975, ix, 279 pp.

The Changing World of Reform Judaism: The Pittsburgh Platform in Retrospect, Walter Jacob (ed.), 1985, xi, 124 pp.

AN AMERICAN RABBINATE

A FESTSCHRIFT

FOR

WALTER JACOB

Peter S. Knobel
and
Mark N. Staitman
Editors

Rodef Shalom Congregation
Pittsburgh, Pennsylvania
Rodef Shalom Press

Published by the Rodef Shalom Press
4905 Fifth Avenue
Pittsburgh, PA 15213
U.S.A.

4905 Fifth Avenue
Pittsburgh, PA 15213
U.S.A.

Library of Congress Catalog Card Number 00 091742

ISBN 0-929699-11-4

TABLE OF CONTENTS

TABLE OF CONTENTS

PREFACE

We acknowledge with thanks the dedicated effort of Nancy Berkowitz who carefully edited this volume. We are grateful to Marianne Fiore and Barbara Bailey for their help with the typescript. Our gratitude is expressed to the Rodef Shalom Congregation which sponsored the 1997 symposium at which these papers were presented and which has made this volume possible.

INTRODUCTION

Peter S. Knobel

Walter Jacob's long and distinguished career as rabbi, teacher, pastor, and communal and international Jewish leader has had a single constant: a deep devotion to scholarship. The breadth of his interests, the power of his intellect, and the vastness of his knowledge are astounding.

When Walter's wife, Irene, suggested a volume in his honor to her brother-in-law, Dr. Herbert Jacob, Walter's late brother, called me and asked me to help organize a *festschrift* for Walter. I was profoundly honored and touched. Herb agreed to edit the volume, and I took on the responsibility of organizing it.

I immediately called Dr. Mark Staitman, Dr. Jacob's successor at Rodef Shalom. Mark not only agreed at once, but he raised the funds and organized the symposium, held in June, 1997, on which this volume of proceedings is based. After Herb's untimely death he arranged for the editing and production of the proceedings. Without his devoted efforts this volume would not have been possible. All of us who cherish and respect Walter Jacob owe Mark an immense debt of gratitude.

This work is, in addition, a tribute from and to Irene Jacob and Herb Jacob. Irene is a scholar and author in the field of biblical plants, garden history, and ethno-botany, often publishing with her husband.

Herbert Jacob was a prodigious scholar in his own right. He was a professor of political science at Northwestern University in Evanston, Illinois, the author of numerous important books and articles, a beloved teacher. Herb Jacob was an active member of

INTRODUCTION

Beth Emet, The Free Synagogue in Evanston, where I have been the rabbi for the last twenty years. He was a friend, a wise counselor, a wonderful human being, and a deeply dedicated Jew. He, his wife, Lynn, and his children have been special and precious friends. His untimely death was a tragic loss for his family, Beth Emet, the Jewish community, the world of scholarship, and me, personally. Herbert and Walter are continuing sources of inspiration.

The goal of this *festschrift* is to reflect on areas of knowledge where Walter Jacob has already made important contributions. Each of the participants, all of whom are friends, colleagues, or students of Dr. Jacob, eagerly agreed to deliver a paper or to respond to papers and to have their work included in this volume as a way of showing appreciation for what they had personally gained from their association with Walter and to further the scholarly projects that are part of Walter's continuing work.

Dr. Staitman's paper offers an overall assessment of Walter's rabbinate by drawing up a set of principles that undergirds it. He provides a model for promoting liberal Judaism and for constructing a model of the rabbinate to be emulated.

Scholarship, compassion, and activism are the hallmarks of the kind of leadership required to continue the liberal Judaism Walter has championed and led. Drawing on an earlier responsum Walter Jacob wrote, I have examined the problem of cloning, building on that responsum as a model and arguing for the permissibility of cloning. No contemporary problem is beyond the type of halakhic examination provided by the hundreds of responses Walter has written along with the Responsa Committee.

Dr. Walter Homolka, who is working with Dr. Jacob to re-store Liberal Judaism in Germany, was ordained by Dr. Jacob and others, on the recommendation of the Leo Baeck College where he had studied, on the day of the symposium. Dr. Homolka's contribution deals with nineteenth-century post-Enlightenment German-Jewish theology. Dr. Jacob's Judaism was nurtured by many of the figures Dr. Homolka cites in his article, which argues that the challenge of the contemporary theologian is similar to that of their nineteenth-century predecessors to provide a balance between continuity and change. There is a straight line between Dr. Jacob's own reflections and those of his intellectual forebears.

Rabbi Debra Pine offers a brief response, drawing on the work of Leo Baeck and Hermann Cohen and fleshing out how the rational must be tempered with mystery.

Irene Jacob, director of the Rodef Shalom Biblical Botanical Garden, discusses the history and uses of papyrus. In addition to supplying important historical material, Irene reminds us that Walter loves to make things grow and that his work in all areas, although rooted in study and reflection, is not ivory tower scholar-ship: he is an activist in every sense of the word.

Dr. W. Gunther Plaut, who shares Walter's German-Jewish background and who succeeded Walter as co-chairman of the Central Conference of American Rabbis' Responsa Committee, discusses Walter's rabbinate in the light of both prophetic Judaism and the *Halakhah* as a counterweight to the civil culture of America. He sees a continuity in the work of Walter Jacob and Dr. Solomon Freehof, Walter's predecessor at Rodef Shalom. It is the continuity of great rabbinates that marks Dr. Plaut's contribution.

Rabbi Andrew Busch's response is a plea to find new ways to open the prophetic message to a generation that does not read poetry.

Dr. Michael Cook, professor of New Testament at Hebrew Union College-Jewish Institute of Religion, writes about Judas Iscariot. His work is an exercise in scholarship aimed at enhancing Jewish-Christian understanding, a task that has occupied a significant portion of Dr. Jacob's rabbinate.

Dr. Eberhard von Waldow, who teaches theology at Pittsburgh Theological Seminary, affirms the value of Dr. Cook's work and reminds the reader that when Judas is used as the focus of anti-Semitism it is not the tradition itself that speaks but the anti-Semitism of the interpreter.

Dr. Mark Washofsky, professor of Talmud at Hebrew Union College-Jewish Institute of Religion, who is Walter's successor as chairman of the Central Conference of American Rabbis' Responsa Committee, analyzes the work of the Orthodox *posek* Moshe Feinstein to provide an understanding of liberal *Halakhah* as *Halakhah* insofar as it participates in the culture of argument, its way of thinking and speaking, that constitutes halakhic reasoning. His important literary analysis sets forth a challenge to all liberal authorities who wish to write responsa.

Rabbi Richard Rheins in his essay seeks to draw out the practical implications of Dr. Washofsky's work as providing a model for Reform responsa.

Moshe Zemer, who, along with Dr. Jacob, directs the Free-hof Institute for Liberal Halakhah and who serves as the *posek* of the Israel Progressive Movement, shows how the reasoning of Maimonides to permit "the lesser evil" is a halakhic precedent that can be used to respond to changing sociological situations. He cites as an example the work of Ben Zion Uziel, former Chief Rabbi of Israel, to permit conversion for the sake of marriage as a "lesser evil" than letting a man or woman live in sin with a Gentile. The needs of the time are important to our own halakhic thinking.

Rabbi Daniel Schiff's response offers a caution and questions Rabbi Zemer's conclusion as perhaps going too far. Rabbi Schiff, however, cites Dr. Jacob's own use of reasoning similar to Maimonides' in the case of adulterers who wish to marry each other. The article and the response provide an interesting intersection of primary values.

One area of scholarly achievement not represented in this volume is the biblical scholarship of Walter's grandfather Benno Jacob. Walter has meticulously translated Benno Jacob's commentary on Genesis and Exodus so that a new generation can learn from this important work. We have also not treated his interest in Jewish art and the Associated American Jewish Museums, which he continues to lead. We have not dealt with his most recent efforts in Germany and the Abraham Geiger College, the first rabbinic seminary in Central Europe since the Holocaust, of which he is president. Those efforts are still unfolding. The accumulated scholarship in this volume demonstrates that the work Dr. Jacob has pursued and continues to pursue is part of the lively conversation about the Jewish future. No thin volume or single symposium can do justice to this amazing human being and to his rabbinate.

INTRODUCTION

It is our hope that those who read this work will want to delve more deeply into the wellspring of accumulated knowledge that Walter Jacob has provided and then will wish to follow his example of a person of intellectual curiosity, meticulous scholarship, and personal and professional activism. May God bless Walter and Irene with continued health and strength that they may enjoy many fruitful and productive years and that the many gardens they have planted will continue to flower. We their friends and students will tend them faithfully.

AN AMERICAN RABBINATE

Mark N. Staitman*

As Dr. Jacob's colleague for more than twenty years, my paper is quite different from the academic papers that constitute the rest of this volume. I wanted to talk not so much about Dr. Jacob specifically, but as a younger colleague who learned from him directly. I wanted to focus on his rabbinate, to try to understand one example of a successful American rabbinate.

Next Shabbat in Cincinnati, young men and women who have spent five years studying at the Hebrew Union College will be ordained as rabbis. At the time of ordination, each will have a hope or an expectation that his or her career will blossom and flourish and that his or her rabbinate will be successful. Yet few have really looked at what makes a successful rabbinate. Every rabbinate is different. Every rabbinate reflects both the individual rabbi and the congregation or organization whom that rabbi serves. It is the unique combination of those two that ultimately allows for success. But I think that by looking at one successful rabbinate, we can draw some principles that apply to all rabbis in terms of understanding what a successful rabbinate is.

The rabbinate today is much different from that of a previous generation. Dr. Jacob's rabbinate has really straddled two very different examples or understandings of what the rabbinate was or was to be. The earlier generation, that of Abba Hillel Silver, of our own Dr. Freehof, was one in which the rabbis for many people was "the Jew." He was the one (and I use the term *he* because there were no women rabbis) that was part of the expectation of what a Reform rabbi was to be. That Reform rabbi was dignified, was scholarly, and was male. That rabbi served as "the Jew" for congregants, and congregants really saw the idealized Jew in that individual. He should be well bred, well read, and a good speaker; he should be one who projected the right image and the right presence to the community. He should be one who inspired, who was pious, who showed people the very best of what a Jew could be, but often was perceived as doing that in place of the congregant. So people could derive great pride from the scholarship of Dr. Freehof, but rarely were themselves drawn to serious Jewish study. They could enjoy seeing him active in the community, nationally and internationally, without themselves feeling that they were called to do the same.

Today's rabbinate is very different. Your rabbi is not a substitute for you, and, if anything, you hear from your rabbis today that it is necessary for you to study, for you to be involved in the community, for you to be doing all those things that raise you to the level of what that ideal Jew ought to be. Dr. Jacob's rabbinate indeed has straddled both of these images of the rabbi— not an easy job.

Now, if you were to ask rabbinical colleagues what really marked Walter Jacob's rabbinate, I think the first thing that most would reply would be his scholarship. I had an opportunity to look through Dr. Jacob's bibliography. I don't know if any of you have ever done that: 1,136 publications since 1955. That is amazing! Few scholars could claim anything close to that. They include, first of all, 26 books; the rest are essays and articles. What are they in? theology, responsa and *Halakhah,* Bible, Jewish history, modern Jewish problems, gardens and botany, and book reviews. Now, that, I think, indicates something particularly important here. From Dr. Jacob's perspective scholarship was not simply learning a great deal about one small area. The breadth covered here is tremendous! You see that Dr. Jacob founded an organization for the purpose of promoting scholarship, the Solomon B. Freehof Institute for Progressive

Halakhah. And then you look at the various boards and committees on which he has chosen to invest his time: the Editorial Board of the Religious Education Journal, the National Commission on Conversion of the UAHC, the International Responsa Committee of the World Union for Progressive Judaism, the Responsa Committee of the Central Conference of American Rabbis, and the American Association of Botanical Gardens and Arboreta. Again, these are varied, and you see the real breadth of his learning; but, equally, each of these demands not just scholarship, but scholarship that is used in some way, that develops a useful product—policy on conversion, research in religious education, the answers to how one as a Jew is to approach specific kinds of problems.

What principle can we draw from this? Well, Dr. Freehof, when talking with young colleagues about preaching, used to say that you ought to think of yourself as a rain barrel. You study and study and study until you fill up the barrel, and ultimately it starts to overflow. That, I think, is an important principle here for any rabbi. To have a successful rabbinate one must continue to study and study seriously. First of all, of course, simply in order to learn what we call *Torah L'shma,* learning Torah for the sake of learning. But more than that, as you look at Dr. Jacob's rabbinate, you see this was a successful transition because study, although important for Dr. Jacob personally, became equally important to the Congregation because of his example. And so, when the Rabbi went from being the one whom the Congregation perceived as acting for them to being the exemplar of what they ought to do and be, the nature of programming in the Congregation changed as well. If you look at the educational program of the Congregation, from the time Dr. Jacob assumed the position of Rabbi of the Congregation until his retirement, you see a steady

3

progression of programs and classes and lectures for the Congregation.

Now I have to tell you, when we as staff here at Temple sat and talked about this symposium and about where to hold it, the first suggestion was the small dining room, and the second was the Falk Library upstairs. In either of those rooms we could fit perhaps 35 to 50 persons. The chapel as it is set up now seats 120. What does that mean? It means that this congregation has become really committed to learning. After all, how many people in any congregation would come to listen to a series of academic papers? At scholarly symposia, one rarely sees many people other than those working in that specific area. The fact that more than 100 of you are here indicates the success Dr. Jacob has had in making that transition, in instilling in congregants that same desire to continue to learn. So, the first principle we might say for a successful rabbinate is that it demands continued, lifelong learning. At Temple we talk about lifelong Jewish learning, but I think the breadth exemplified by Dr. Jacob's study helps us see that it is not simply Jewish learning.

A second area, if you were to ask Dr. Jacob's colleagues what it is that has marked his rabbinate as successful, would be that in a sense it represents them. After all, Dr. Jacob, as the chairman of the Responsa Committee or being responsible for the kind of quasi-halakhic decisions and positions that the Reform movement takes or as president of the Central Conference of American Rabbis, really has been the representative of the Reform rabbinate, and, frankly, for much of the rabbinate in the Reform movement in general, in places like the Conference of Presidents of American Jewish Organizations. Look at the edited list of organizations with which he has been involved: he has served on the boards of The Pittsburgh Pastoral

4

Institute, Project Equality of Western Pennsylvania, The United Cerebral Palsy Association of Pittsburgh, Friends of Phipps Conservatory, Pittsburgh Chamber Music Society, WQED, The Epilepsy Foundation of America, The William and Mildred Orr Compassionate Care Center, The Religious Education Association, the Pittsburgh Race and Religion Council, The United Jewish Federation of Pittsburgh, The American Jewish Committee, the ADL of Pittsburgh, Community Day School, the Pittsburgh Jewish Chronicle, the Central Conference of American Rabbis, the UAHC, and the World Union for Progressive Judaism. This list represents about every third organization: I simply divided them between non-Jewish and Jewish organizations and took every third or fourth.

Now, what does it mean to be a representative? In a sense, it is a reflection of that old-style rabbinate. In other words, that one served as the representative of the congregation, of the Jewish community, of the American Reform rabbinate in a particular sphere, in a particular area. And that, of course, has always been important in American Jewish life. From the earliest days of the Reform movement in America there has been a sense that the rabbi had an obligation to do what the congregant could not do. The congregant was out involved in commerce and in business, and the rabbi needed to be the one who ensured that the communal structure, both Jewish and non-Jewish, reflected the values of liberal Judaism. That was particularly important when what for the non-Jewish world was known as social gospel and for Reform Judaism, prophetic Judaism, in the days when that was the hallmark of our liberal religious movement. So the rabbi really served on boards and committees, not just to do the work, though that was important, but to represent all those people who could not be a part because they perceived their role as being involved in their businesses in order to enable the Jewish community and the rabbi to do these things.

But you know, that is really only a piece of it. If you look at what Dr. Jacob was able to do as he served on those boards, it goes far beyond simply representing a congregation or a community. Look, for example, at the Religious Education Association of America, an organization of religious educators from all the various religions and religious movements in the United States. This is not a Jewish organization. Dr. Jacob served not only on the board, but also as president of the Religious Education Association and, from the time he became an officer, the nature of the organization began to change. Jewish educators became much more involved, issues of understanding each other—interreligious ecumenism—began to appear as part of the journal the organization published. In other words, the values of Judaism began to be manifest in the organization. That made the organization much more hospitable to many more people, and thus it could grow. Or, if you look at our own United Jewish Federation, think of how Federation dealt with issues of pluralism twenty-five years ago and how it deals with them today. It is radically different. Twenty-five years ago, Dr. Jacob preached a sermon (it actually is a little longer than that; I believe it is closer to thirty-five years ago) on The United Jewish Federation and was mildly critical. He said in his sermon two things that by today's standards we would find moderate at best:

1. That Federation needed to be more sensitive to synagogues.
2. That it needed to look at the role of non-Orthodox Judaism in Israel.

Now, I will not recount to you the pressure that Dr. Jacob encountered as a result of that sermon. Today, one could not be a credible Jewish leader in the Federation movement and not address those issues. What has happened? Well, in part, society has changed, and, in part, the Federation movement has changed. I think, locally, if you look at what it meant for a liberal rabbi to be able to raise issues and to raise them quietly in various forums and still serve on the board of the organization, you will see that Walter was not only able to serve as a representative, but also to bring Reform values slowly and patiently, and with a good deal of work, to a diverse organization. And we have seen him bring that ability to virtually all these organizations. A successful rabbinate demands the capacity to represent the congregation and the Jewish people to the community. It requires that the rabbi be able to offer help and advice that influences the community and imparts the values of liberal Judaism to those organizations. It is the recognition that one represents more than one's self but is always true to the values that make up who and what you are. So, though it is difficult, and though it may take years of patient work, that aspect of representing and, through that aspect, helping to bring about change is, I think, critical to a successful rabbinate.

Now, obviously, every rabbi, to have a successful rabbinate, has to understand what it means to serve a congregation. The rabbinates of an earlier generation took the idea of being a pastor as a part of the rabbinate, but not necessarily a principal part of the rabbinate. Serving a congregation, at least in part, involves things that to the traditional rabbinate are completely foreign—not in the sense that individuals do not do it, but in the sense that it is considered obligatory for the rabbi. All of us are required to visit the sick, but the complaint comes when the rabbi fails to visit. All of us are required to

7

comfort the mourner, but the rabbi especially. All of us should be visiting shut-ins, but for the rabbi it is a particular duty. That aspect of being a pastor is one piece; preaching is another. The preacher traditionally tries to do two things: he tries, of course, to teach, but, equally, he tries to motivate people to change. Today, that happens in part through preaching, but equally through involvement in other aspects of worship. In serving the congregation, the rabbi has to be a teacher, but also, especially as the rabbi of a liberal congregation, he has to be able to administer change, to be able to help the congregation move from where it is to where it could be.

Well, let's look for a moment at this particular rabbinate. When you talk with congregants about Dr. Jacob's rabbinate, what stands out for most are life-cycle events, that Dr. Jacob was there at a bris, was there at a funeral, officiated at a wedding, visited the hospital, made a shiva call.

He is often referred to as "quietly compassionate," and I think that is a fair and accurate description. I don't mean to embarrass you, Walter. Not every rabbi has to be quiet, but every rabbi should be compassionate. Every rabbi has to be involved in the lives of congregants without being intrusive, has to be able to help congregants move through various times of their lives without their really feeling that he or she is pushing or standing off too far. That is not a skill; that is an art. As with most arts, however, skills are involved, and one can learn them and apply them well or poorly.

This idea of the rabbi using worship as a way of helping people learn and change is something that certainly has happened in this particular rabbinate. If you look in front of you, those of you who are not in the front row, you will find prayer books. If you look at those prayer books, you will see that for most of you they are different from the prayer books with which you grew up. You grew up in this congregation with *The Union Prayer Book* and then *The Union Prayer Book,* revised, and then *The Union Prayer Book,* newly revised. We were among the last of the congregations to make the transition from that to *Gates of Prayer.* We did that slowly for a number of reasons, not the least of them being that the editor of *The Union Prayer Book,* revised and newly revised, was our own Dr. Freehof, and there was a respect for Dr. Freehof, a real love of Dr. Freehof. We were not going to make a change in a prayer book that would in any way be offensive to him. But look at what we were able to do. We were able to slowly change prayer books here in this chapel and then ultimately in the sanctuary.

And it is not simply prayer books. You know, it is not that many years ago that we added a cantorial soloist. For those of you who do not remember, it was approximately 1978, not quite twenty years ago. Now it seems as if we have always had a cantorial soloist. Well, part of that is the trick that memory plays. I love to tell this story of when we restored the sanctuary. That first Rosh Hashanah, I stood just inside the door to listen to people as they came in. One couple came in, looked around, and the husband said, "Those things over the pulpit," pointing to the glass baffles that keep the sound from going into the dome, "those are new," which they were. His wife said, "No they're not, they've always been here." He said, "No, no, I never saw those before, they are new." She said, "You're wrong. When I was a little girl in Sunday school, and bored, I used to look up there to see if they were dusty." Well, some of us adapt to change rather quickly, some do not, and some do not even recognize it. But this idea that one needs to use worship as a way of helping people change is something that Dr. Jacob has been extraordinarily successful with.

9

Administering change, bringing about innovation, is perhaps the most difficult part of serving the congregation.

If you look at change in this congregation, it has happened in a rather remarkable way. Think of the Biblical Botanical Garden. It is only eleven years old, much longer in planning, but in reality, this is the eleventh season; or the Gallery, which we have had for only a few years; or the Museum, which Dr. Jacob began. All these mark innovation. They mark for this congregation real change, but handled without tumult, without difficulty. That managing of change is important, and I think we can say that one principle of a successful rabbinate is that it adds to the quality of life of the congregation. That it sets an example of *klal yisrael,* of the real love of fellow Jews, of Talmud Torah, of encouraging study, and *avodat halev,* of trying to help people to find meaning in worship. It builds on the strength of the congregation and it adds to those strengths, based on the strengths of the individual.

One last area that one rarely sees in the rabbinate truly marks this rabbinate as different and as successful. It is the ability to bring one's outside interests into the congregation for the benefit of the congregation as a whole. Let me give you some simple examples of this. Dr. Jacob, I learned quickly (in fact I learned it the time I first interviewed with him), was interested in gardening, passionately interested in gardening. The first time I was at his home I saw a beautiful garden. Now, gardening is not necessarily a Jewish interest. Dr. Jacob and Irene have a real interest in travel, and have done a good deal of that. They have an interest in collecting. Now think of those and think of how Dr. Jacob has been able to take these personal interests and make them a part of his rabbinate for the benefit of the congregation. His love of gardening led to his and Irene's establishing

10

the Biblical Botanical Garden, a truly important institution within this congregation, one that has involved hundreds of congregants who might not otherwise participate in many other aspects of Jewish congregational life, and brought to the congregation the thousands of visitors who come every summer to see the garden.

Dr. Jacob has taken his interest in travel and used it as a way not only of educating the congregation, but of motivating others to travel. After all, Dr. Jacob, is, I believe, the only rabbi of the congregation to lead a trip to Israel from this congregation. His interest in collecting has led to the creation of the Jewish Museum within the congregation, but equally to the establishment of a new organization, The Associated American Jewish Museums, a group of small congregationally based museums that now can promote the building of collections of Judaica, not just in major cities, not just in Chicago or New York, but any place there is a synagogue. That really is a tremendous success.

To take one's interests and find a way of making those a part of congregational life and, through them, to enhance the life of the congregation means there is a principle here that says a successful rabbinate recognizes the unique qualities of the individual rabbi and allows the interest of the rabbi to be manifest in the life of the congregation.

So what then ought these young people that will be ordained on Shabbat be keeping in front of them as basic principles as they begin their rabbinate? First, a continued learning. They need to really love learning, to love both Jewish and general learning, and they need to make that a part of their lives if they are going to be successful in their rabbinate. They need to have a capacity to represent the

11

congregation and the Jewish people without ever sacrificing their own values. They need to be able to be themselves and at the same time to be honest representatives. They need to develop the quality of life of a congregation by setting an example of *klal yisrael,* the love of fellow Jews of Talmud Torah, of encouraging fellow Jews to study, to learn, and (Hebrew) of finding meaningful ways to worship. And fourth, they ought to find a way to make their own unique qualities as individuals, their own interests, those that make them not just rabbis, but well-rounded human beings, a part of their rabbinate and through that manifest in the life of the congregation.

These are principles I believe we learn from Dr. Jacob's rabbinate and yet they can help all of us as his colleagues ultimately to develop a successful rabbinate.

---

* The following remarks of welcome were given at opening of the symposium on June 1, 1997: "The symposium came into being through Dr. Jacob's brother, Herbert, of blessed memory. Dr. Jacob was beginning to prepare for his retirement; Herbert suggested to Irene Jacob that an appropriate gift to a rabbi who is retiring, something other than a watch, would really be a *Festschrift.*in honor of this scholarly rabbi. Irene brought that suggestion to me and to Bart Cowan, the president of the Congregation, and we somehow kept this secret from Dr. Jacob until his retirement dinner in October 1996, no easy feat.

After Herbert's death, Peter Knobel, Herbert's rabbi, offered to play a major role in the production of the *Festschrift.* He has been a wonderful colleague to me, to Dr. Jacob, to all of us in the rabbinate, and he made this symposium a reality and I am grateful. We ought, of course, to thank the Board of Trustees of Rodef Shalom Congregation for helping to create this marvelous expression of thanks for Dr. Jacob's rabbinate here at Temple and for publishing this *Festschrift.*

We want to extend our thanks to Bart Cowan, Jeff Herzog, administrator of the Congregation, Rabbis Debra Pine and Andy Busch, who have helped to make this a reality; Marianne Fiore and Chris Benton of the staff of Rodef Shalom, who have worked so hard on this; and to all those who offered to write for this *Festschrift*. Many papers came on time, so I think that itself says something about the way colleagues feel about Dr. Jacob.

Our thanks, of course, to the respondents who will speak following five of the papers and to the Congregation itself, which not only underwrote the symposium and the *Festschrift*, but also always insisted that its rabbis develop well-rounded rabbinates and has expected all of us to take study seriously. So this symposium and this *Festschrift* are not only a way of honoring Dr. Jacob and his rabbinate, but are also a superb indicator of the kind of commitment that Rodef Shalom has to Jewish study."

IS ONE OF ME ENOUGH?
To Clone or Not to Clone:
That Is the Question

Peter S. Knobel

Technological advances are constantly and with increasing rapidity transforming science fiction into ordinary living. This is especially true in biotechnology, which has made it possible for us to cure diseases and treat conditions that were fatal only a few short years ago. Our ability to prolong life and postpone death present enormous ethical challenges. Greater longevity is a blessing for some and a curse for others. From the beginning to the end of life, the impossible has become reality. From conception outside the womb to a transplantation of a heart, we are witness to and recipients of medical miracles.

These developments raise numerous ethical questions. For example, how do we distribute costly procedures fairly in a world of unequal distribution of wealth? In a world of limited resources, are these medical miracles too expensive when measured against other basic needs? If one person has to die so that another can live, how do we prevent the murder of one to save the other? How will greater longevity affect our understanding of marriage? How does greater longevity affect the relationship between parents and children, especially when people must care simultaneously for their own children and their aging parents. The manner in which we respond to these and a myriad of other questions will determine the quality of the society we create.

As Jews, we are the heirs to a rich ethical tradition enshrined in the panoply of our sacred texts. Over the years, individual rabbis and, now, committees of rabbis, seek to respond to ethical and ritual inquiries in carefully reasoned reflections on these texts. Rabbinical texts often failed to directly address the problem that the rabbinic decisor was expected to adjudicate because the specifics of the situation were unknown to previous generations. This difficulty increases with increasing rapidity as the pace of technology extends the range of the possible. He, therefore, and now she, use analogical reasoning to extract principles that apply to the new situations.

Most of the decisions have been reactive rather than anticipatory. Professor Anne Reichman Schiff, in a probing article on artificial insemination by donor, has written:

> The law's response to the new reproductive practices to date has generally been reactive rather than proactive. Too often the legal approach in this area has been one of "crisis management," in which laws are formulated in response to specific fact situations that require speedy resolution. This path has failed to acknowledge that what is required is a paradigmatic shift in legal thinking. What is needed today is a coherent legal framework that is comprehensive in scope and sensitive to the ethical and societal impact of this reproductive era.[1]

Her observation applies not only to secular law but to the legal and ethical probings of liberal Jewish thinkers. A progressive *Halakhah* not only must answer the questions asked but also must anticipate the scientific and societal developments that are largely unprecedented and establish a framework for determining what is obligatory, permissible, and prohibited.[2]

Rabbi Dr. Walter Jacob has been in the forefront of those who have used the insights of the *Halakhah* to help Jews face the conundrums. His many volumes of responsa as well as the thousands of questions he has answered in writing and orally are a treasure trove of practical guidance for individuals and for the Jewish community. In this paper I wish to address a question that Dr. Jacob addressed in Responsum 20, "Genetic Engineering," dated February 1978, in his volume *Contemporary Reform Responsa.*[3]

Long before Dolly was a glint in her creators' test tube, Walter Jacob was being asked to speculate about what if...? The responsum deals with what is the latest, and now understood to be in some ways the most striking and controversial, breakthrough in reproductive technology – cloning.

The birth of Dolly the sheep in Scotland has created a fire storm of conflicting opinions. For some it is a great boon; for others it is the realization of their worst nightmare. If we can clone sheep, the argument goes, it will not be long before we can clone human beings. Although we have many technical hurdles to overcome, the cloning of humans is more than Frankensteinian fantasy.

Many voices have called for a ban on cloning of humans and a halt to federally funded research. We wonder: Are we on the verge of a new era of medical progress and economic prosperity or is this the beginning of the end of human life as we know it? If we can reproduce ourselves exactly from a single cell, are we in danger of disconnecting reproduction from love and as well from sexual intercourse? What will constitute a family in this brave new world? Who should be cloned? Imagine a world of thousands of Einsteins or Michael Jordans? Or Adolph Hitlers as imagined in the novel *The Boys from Brazil.*

Such selective breeding presents us with the potential dangers of cloning on the basis of social worth, that is, societal need, economic gain, or diabolical plan. This represents the ultimate "commodification" of individuals: clones for sale manufactured on demand.

Selective breeding conjures images of Nazi eugenics. Because a technology is subject to misuse and abuse does not, however, in and of itself, justify banning it. Selective breeding of animals and plants as well as newly created microbes and species has created heartier crops, more efficient techniques for producing new medicines, cows that give more milk. Genetic engineering and new reproductive techniques have had innumerable positive results and will prove increasingly beneficial in the future.

Our desire to improve on nature is an example of the creativity that we share with God. The question is, How far should we go?[4] Azriel Rosenfeld in his article "Judaism and Gene Design," after discussing the clear permissibility of genetic surgery to correct serious defects prenatally, even if the surgery puts the fetus at risk, suggests,

> Our sages recognize, and perhaps even encourage, the use of prenatal (or better, pre-conceptional influences) to improve one's offspring.

He then cites a very interesting story about the sage R. Yohanan:

> R. Yohanan used to go and sit at the gates of the place of immersion, saying: "When the daughters of Israel come out from their required immersion, they look at me and may have sons who are as handsome as I, and as accomplished in Torah as I.[5]

The women, having seen R. Yohanan and now in a state of ritual purity, would return and have sexual intercourse with their husbands. The resulting children would be beautiful and have the capacity and desire to become learned in Torah.

Rosenfeld says further:

> This concept might well be extended to allow the use of gene-surgical techniques to produce physically and mentally superior children.

This certainly smacks of eugenics. Although it can be couched in phrases like *tikkun olam* or divine human partnership in perfection of the world, it is fraught with danger. A good thing — namely, to correct a serious illness or physical defect — is transformed into selective breeding. To deliberately breed for intelligence or physical beauty may be "playing God" in a negative sense of that term.

Rosenfeld continues:

> On the other hand, turning a person into a monster by surgical means would very likely be forbidden, unless it was necessary to save his life, and creating a monster through gene surgery might thus also be forbidden.[6]

The word "might" is disturbing. Although the issue of eugenics raises significant concerns, let us return to an earlier question from a Jewish point of view: Is it permissible to clone human beings? If it is permissible, under what circumstances and with what safeguards?

I now wish to return to Dr. Jacob's responsum. His questioner asks:

> Would a person produced through genetic engineering rather
> than natural reproduction possess a soul? Does a clone have
> a soul?

Dr. Jacob discusses Jewish views of ensoulment and cites the legend of the *golem,* a creature created of wood or clay through the use of magical incantations and the insertion of the divine name in its mouth or the placement of the name on its forehead. In determining the status of the clone, he cites a responsum of Zevi Ashkenazi and Jacob Emden, who rule that a *golem* cannot be counted in minyan, implying that a *golem* is not fully human and therefore has no soul.

In two very intriguing recent articles[7] Professor Byron Sherwin explores in depth the status of the *golem* and the moral implications of the *golem* legend. He points out that in many versions of the *golem* legend the word *golem* is not used but rather "a man created by means of *Sefer Yetzirtah.*"[8] He makes a distinction between artificial life and artificially created life. He makes a distinction between *golem*s of the past and modern *golem*s. He analogizes the clone with a fully developed *golem* and points out that medieval texts use the term *golem* for embryo; he also explores the *midrashim* that Adam was originally created a *golem* and only at the final stage of creation becomes fully human. We will return to Dr. Sherwin's articles later in the paper.

Dr. Jacob continues:

> We are, however, concerned with an entirely new being which might conceivably begin its life in a test tube from a fertilized *ovum* or a variety of genetic material and would be capable of sexual reproduction. We shall not discuss the desirability of such an undertaking, but at some time in the future it will, undoubtedly, occur with or without approval. We could well consider such a being to have a soul. It will have been formed from human material despite all genetic alterations. Its development will have taken place in an artificial environment rather than the womb, but at some point it will emerge as human being. Hopefully, it will then not be enslaved to its maker or master, but will develop independently as other human beings. Unless such possibilities of independent intellectual and moral development are genetically removed, this would be a human being.

Walter Jacob raises a number of important issues, the most serious of which deals with the status of a clone as a human being. If a clone is not granted the status of human being, it could become a being enslaved to its creator like the *Golem* of Prague, or it could potentially become simply a source of spare parts for its older sibling.

A couple recently conceived a baby for the purpose of providing a bone marrow transplant to an older child. Although it seems clear to me that such an act would constitute an act of *pikuach nefesh* and therefore permissible, there are some significant medical concerns, especially about the younger sibling's lack of ability to consent to a procedure that has some risks. There are also grave psychological concerns whether the procedure succeeds or fails. We must also be concerned about the precedent that this establishes and how much risk a parent could subject a minor to for the benefit of another child or, for that matter, for the benefit of the parent.

The issue is similar to whether a person is required to donate an organ to save the life of a person who needs it. Dr. Solomon B. Freehof concludes, following an opinion of the Tzitz Eliezer, Rabbi Eliezer Waldenberg, an individual who is an acceptable donor is not duty bound to donate the organ; such an act would be an impermissible wounding of the body:

> A person is certainly not required by law to donate an organ of his body in order that it may be planted into the body of another. If he is endangered by the removal of the organ, then he is actually forbidden to risk his life. Of course if the danger to his life were minimal, it would be a good deed; but otherwise one should not endanger his life in this way because one life – in this case his own – is as valuable as the life he wishes to save. Waldenberg then uses the Talmudic dictum, "What makes you think that his blood is redder than yours?"... Its meaning is clear.... Every life is as equally valuable as any other life.[9]

A second point Walter Jacob makes in dealing with the status of a clone as a human being is, "Unless such possibilities of independent intellectual and moral development are genetically removed, this would be a human being." The possibility of manufacturing human beings that Aldous Huxley describes in his *Brave New World* is the ultimate nightmare – we could create humans without mothers or fathers. We could create a society of all males or all females, genetically identical, genetically manufactured and conditioned to perform specific roles. Imagine, as Huxley did, human reproduction removed both from sexual intercourse and from gestation inside the mother, a society that produces individuals according to a central plan that decides what society needs and deliberately adds formaldehyde to developing embryos to produce a class of menial workers.

Huxley's vision should serve as a constant reminder of the dark side of technology. As in the legend of the *Golem,* although the *Golem* of Prague was created to protect the Jews of Prague, one Friday night without explanation it began to destroy the ghetto. Fortunately, Rabbi Judah Loew, its creator, had the power to destroy it. Yet, when the cat is let out of the bag....

If, on the one hand, we could clone a single organ that was a perfect match and would be in unlimited supply, what a boon it would be to people who require transplants. If, on the other hand, we clone an embryo, use it, and then abort it so it can serve as a source of spare parts, we have entered a moral wasteland. It is not clear that under Jewish law such a scenario would be prohibited.[10] As we develop the techniques for cloning human beings we will have to consider many factors: What would constitute good results and bad results? What do we do with our mistakes?

I wish to repeat that genetic engineering, cloning, artificial embryonization, artificial insemination, in vitro fertilization all have their positive side even if darker possibilities always remain. This was recognized by the rabbis in their discussion of artificial life. The character of the creator is crucial. Judaism accepts the concept that scientific experimentation as morally neutral; but it demands of the scientists that they be responsible for the results of their experiments. Scientific research can be understood as having Faustian potential for the demise or domination of humankind, or it can be viewed as one more expression of human creativity. It is either the work of the devil in which one seeks to supplant God, or it is an example of *imitateo Dei,* one aspect of what it means to be created in the image of God. As Byron Sherwin notes,

> Classical Jewish literature stresses these features of the creative act...moral, technical and intellectual prerequisites of one who would deign to create life. Furthermore, Jewish literature refuses to sever creature from creator. Not only is the creator responsible for what the creature does but the creator is responsible for what the creature becomes. The creature reflects not only technical skill but the moral nature of its creator.[11]

The role of the scientists and regulators as well as the distributors of this technology are crucial. As we move ahead in these areas, we must not panic, as I believe has been the case in the early reactions to the cloning of Dolly, but we must anticipate both the positive possibilities and the worst case scenarios and try to institute checks and balances. Walter Jacob in his responsum also reminds us that, from a practical perspective, banning cloning will not work. We must therefore be concerned about its regulation.

A similar statement was made by Rabbi Immanuel Jakobovits in the 1975 edition of his *Jewish Medical Ethics.* He writes:

> It is indefensible to initiate uncontrolled experiments with incalculable effects on the balance of nature and the preservation of man's incomparable spirituality without the most careful evaluation of the likely consequences beforehand.... "Spare-part" surgery and "genetic engineering" may open a wonderful chapter in the history of healing. But without prior agreement on restraints and the strictest limitations, such mechanization of human life may also herald irretriev-

24

able disaster resulting from man's encroachment upon nature's preserves, from assessing human beings by their potential value as tool-parts, sperm-donors or living incubators, and from replacing the matchless dignity of the human personality by test-tubes, syringes and the soulless artificiality of computerized numbers.[12]

How we get prior agreement when it is clear that we are dealing with a worldwide phenomenon with broad economic and political implications is no easy task. The fact that we can now, in this country, patent new organisms raises questions of ownership and use. We must face the complexity caused by our progress. To withdraw Federal support for research will merely place our heads, ostrichlike, in the sand.[13]

I wish now to turn to an issue that is sometimes lost in these discussions. Although the clone may be genetically identical to its progenitor, it is not the same person. Personal identity is a combination of genetics and experience. Genetic predisposition is not necessarily destiny.

Man [sic], as the delicately balanced fusion of body, mind and soul, can never be the mere product of laboratory conditions and scientific ingenuity. To fulfill his destiny as a creative creature in the image of his Creator, he must be generated and reared out of the intimate love joining husband and wife together, out of identifiable parents who care for the development of their off-spring and out of a home which provides affectionate warmth and compassion.[14]

The Talmud says:

There are three partners in man: the Holy One, blessed be He, his father and his mother. His father supplies the semen

25

of the white substance out of which are formed the child's bones, sinews, nails, the brain in his head, and the white of his eyes. His mother supplies the semen of the red substance out of which is formed his skin, flesh, hair, blood, and the black of his eye. And the Holy One, blessed be He, gives the spirit and the breath, beauty of features, eyesight, the power of hearing, the ability to speak and walk, understanding and discernment. [15]

The complexity of what constitutes an individual person ought not be lost. We know this from studies of identical twins. The Talmudic adage, that when God creates He makes a die, and each coin He stamps out is different, unique, but when a human does the same each coin is the same, ought to remain a reminder that personhood is more than a collection of genes. A clone is not a copy of me now. It is a genetic duplicate that is yet to have a history.

An interesting talmudic passage may be read to suggest that Eve was a clone of Adam, and only after the creation of both Adam and Eve does sexual union become the norm:

He said to them, "At first Adam was created from dust and Eve was created from Adam's rib. From that time on [man propagates] 'in our image, after our likeness.' [That means] a man must have a woman, a woman must have a man, and both must have the divine presence [together with them in order to propagate]."[16]

Sexual union is the Jewish norm in which reproduction is an important *mitzvah* that permits us to use all our technological ingenuity; the use of technology remains the exception and not the norm. In fact, the use of technology to replace intercourse would

26

be prohibited except where fertility or genetic problems make it a necessity.

The Talmud emphasizes that a human being is both body and soul. The question of ensoulment, although interesting, does not seem to be crucial for the status of potential life or actual life, and it is clear that when a clone emerges from the womb it has a soul:

> Antoninus said to Rabbi: "The body and the soul can both free themselves from judgment. Thus, the body can plead: 'The soul has sinned, [the proof being] that from the day it left me I lie like a dumb stone in the grave [powerless to do aught].' Whilst the soul can say: 'The body has sinned, [the proof being] that from the day I departed from it I fly about in the air like a bird [and commit no sin].'" He replied, "I will tell you a parable. To what may this be compared? To a human king who owned a beautiful orchard which contained splendid figs. Now, he appointed two watchmen therein, one lame and the other blind. [One day] the lame man said to the blind, 'I see beautiful figs in the orchard. Come and take me upon your shoulder, that we may procure and eat them.' So the lame bestrode the blind, procured and ate them. Some time after, the owner of the orchard came and inquired of them, 'Where are those beautiful figs?' The lame man replied, 'Have I then feet to walk with?' The blind man replied, 'Have I then eyes to see with?' What did he do? He placed the lame upon the blind and judged them together. So will the Holy One, blessed be He, bring the soul, [re]place it in the body, and judge them together, as it is written, *He shall call to the heavens from above, and to the earth, that He may judge His people: He shall call to the heavens from above — this refers to the soul; and to the earth, that He may judge His people — to the body.*"[17]

27

The human being is a combination of body and spirit, heredity and education, nature and nurture. As Rosenfeld remarks, "Spiritual heredity is at least as important as the physical,"[18] citing the following three talmudic passages. (In our context the sexism of the passage is disturbing but the point is clear.)

> One who raises an orphan in his house is regarded by Scripture as if he had given birth to him. One who teaches his friend's son Torah is regarded by scripture as if he had begotten him.[19]

> A father endows [zokheh] a son with beauty, strength, wealth, wisdom and longevity.[20] But the sages say: "Until he comes of age his father endows him, thereafter, he endows himself."[21]

He concludes:

> As we move into an era of genetic engineering when fathers [we would add mothers] may be able to choose and control the qualities of their children, let us hope that we don't forget our ultimate dependence on the merit of our forefathers [sic.; foremothers not in the original] and on our Father in Heaven.[22]

This leads, however, to a consideration of our role in the universe. It can be argued that God deliberately left the world incomplete for us to complete. In Reform Judaism our concept of tikkun olam means that we will use our God-given talent as being created in the divine image to correct the flaws and repair the breaches in creation. Our creative ability is what we share with God. The Talmud teaches that our ability to create is limited only by our sinfulness:

> Raba said, If the righteous desire it, they could create worlds, for it is written, *"But your iniquities have distinguished between you and your God"* [Isa 59:2]. Rabban created a man and sent him to Rabbi Zera. Rabbi Zera spoke to him [the artificially created man], but received no answer. Thereupon he [Rabbi Zera] said to him [the artificially created man]: You are a creature of the magicians. Return to your dust.

> Rabbi Hanina and Rabbi Oshaia spent every Sabbath studying the *Sefer Yetzirah* [The Book of Creation] by means of which they created a third-grown calf which they ate.[23]

The artificially created man is flawed, not fully human, as the commentators discuss,[24] and therefore Rabbi Zera is permitted to kill him without being subject to the charge of murder. The flaw, however, is only because of the limited righteousness of Rabba. This does not mean that a more righteous person might not be able to artificially create a human being. In the meantime, the Talmud reports with approval the fact that Hanina and Oshaia produce and eat a third-grown calf by means of the same book. It is clear that creativity is a trait we share with God.[25]

Elliot Dorff, one of the leading Conservative rabbinic experts on medical ethics, in his recent testimony before the President's National Bio-Ethics Advisory Committee, reminds us:

> Adam and Eve are put into the garden to *"work and preserve it"* [Gen. 2:15]. As long as we preserve nature then we have the right and the duty to work with it to fulfill human needs. In a parallel talmudic phrase we are God's partners in the ongoing act of creation when we improve the human lot in life.[26]

David Lilienthal, our colleague in the Netherlands, reports the following from R. Evers, a Dutch Orthodox Rabbi:

> The Bible (in Leviticus 19:19) prohibits the cross-fertilization of animals and plants, but in my opinion that prohibition does not apply to cloning. Nachmanides (1194–1270) writes concerning this text: "He who grafts or cross-fertilizes two sorts, changes the Creation. By this he implies that the Creation is imperfect." However, the scientist who clones has no intention of changing the Creation; he only wants to multiply characteristics that are wanted. In the midrashic literature, many sources point out [that] God intentionally created the world imperfect, so as to give the human being the opportunity to perfect the world as God's partner.[27]

An interesting aside reported in a number of places but also stated by Rabbi Evers is:

> Another argument why cloning is not prohibited by Biblical Jewish law is [that] the action takes place on the microscopic level, invisible for the human eye. In a famous responsum, Rabbi Moshe Feinstein, the leading American rabbi of this century, decided that microscopic facts do not count in Jewish law. We are not allowed to eat "swarming" animals, but this does not mean that we should stop breathing because there are all kinds of microbes circulating in the air. Cloning takes place on the microscopic level and seems permitted according to Biblical norms.

An issue much in the minds of ethicists is the concept of "playing God." What are the limits of the use of human power? This is an issue the book of Genesis already addresses and is cited as a matter of concern by Rabbi Elliot Dorff. He said, referring to human hubris as described in the story of the Tower of Babel (Gen. 11:1–9),

> There is a boundary between what we do and what God does, that God refuses to allow a situation in which nothing that people may propose will be out of their reach. Moreover, even when we accomplish things within the proper bounds for human beings, we must take due note of God's role in our achievement, for the essence of human hubris is to brag that "my strength and the power of my hand accomplished these things" (Deuteronomy 8:11–20).[28]

Gershom Scholem, in his article "The Idea of the *Golem*," translates two midrashic texts expressing the concern that as we become technologically more astute, we begin to believe in our own omnipotence. They worry that the worship of humankind will replace the worship of God.

> Ben Sira wished to study the book *Yetsirah*. Then a heavenly voice went forth: You cannot make him [such a creature alone]. He went to his father Jeremiah. They busied themselves with it, and at the end of three years a man was created to them, on whose forehead stood *emeth* as on Adam's forehead. Then the man they made said to them God alone created Adam and when He wished to let Adam die He erased the *aleph* from *emeth* and he remained *meth*, dead. That is what you should do with me and not create another man lest the world succumb to idolatry as in the days of Enosh. The created man said to them, Reverse the combinations of letters [by which he was created] and erase the *aleph* of the word *emeth* from my forehead and immediately he fell into dust.[29]

31

In a pseudepigraphon attributed to the Tannaite Judah ben Bathyra, we read:

The prophet Jeremiah busied himself alone with the *Book Yetsirah*. Then a heavenly voice went forth and said: Take a companion. He went to his son Sira, and they studied the book for three years. Afterward they set about combining the alphabets in accordance with the kabbalistic principles of combination, grouping, and word formation, and a man was created to them, on whose forehead stood the letters *YHWH Elohim Emeth*. But this newly created man had a knife in his hand, with which he erased the *aleph* from *emeth;* there remained: *meth*. Then Jeremiah rent his garments (because of the blasphemy: God is dead, now implied in the inscription) and said: Why have you erased the *aleph* from *emeth?* He replied: I will tell you a parable. An architect built many houses, cities, and squares, but no one could copy his art and compete with him in knowledge and skill until two men persuaded him. Then he taught them the secret of his art, and they knew how to do everything in the right way. When they had learned his secret and his abilities, they began to anger him with words. Finally, they broke with him and became architects like him, except that what he charged a thaler for, they did for six groats. When people noticed this, they ceased to honor the artist and came to them and honored them and gave them commissions when they required to have something built. So God had made you in His image and in His shape and form. But now that you have created a man like Him, people will say: There is no God in the world beside these two! Then Jeremiah said: What solution is there? He said: Write the alphabets backward on the earth you have strewn with intense concentration. Only do not meditate in the sense of building up, the other way around. So they did, and the man became dust and ashes before their eyes. Then Jeremiah said: Truly, one should study these things only in order to know the power and omnipotence of the Creator of this world, but not in order to really practice them.[30]

Sherwin concludes:

In the kabbalist view of *golem* making, two contradictory motifs meet. Here the story is reinterpreted as a moralistic legend and a warning becomes more profound. To the Hasidim, the creation of a *golem* confirmed man in his likeness of God; here thanks to the daring amplification of the inscription on the *golem*'s forehead it becomes a warning: in the real and not merely symbolic creation a *golem* would bring with it the 'death of God'! The hybris of its creator would turn against God.[31]

The *golem* of Prague had to be destroyed by its creator because it attacked the Jewish community it was created to protect. The temptation of the Jews of Prague to reawaken it from its sleep in the attic of the Altneuschul was powerful, especially in times of trouble.

Sherwin recounts that 150 years after Judah Loew consigned his dead *golem* to the attic of the Altneuschul, no one dared try to enter the attic and revive the *golem*. Ezekiel Landau, a late eighteenth-century successor of Loew, decided to try. He prepared himself spiritually with prayer, fasting, repentance, and ritual immersion. He ascended wrapped in his tallit. But as he ascended he was seized by an overwhelming dread, and he descended without entering the attic. Landau decreed that entering the attic was forbidden even to the chief rabbi of Prague.[32]

Sherwin speculates on what he feared. I believe it is a warning that we can never be sure what forces we unleash when

33

we create life. We should approach these new abilities with the proper awe and not without some fear.

In an interesting contrast to Sherwin's view, Rabbi Evers suggests that clones are not to be analogized to the *golem* of Prague. He writes:

> If it in the future becomes possible to let embryos grow to full-grown and healthy babies artificially and entirely outside the uterus, which may become possible when the cloning techniques of humans develop further, then the Jewish sages have already now decided that such clones in any case cannot be compared to the legendary "*Golem* of Prague," which was not regarded as human since it was created in a super-human manner [the original sentence is also impossibly long. D.L.]. From the Jewish point of view, cloning is in principle a natural process, whereby the modern technique only offers a helping hand.[33]

Sherwin points to a dispute between Gershon Hanokh, who argues for the full human status of *golem,* and Judah Loew, Zevi Ashkenazi, and Jacob Emden, who argue against it:

> In making his claim that a *Golem* might be considered human, Gershon Hanokh articulated his disagreement with the position of Judah Loew of Prague and others, who maintained that a *Golem* could never have all of the human characteristics, and hence, could never be considered a human being. For Judah Loew, and for others previously noted, a human artifact could never be a human being. Gershon Hanokh's view is willing to eradicate any absolute distinction between humans and *Golems*. For Gershon Hanokh, a *Golem* that meets certain prerequisites can be considered human. Judah Loew, on the other hand, would insist upon a firm line of

34

demarcation between humans and *Golems*. For Loew, a *Golem* by definition cannot be considered a human.[34]

The daring late Hasidic master Gershon Hanokh Leiner of Radzyn, in his controversial *Sidrei Taharot,* went even further than the *Sefer ha-Bahir*. Gershon Hanokh agreed that Rabbi Zera was justified in killing Rabbah's *Golem* because it lacked intelligence and consequently was regarded "as an animal in human form and it is permissible to kill it." However, he added, if an intelligent *Golem* had been created, "he would have the legal status of a true man...even as regards being counted in a *minyan*...and he would be the same as if God had created him." Thus, Gershon Hanokh admitted the possibility of considering an artificially created being, who had all the normal human traits, including intelligence, as a human being. Gershon Hanokh would grant human personhood to such an "artificially" created human being. Destroying such a *Golem,* it would follow, would be murder.[35]

How a human being is created does not change his or her status. Artificially created life is not artificial life. In slightly different language this is the point that Walter Jacob makes near the end of his responsum, that the newly created being will have a soul and be entitled to full protection.

There are other important, ethical questions such as cloning used for gender selection, and, as Rabbi Evers points out,

If people will be cloned, a surplus of men could arise. From research in the United States it appears that many parents-to-be have a clear preference for boys. This preference is mainly present among couples who only want one child. If the cloning techniques in the future were to lead to a situation wherein parents can choose the gender of the child, the percentage of boys will rise considerably. This would lead to a situation

35

in which many men would not be able to marry. This pros-
pect clashes with the Jewish "Weltanschauung." The prophet
Ezekiel says that the world was created in order to be populated. A distorted men-women proportion would prevent this.

Even at these early stages it is necessary to worry about the potential misuse of technology.

It is clear in Jewish law that we are permitted to go to great
lengths to heal or to preserve human life. One not only is permitted, but is required, to perform prohibited activities on Shabbat to
save a life. It is equally clear that although cloning would not be
the preferred technique for solving the problem of childlessness,
since *peru uvrevu* is such an important *mitzvah,* it would be permitted. Yet, it also raises many of the same ethical issues as the other
new reproductive techniques. Since the cloned embryo would still,
for the conceivable future, have to be implanted into a woman's
womb, issues of maternity as well as the potential exploitation of
women who are paid to be hosts for clones require consideration.
Hertz rent-a-womb could become a profitable and exploitative
enterprise. One must therefore ask whether adoption is not preferable to cloning.

There seems also to be little doubt that in a case of *pikuach
nefesh,* where the clone's rights would be protected, cloning would
not only be permitted but might be required.

Rabbi Evers has raised another issue, concerning resurrection of the dead. He writes:

It is remarkable to what extent the modern technique places
the prophetic promises for the future within the context of the

human reality. In Ezekiel chapter 37, the dead in the valley of Dura are brought back to life, which is understood as a foretaste of the final revival of the dead. This revival of the dead is the last of Maimonides' Thirteen Principles of Faith: "I believe with perfect faith the dead will be revived at a time which God will decide." It is striking that it is possible, through the cloning technique, to reproduce a new human being from only one cell. The Talmud says that there always remain a number of cells of every person who was ever buried, which then form the raw-material for the revival. The belief in the resurrection of the dead was until recently only something in the distant future. But these modern techniques show us that this no longer is impossible. The real benefit of the development of the cloning technique is the fact that even the most inveterate atheist can again believe unconditionally.[36]

The desire for scientific verifiability is constant, especially for a religion that asserts that God acts in history. Only last week a leading Conservative thinker, Rabbi Neil Gillman, published a new book, in which he writes,

> At the end of days God will bring my body and soul together and I will be reconstituted as I was during my life on earth.... I insist that resurrection affect all of me in my concrete individuality because I understand the central thrust of the doctrine of the afterlife as establishing the everlasting preciousness to God of the life I led here on earth.[37]

Our finitude remains a central issue for most of us. Although our limited life span may teach us to number our days so we grow wise in heart, death is still the great enemy and immortality a fervent dream. Reform theology denies bodily resurrection while supporting immortality of the soul. Increasingly, within Reform Judaism, we remind ourselves that we are embodied. To use Gillman's wonderful phrase, I am my body. Without my body there is no me. It is interesting to note that this discussion about resurrection of the dead is taking place at a moment in Reform Jewish history when some have suggested that it is time to restore the concept *mechaiyei meitim,* resurrection of the dead, officially to our liturgy. and it is ironic that we should be discussing this in Pittsburgh, because it was the Pittsburgh Platform of 1885 that explicitly excluded it from Reform Jewish theology. Some may find it tempting or comforting to know even if I am no longer around my genetic duplicate will be around. It presents us with the danger of what Elliot Dorff has called self-idolization. The central question is, Is one of me enough? I think that answer in most cases must be, yes.

In 1978, when Walter Jacob first discussed these matters, the technology was not nearly so advanced as it is today, and we still have a way to go before human cloning will be a reality. Dr. Jacob was rightly concerned that newly created life might be exploited and that we had to be prepared to recognize the rights of sentient beings created artificially. He rightly points to the legend of the *golem* as the place to begin our consideration. He also distinguishes between permissibility and desirability. A human being no matter how created is a human, and potential life is potential life, to be destroyed only after due consideration.

In summary, cloning will take place.[38] As with any new technology, its full implications cannot be known at the outset. Although from a halakhic point of view, it is certainly permissible, there are significant concerns. Human hubris knows no bounds, and the Huxley fantasy of technology run amuck is certainly a warning. It is important that we conceive of possible uses of cloning and explore their ethical implications. To fail in this endeavor is to ignore our role as *betzelem elohim* and divine partners in the completion of the world. To fail in this endeavor is to fail to recognize our ever present temptation to play God and, like Prometheus, not only to steal the fire but to supplant God. Safeguards are important. National and international governmental regulation will certainly be required, but the results will ultimately depend on the scientists and the institutions that will do the cloning and provide the services. Technology may be morally neutral, but scientists may not be. Must we do everything that we can do?

I close with my thanks to Walter Jacob for teaching us how to think Jewishly and for providing us with guidance along the slippery slope of decision making. May God grant him and Irene many more years of good health and blessing. We all look forward to his continually teaching us in the years ahead.

Notes

1. Anne Reichman Schiff, "Frustrated Intentions and Binding Biology," *Duke Law Journal* 44:3 (1994), p. 570.

2. Prof. Byron Sherwin of the Spertus Institute of Jewish Studies, in an April 16, 1997, address to the Chicago Board of Rabbis, states, "Just about any halakhic problem may be presented in the following way: here are three relevant categories. Which one applies in this case before us? These three categories are *hovah, assur,* and *reshut.* These categories may be viewed as a spectrum. On one side is *hovah* — the action is prescribed, required. On the other is the opposite, *assur* — the action is proscribed — forbidden. In the middle is a spectrum of possibilities where, under certain circumstances, the action is permitted. This simple structure, it seems to me, can be applied to about any issue from *kashrut* to abortion, from issues in business ethics to sexual ethics."

3. Walter Jacob, "Genetic Engineering," Responsum 20, *Contemporary Reform Responsa* (1987), pp. 32–34.

4. Azriel Rosenfeld, "Judaism and Gene Design," *Tradition* (Fall 1972). Reprinted by Fred Rosner in *Jewish Bio-Ethics* (1979), p. 403.

39

IS ONE OF ME ENOUGH?

5. *Berakot* 20a.

6. Rosenfeld, in Rosner, *Jewish Bio-Ethics,* p. 403.

7. Byron Sherwin, "Moral Implications of the *Golem* Legend," in his *In Partnership with God: Contemporary Jewish Law and Ethics* (Syracuse: Syracuse University Press, 1990), pp. 181–207, and "The *Golem* of Zevi Ashkenazi and Reproductive Biotechnology," *Judaism* 44: 3, pp. 314–22.

8. Sherwin, "Moral Implications," p. 194.

9. Solomon B. Freehof, *American Reform Responsa,* (New York: CCAR, 1983), p. 249.

10. The status of the fetus as potential rather than actual life as well as the time of the abortion would be factors in decision making. A full discussion of this matter, however, will take us too far afield for this paper.

11. Sherwin, "Moral Implications," p. 204.

12. Immanuel Jakobovits, *Jewish Medical Ethics* (New York: Bloch, 1975), pp. 261–66.

13. The decision to withhold Federal research grants and to prohibit cloning will just drive the research underground or abroad. Our best hope is to support it with the appropriate safeguards.

14. Jakobovits, *Jewish Medical Ethics,* pp. 251–66.

15. *Niddah* 31a.

16. *Yerushalmi Berakhot* 9:1.

17. *Sanhedrin* 91ab.

18. Rosenfeld, in Rosner, *Jewish Bio-Ethics,* p. 407.

19. *Sanhedrin* 19b.

20. *Edduyot* 2:9.

21. *Tos. Edduyot* 1:14.

22. Rosenfeld, in Rosner, *Jewish Bio-Ethics,* p. 403.

23. *Sanhedrin* 65b.

24. Sherwin, "Moral Implications," According to the *Sefer ha-Bahir,* Rabbah's *golem* did not have the power of speech because it was not created by the completely righteous. Had it been so created, however, it would have had the power of speech and would have been intelligent. Hence, the inability to create an intelligent *golem* indicates a flaw in the creator of the *golem* that is reflected in the *golem* he created.

25. Sherwin, "Moral Implications," p. 196.

26. From a typescript of Dr. Dorff's March 14, 1997, Testimony before the National Bio-Ethics Advisory Committee.

27. Translation of the text of an article in the Dutch Christian Daily newspaper *Trouw,* March 7, 1997, by R. Evers, rabbi of the Dutch Orthodox Union and Rosh Yeshova at the Nederlandsch Israëlitisch Seminarium in Amsterdam.

28. Dorff, Testimony.

29. As quoted in Gershom Scholem, *On the Kabbalah and Its Symbolism,* "The Idea of the Golem," (New York: Schocken Books, 1965), p. 179.

30. Ibid., pp. 180–81.

31. Ibid., p. 191.

32. Sherwin, "Moral Implications," p. 184.

33. See n. 27.

34. Sherwin, "Moral Implications," pp. 202–203.

35. Ibid.

36. Evers, Translation, 1997.

37. Neil Gillman, *The Death of the Death of God: Resurrection and Immortality in Jewish Thought,* p. 274.

38. Sherwin concludes his presentation to the Chicago Board of Rabbis with the following five statements:

1. Cloning of plants and animals in certain circumstances aimed at improving the health and well-being of human beings is permitted and perhaps obligatory.

2. Cloning of human beings is not necessarily forbidden. There is no explicit *assur*. The Rashba established a principle in Jewish Law that that which is not explicitly forbidden may be considered permitted. Cloning is therefore not forbidden, but is a matter of *reshut*, meaning it is permitted but under certain restrictions.

3. Analogy is a normal practice used to expand legal precedents. Using analogical thinking, we can relate issues of the artificial creation of life to the *golem*. Creation of *golems* is permitted. A *golem* at a certain stage in its development may attain human status.

4. Cloning is a natural phenomenon. As such, technological cloning is not the creation of artificial life but the artificial creation of life. Cloning is not new; what is new is the ability of scientists to control the process of cloning.

5. The cloning or bio-engineering of certain kinds of mixed species like a goat/sheep that has already been done, or a monkey/man would be forbidden by certain biblical restrictions against mixing species.

JEWISH THEOLOGY AS A PRODUCT
OF CULTURAL INTERCOURSE
A History of Jewish Thought in Post-Enlightenment Germany

Walter Homolka

The definition of what "religion" as a term could mean for a specific faith at a specific time depends heavily on the sociological climate in which the theological task is set:[1] "society" and "religion" are in a state of interaction; Jewish theology is highly contextual.

Jewish theology has always been determined by the distinctive social environment in which it developed its particular character. Especially in times of open cultural interchange, one can detect a self-conscious act of intellectual reflection on the content and character of Jewish faith. During the centuries of its biblical and talmudic development, the sort of reflective abstraction and intellectual questioning that are characteristic of philosophy and theology may be less pronounced. But even then, intellectual modification of some sort was a necessary tool to preserve continuity and at the same time allow certain changes.[2] Eugene Borowitz rightly points out that "Jewish theology is the product of social hybridization."[3] One can claim that the dramatic changes in the aftermath of the Enlightenment and the emancipation of European Jewry created a sort of social hybridization to a much more radical extent than ever before.[4] By concentrating on some of the major trends, I will try to present a picture that communicates something of the contextualism of German Jewish theology as a whole and the interaction of Jewish and Christian thinkers from the Age of Enlightenment until after World War II.

THE ENLIGHTENMENT AS THE BEGINNING
OF JEWISH EMANCIPATION AND INTEGRATION

By opening the gates to its environment, itself in the process of intense transformation, the emancipation period had put an end to the Jewish Middle Ages, when over the centuries the impact of time and circumstance on the Jewish spirit can be considered to have been only marginal. Among nineteenth-century German Jews liberal theology was concerned mainly with theological reflection on the integration of Judaism into the framework of modern culture.[5] Legal emancipation presented one paramount task: to prove that the religious value of Judaism was sufficiently strong and unique in character to justify Jewish nonconformity. If the enterprise were to succeed, however, all Jewish theological endeavor to prove this value would have to be judged by two criteria. Theology had to give answers within the modern social situation from which it arose. (We can expect it, therefore, to show certain affinities to the prevalent thought forms and determinative ideas of its non-Jewish surroundings.) Yet the Judaism so conveyed must also remain authentic enough to merit the description "Jewish." Determining what was acceptably modern and yet authentically Jewish turned out to be a substantial task for any Jewish theology that intended to be modern in its time.

The first great theoretician of modern Jewish thought, Moses Mendelssohn, provides us with a good example of the apparent tensions this task created. The content of Mendelssohn's faith is fully modern in its emphasis on the universality and rationality of the human spirit. Yet it also affirms a particularistic and supernatural revelation of the law at Sinai — on which his apparent orthopraxis seems to be based — that would allow no change in the boundaries defined by tradition. Since the two levels cannot be harmonized, the need for integrity makes this approach to truth on two levels unacceptable. Once Kant had established the first of his great critiques, humankind's thinking about the spirit and the soul had changed in such a revolutionary way that Mendelssohn's conception no longer seemed to make sense. The belief in supernatural revelation was no longer accepted, and the ability to prove religious truth by metaphysical means was admitted.[6]

Most Jews of later generations adapted their Jewish observance to this change in an attempt to sustain their affirmation of Judaism during the transition from the ghetto to the social realities of modern life.[7] Despite the departure from tradition, they still felt that they remained faithful to their Jewish past. Their modernization of rite and practice stood in conscious opposition to the way of Jews who adopted Christianity.

In an acceptable Jewish theology, however, this strategy would have to be explained. In this way the demand for an authentic Judaism within changed social and political conditions called for a standard of legitimate modification of the old without loosening the bonds to the religion of their ancestors.

To sum up: Jewish liberal theology in the nineteenth century faced the challenge of integrating Judaism into the framework of modern culture. Jewish society was no longer limited to a more or less segregated life in the ghettos but was offered the chance to partake of all aspects of the social, cultural, and economic life of Christian society. This process of overcoming traditional social limits demanded a new interpretation of Jewish religious life. Jewish nonconformity had to be justified by proving the religious value of Judaism. It was liberal theology that took on this task: Jewish scholars used contemporary scholarship to reinterpret Jewish tradition in a modern way.

WISSENSCHAFT DES JUDENTUMS AND THE HEGELIAN "IDEA"

The earliest strategy for bringing the Jewish Middle Ages to an end was the *Wissenschaft des Judentums* as a historical discipline.[8] In their program for the new learning, Zacharias Frankel[9] and Heinrich Graetz had attempted a history of Jewish law and custom, critical in its methods and based on the model of contemporary scholarship but essentially positive in its appreciation of Jewish tradition. They hoped that once the development of the Jewish "idea" as a historical process had been grasped, its essence would emerge clearly, free of the bonds of tradition that seemed to impede access to the world of modern Europe.[10] This approach, however, failed to do justice to the attempt to delineate the historical reality of Judaism insofar as it was guided by a preconceived idea of what Judaism ought to be in order to meet the standards of nineteenth-century religious thought. In well-known Hegelian fashion society saw the historical process as culminating in the concepts of classical Reform with its "fathers" Samuel Hirsch, Samuel Holdheim, Salomon Formstecher, Ludwig Phillipson, and, above all, Abraham Geiger.[11]

In spite of his professed interest in history, Abraham Geiger's reading of Jewish history was dominated by the motives of his own age. The rise of the modern world was seen as opening up for Jewry many contacts with its environment. In Geiger's view this created the possibility that Judaism could become the classical representative of a religion that was rational and therefore universal. In his idea of an abstract doctrine, the standard according to which Geiger had assessed the epochs of Jewish history, his

46

theology seems — as some critics claimed — somewhat unhistorical and dominated by the spirit of the enlightenment.[12]

The intention of Geiger and his allies was to reduce the possible tension that derived from both religious and national differences *(Dejudaisierung)*. The main theme stayed the same as in Mendelssohn's time: how to retain a distinctive Jewish identity while at the same time attempting to acculturate to a country that defined itself increasingly in national terms.

In the late nineteenth century the naive belief that history manifested the inevitable progress of the "Idea" became more and more problematic and doubtful. Perhaps the most significant reason is that Ranke, Sybel, and Niebuhr introduced a new methodology of historiography that revealed the failure of former historico-philosophical constructs to satisfy the requirements of historical scholarship. Owing to the romantic emphasis on individuality, it also became common to declare that abstract ideas cannot describe particularity.

This downfall of the Hegelian metaphysics of history[13] did much to discredit the classical Jewish Reform theology of the kind Abraham Geiger presented. Geiger and his contemporaries had erred in projecting their own "fundamental idea" *(Grundidee)* of Judaism into their reconstruction of history. They were at least guided, however, by a more or less philosophical concept of Judaism. They also avoided the pitfalls of historicism by bringing to the study of Jewish history a clear, albeit somewhat arbitrary, conception of the ultimate goal and nature of Judaism.

Nonetheless, they did not try to derive a concept of Judaism from a reading of history but read history in the light of a preconceived "idea." They no longer felt the inner connection between *Wissenschaft des Judentums* and the new theology of Judaism that Geiger had conceived to be self-evident.

In its later development the *Wissenschaft des Judentums* lost its sense of purpose and direction, dissipating its energy in detailed research and without a guiding vision that could impart unity to such efforts.[14] Theology, bereft of a philosophical principle to underpin it, ran the danger of moral breakdown.

By contrast, the Breslau conservative program, which combined traditional Jewish law and freedom of research, was designed to obtain genuine contact with the contemporary world without sacrificing authenticity. Leo Baeck, the great Jewish thinker of the twentieth century, should be seen in this line of thought.

LIBERAL JEWISH THEOLOGY AND THE JEWISH NEO-KANTIAN REVIVAL

In the wake of emancipation, the task of Jewish philosophers and theologians was to draw a line beyond which assimilation could not proceed. Nonetheless, explicit Protestant thought had a tremendous influence on Jewish theology. It seems paradoxical that the conflict between German Judaism and Protestantism derived from a shared set of values and common political goals, a rather similar set of aesthetics, and a common way of life. This created a peculiar and ambivalent situation in the decades around 1900, when the affinity of Jewish thought for the Protestant Zeitgeist appeared to be symptomatic of liberal Judaism in general and included close friendships between representatives of the two camps.[15]

Under the Second German Empire liberal Protestantism, in particular, saw a profound change.[16] Both the institutional framework of the church and its social organizations saw a decline in both dedication and quantity. Yet, liberal Protestantism became an important pillar of Imperial Germany's nationalism, and it shaped the way of life of the intelligentsia and the upper middle class *(Bildungsbürgertum)*.[17] Rudolf von Bennigsen, the leader of the Protestant League *(Protestantenverein)* and one of the leaders of the National Liberals, described this new orientation:

> As originally conceived, Protestantism was separate from political life. Yet already in Luther's time it had become clear that just as the German states could not exist without Protestantism, so this religion could not exist in a political vacuum.
>
> Now, since the formulation of the spiritual foundations of liberal Protestantism, it has become even more evident that "Christianity is not merely a matter of sermons; ...it is a part of the 'personality-idea' *[Persönlichkeitsidee]* inherent in the concept of German national citizenship...."[18]

At the turn of the century, Martin Rade, one of the liberal Protestant leaders of the Second Reich and editor of their main weekly, *Christliche Welt,* critically defined liberal Protestantism as a system of opinions and beliefs that had turned from a religion into a science and then into a secular theology that was fully capable of serving as the main support of the new German nationalism:

> Liberal Protestantism has been transformed from a religious to a secular ideology with a religious aura, and from a framework for the beliefs of individuals to a framework for a national culture with an aura of holiness....

> Today this is the ideology of the German nationalist, of the German intelligentsia and of all who rise up against atheistic socialism, on the one hand, and against conservative clericalism, on the other....[19]

This also meant a profound change of perspective within the organized Jewish community in the Second Empire. From the beginnings of liberal Protestantism until the 1880s, many German Jews had believed that this movement safeguarded the realization of Jewish legal and social emancipation. Already, Schleiermacher's *"Briefe bei Gelegenheit der politisch-theologischen Aufgabe und des Sendschreibens jüdischer Hausväter, von einem Prediger außerhalb Berlin"* had shown the intention of liberal Protestantism to establish an independence of civil liberties from baptism into the Christian Church.[20] Rabbi Joseph Eschelbacher expressed this attitude even as late as 1884, when he stated:

> The conservative Protestants constitute at once a social, political, economic and religious bloc that is closed to the social integration of German Jewry.., whereas the liberal Protestants...together with the Jews of Germany...are proponents of the Constitutional State *[Rechtsstaat]* founded upon the principle of natural and secular law, upon that rationalism that is shared by all mankind...and upon the equality of all men, an equality not dependent upon ethnic origins or the religious faith of the individual.[21]

The Protestant section of the population was considered to represent the more advanced tendencies in cultural, scientific technical, and political life. For obvious reasons this attracted the sympathies of Jewish intellectuals. This is why the theological argument to preserve Jewish separatism had to be established mainly against *liberal* Protestantism. It was Martin Phillipson, another major Jewish spokesperson, who asserted in 1903 that liberal Protestantism was likely

> to prove extremely dangerous to the continued existence of a Jewish community seeking to attain full integration within German society without, at the same time, ceasing to be Jewish...for, following in the footsteps of Professor Theodor Mommsen, they demand of us that we give up our Jewish distinctiveness, both spiritual and communal....
>
> Furthermore, from their viewpoint, equality *[Gleichheit]* does not mean that all men are of equal value and consequently have the right to be different from one another...[but rather] for the liberal Protestants and the liberal nationalists, equality means equalization *[Gleichmacherei]*...and, moreover, equalization within the framework of Christian society. This is a framework that threatens us as a new Leviathan.[22]

After Adolf von Harnack published his lectures *What Is Christianity?* at the beginning of the twentieth century,[23] the leaders of German Jewry came to realize that the liberals' insistence on the separation of church and state by no means indicated any willingness to dispense with the establishment of an authoritative Christian ethic and a publicly Christian conduct of life.[24] Harnack and Ernst Troeltsch claimed it was the great achievement of the Lutheran Reformation and, to an even greater degree, modern Protestantism, including Pietism, to encourage the view that the Gospel provided no straightforward answers to the problems of everyday politics.

The state operates within its own moral framework. This morality, however, was seen as rooted in Christianity, so that the nationalism of the Second Empire could appear to be essentially

Protestant nationalism, and even the glory of the fatherland could be seen as essentially Christian in character.[25]

The Jewish answer was clear: such a liberalism would be a despotism of unification, and it could definitely lead to the suppression of individualism and the freedom of religion and conscience. It would encourage the individual to abandon individual ethical values, until finally a "political-social mush of the masses" *(politsch-sozialer Brei aus den Menschenmassen)* would result.[26]

Beyond this vital yet tactical question of separation of church and state lay the deeper difference that theological thought derived from Martin Luther's emphasis on faith. This did not foster sympathy with a people shaped and preserved by the belief in an everlasting divine commandment.[27] There was a certain amount of overlap, however, in the conscious association of values of faith with human activities in this world. Conservative neo-Lutheranism claimed its spiritual inheritance as the very root of culture and civilization.[28] One result of this tendency of bringing faith into the modern world was the interpretation of Kant's autonomous ethics as a specifically Protestant teaching.

Hegelianism no longer provided the basic framework for ideological debate between liberal Protestants and liberal Jews. Rather, historical research and the neo-Kantian ethics laid the foundation for both a new convergence and a new rivalry between the two camps. Interestingly enough, it was usually Jews, in philosophy as in politics, who argued in favor of a return to Kant.[29] During the 1870s, when neo-Kantianism in philosophy and Protestant theology was only in its beginnings, the Breslau rabbi and teacher at the Theological Seminary,[30] Manuel Joel, declared the Königsberg thinker's critical philosophy to be the given basis for the theoretical understanding of monotheistic religion.[31]

On the intellectual stage, in this critical situation Hermann Cohen had attempted to carry out this program philosophically and — in Jewish terms — to restore the "infinite" gap between ideality and reality, *noumenon* and *phenomenon*. Through his influence twentieth-century Jewish theology in Germany was able to liberate itself from a sterile historicism and recovered the almost lost domain of the absolute, of truth, and of faith in a truth by allying itself to the revival of Kantian thought.[32] Cohen, however, did not primarily intend to offer an apology for religion. He must be seen as a philosopher for whom intellectual and academic concerns were paramount. This makes his achievement of a new philosophy of Judaism even more remarkable.

Cohen went on to elaborate the Kantian concept that ethics provide the key to understanding human beings and organizing society. Duty itself, not its fulfillment, is at the heart of humanity's existence. It is an eternal task whose accomplishment grows steadily in reality yet remains infinitely distant and incomplete.[33] That task must nevertheless be carried out in the real world. Otherwise, it would remain on a purely conceptual or imaginative level.

If the ethical task is to be accomplished, however, the ethical domain has to be linked to nature. Continuity is achieved only if the system contains an idea that transcends both the realm of ethics and the realm of nature so that they can maintain their respective integrity and individual structures but that is comprehensive enough to establish a harmonious relation between the two realms. This makes the idea of God a rational necessity for Cohen's system: a God who is one and unique and has primary significance for humankind by being the foundation and the rationale of ethics.

Thus, in *Religion der Vernunft aus den Quellen des Judentums,*[34] the permanent ingredients of Judaism can be identified: its ethics and its understanding of God are considered its lasting and unique characteristics. Judaism is presented as the classic representation of the religion of reason. Cohen recognizes the need for ceremony and ritual; that is, the bulk of nonethical commandments of the tradition *(Ritualgesetze).* But certainly any such acts are of lesser importance when compared to ethical duty. Ethics, according to the neo-Kantians, enabled humankind to order life according to an a priori system of principles. Cohen's criterion of continuity in change becomes apparent: ethical duty is paramount, whereas nonethical activities might be valuable or useful but not permanently or absolutely obligatory. The uniqueness of Judaism is based on the importance that ethical monotheism enjoys.

Defining ethical monotheism as the center of Jewish faith also opens up the possibility of declaring Judaism superior to Christianity. God's unity and uniqueness appear to be compromised by the Christian doctrines of the Trinity and the Incarnation. And although Christianity certainly incorporates a specific morality, it seems to have been marginalized by the predominant emphasis on faith.[35]

At the end of the nineteenth century, the executive committee of the *Rabbinerverband Deutschlands* (the association of non-orthodox rabbis in Germany) put it this way:

As long as liberal Protestants continue to adhere to the tradition of the Incarnation, the redeeming power of Jesus, and the abolishment of the Law as a fundamental spiritual and ethical principle,...Christianity will not be free of elements that cannot meet the scrutiny of reason,...and it is our task to contribute freely from the storehouse of pure monotheism — and hence the storehouse of the purest morality — to human culture in general and to our German culture in particular.[36]

To sum up: the neo-Kantian revival was quite successful among Jewish theologians at the turn of the century and beyond. They considered it a proper way to define the Jewish faith in the new situation of the Second German Empire, with its growing nationalistic ideology that expected uniformity above all else.

The implicit attack on the concept of individual responsibility and everyone's ability to shape his or her life, however, did not foster sympathy among a people preserved by the belief in an everlasting divine commandment. Many considered it the task of German Jewry to uphold the concept of individualism and a rational-critical outlook that gave credit to the insight that equality was not at all synonymous with homogeneity and egalitarianism and that freedom could not mean total assimilation into the ambient nationalistic culture.

For modern Jewish theology it meant a twofold reorientation: firstly, a regeneration of the old apologetics under new conditions and, secondly, for the first time, a historico-critical investigation of the origins of Christianity with the intention of relativizing it as a historical phenomenon.[37]

JEWISH THEOLOGY AS A PRODUCT OF CULTURAL INTERCOURSE

FRIEDRICH D.E. SCHLEIERMACHER
AND THE DEVELOPMENT OF HISTORICAL THEOLOGY

The possibility of evaluating religious tradition in its historical context had been opened up by Christian theology itself. From the end of the eighteenth century to the beginning of the nineteenth, liberal Protestantism was essentially an ethical-theological movement and a school of historical theology under the leadership of Friedrich Daniel Ernst Schleiermacher and Christian Baur and, later, within the framework of the *Jüngere Tübinger Schule*.[38] Schleiermacher is most certainly also a source of influence on Jewish theology. Leo Baeck takes great pains to make certain that his reliance on the sense of religious consciousness is not confused with that of Schleiermacher, which is a good reason to think he was not oblivious to his debt. In his *Glaubenslehre* in 1821, Schleiermacher had laid down the fundamental principles from which most later liberal Protestant thought developed its method. He sought to exhibit the kernel of Christian belief as grounded in the experience of a human being's religious consciousness of redemption through Christ. Schleiermacher interpreted religion not in terms of practical reason, but in terms of man's self-consciousness, particularly that self-consciousness that Schleiermacher identifies as religious consciousness. This reliance on religious experience made the conception of the immanence of God the main focus of nineteenth-century theologies.

In the later nineteenth century the theology of Albrecht Ritschl showed less interest in metaphysics but stressed the conquest of nature by the spirit and emphasized the moral content of faith as an essential key for theology.

56

Thus, liberal theology allied itself with the ethical aspirations of nineteenth-century liberal doctrines of historical progress and the need for social reconstruction. Schleiermacher and Ritschl had separated theology from philosophy as natural theology so that theology became "autonomous," but at a high price. Once the principle of the independence of faith from reason was affirmed, a historical theology developed that was then confronted with the crisis of historicism.

JUDAISM AND DIALECTICAL THEOLOGY

In the early 1930s, with the crisis of historicism, the call for an authentic Jewish theology became urgent. The period was one of bewilderment and unrest. It was the time when Karl Jaspers wrote his portrayal of the growing uneasiness and alienation of modern humankind.[39] In 1926, Martin Heidegger published his *Sein und Zeit,* the most authentic and compelling document of secularization, showing a humankind that had lost the sense of eternity and interpreting existence as *Sein zum Tode.* In 1932 Hans Joachim Schoeps expressed this mood of despair in his *Jüdischer Glaube in dieser Zeit.* In his negation of anthropocentric idealism, Schoeps looks like a truly Barthian theologian, introducing only slight modifications to meet Jewish requirements.

Around the same time, Martin Buber convened a meeting of Jewish theologians at the office of the *Reichsvertretung der deutschen Juden* in Berlin. He proposed the publication of an anthology to be titled *Beiträge zu einer jüdischen Theologie* — a book that was never written. Alexander Altmann, however, preserved the proposed Table of Contents:[40]

57

JEWISH THEOLOGY AS A PRODUCT OF CULTURAL INTERCOURSE

I. Distinctions
1. The Problem of Power
   The Claims of the State
   Absolutism of State and Church
   The Relation of Judaism and State and the
   Claim of Absolutism
2. Messianism and Progress in Society
3. Religion and Culture
   True and False Universalism
   Judaism's Mission
Excursus A: Judaism and Dialectical Theology

II. Elements
1. History and Tradition
2. The Double Aspect of Teaching and Law and
   the Role of the Authority of Tradition
3. The Significance of the Bible
   Biblical Scholarship
   Biblical Message
4. Prayer
5. Sin and Atonement
6. Death and Afterlife
Excursus B: The Concept of "System" in Jewish
   Theology

III. Paths
1. Sects and Trends within Judaism
2. Forms and Methods of Jewish Education
3. Theology as a Profession
4. Religious Judaism and its Part in the Solution of the
   Problems of the Age

58

A clear picture emerges, particularly from the first part —
Abgrenzungen (Distinctions) — of the state of Jewish theological
thinking at this stage. In the first place was the question of the
relation between religion and the state. Then, was the problem of
Messianism versus the ideology of progress, which is linked with
the problem of religion and culture. The liberal theology of the historical school culminating in Harnack's account of Christianity had
left a spiritual void and called forth the "theocentric theology" of
Erich Schaeder, Tillich's doctrine of *Kairos,* and the "Dialectic
Theology" of a Karl Barth and a Friedrich Gogarten. Dialectical
theology deeply undermined the liberal concept of religion as one
of the elements of culture *(Kulturprotestantismus)*. It had expressed
the view that the crisis of modern humanity resulted from the abso-
luteness with which it had invested culture. In the place of human-
made culture it put the Word of God.

This radical questioning of culture constituted a challenge
to both liberal and orthodox Jewish theology. A belief in the religious value of human culture had been deeply ingrained in Jewish
thinking. Hence, it became necessary to examine the question
posed by dialectical theology from a Jewish point of view.[41]

Leo Baeck, whose work still influences contemporary
Jewish thought, undertook the task of defending liberalism against
dialectical theology. In 1932, in an essay titled *Theologie und
Geschichte,*[42] Baeck expressed his own view of the legitimate possibilities of a Jewish theology. Turning to the particular project of
a Jewish theology, Baeck warned against transferring to Judaism
theological concepts, terminology, and methods peculiar to Christianity.[43] These would undoubtedly distort any description of Judaism, just as Adolf von Harnack, his contemporary, had pointed out
in dealing with the Catholic Church and Gnosticism:

> To encounter our enemy's thesis by setting up others one by
> one, is to change over to his ground.[44]

For Baeck, the two elements of Revelation and Church constitute the nature of theology in Protestantism. Critical reflection on the Word that constitutes the Church is interpreted as the main function of theology. Baeck insists that this notion has no comparable validity in Judaism. Since Judaism does not know dogmas in the accepted sense of the word, Jewish theology has to be undogmatic.[45] It can be a theology only of its teachers, not the theology of a Church administering the symbols of the Faith. Hence, Baeck's definition of a Jewish theology interprets it as "reflection" *(Besinnung)* not on the Word of Revelation but on the history and tradition of Judaism. The concern of a Jewish theology is not recourse to revelation but to the Jewish idea, the eternal task, the way, the future.

In this sense, Baeck claims, Judaism can remain true to its history and yet can overcome the pitfalls of historicism. It avoids historicism by seeking the abiding element, the specific character, the essence and idea of Judaism. And it does full justice to history by discovering this idea in the actual field of history and tradition. Baeck uses the following formula:

> The teaching of Judaism is its history, and its history is at the
> same time its teaching.[46]

This calls to mind Franz Rosenzweig's thesis, "The history of the Jewish people is God's revelation."[47] Baeck, however, opposes any traditional notion of chosenness. All human beings can know God, and some everywhere do. The Jews were chosen only in the sense that when they were confronted with God's command to be human as all people are, they chose to respond as a people.[48]

But it should not surprise us too much: Baeck shares quite a few analogies of thought with the existentialist branch of neo-Kantianism. We can trace both to the same root: Hermann Cohen. Leo Baeck's cast of mind is in many ways different from Cohen's, yet it bears the unmistakable signs of Cohen's influence.[49] It is remarkable how often Baeck uses the terminology of Immanuel Kant in the continuation of Jewish neo-Kantianism.[50] He speaks of "moral action" *(sittlichen Handeln),*[51] of "heteronomy" *(Heteronomie),*[52] of striving for "bliss" *(Glückseligkeit)* as an antithesis to "morality" *(Sittlichkeit),*[53] and of "advice for the conscience" *(Gewissensratschlägen),*[54] the "commandments of practical reason" *(Geboten der praktischen Vernunft),*[55] and the "categorical imperative" *(ketegorischen Imperativ).*[56]

This might raise the question of to what extent Baeck is really arguing in full accordance with Jewish rabbinic tradition, though he must first be cleared of the accusation that he argues simply in the philosophical manner of the Enlightenment. Rather, one should say that he uses this system of contemporary thought and its terminology to present his Jewish standpoint. Furthermore, Baeck's addition of a new principle of explanation like religious consciousness to complement the ethical does not actually strengthen the neo-Kantian line. Once anything beyond the Kantian sense of the legitimately rational is admitted as a basis for consideration and judgment, the sufficiency of the neo-Kantian explanation is repudiated. Cohen himself felt a warm friendship for Baeck and saw in him the appropriate successor of his work. Indeed, no other theologian among Cohen's disciples shows a comparable understanding of what Cohen's idea of the "eternal task" means in terms of religious thinking. It is the axis around which Baeck's own highly personal thinking revolves.

Nonetheless, to the devout there remains an unbearable distance between what philosophy says religion ought to be and what religion knows as its reality. Against the neo-Kantian background Baeck now introduced the subjective level of religion as experienced and interpreted by Jewish believers into his explanation of Judaism. Whether he ever openly admitted this major methodological departure is another matter. Baeck was incapable of joining the existentialists under Rosenzweig's leadership and of going along with their audacious and, at times, risky explorations. He remained too indebted to Cohen for that, but he nevertheless transcended Cohen's conceptuality in using Schleiermacher's category of religious self-consciousness:

> Divine love, this all-embracing divine attribute, is paralleled within man by a basic religious feeling that is the inmost source of all faith and all religious sentiment, all receptivity and openness toward God. It is humility, which is nothing else than the awareness of the immeasurable Divine love.... It combines apparent opposites...the feeling of standing before God as little and insignificant, and without merit; but also the firm personal confidence that one is God's child in Whom one has the rock and support of existence; that one can always hope for His kindness – to be unutterably insignificant before God and yet also unutterably great through Him.[57]

Religious experience testifies to what lies beyond the ethical, to the God who has the right to issue imperatives and make them categorical. Reason cannot reach such a realm, as powerful as it may be in all other ways. It should not be surprising, therefore, that paradox and dialectic are major motifs in Baeck's thinking. Cohen's idealism lives on more strikingly[58] in Baeck's dissociation from Schleiermacher's religion "as absolute dependence"[59] But for Baeck ethics without this mysterious root in God is mere moralism. Reason cannot touch this root, but it is nevertheless present in the consciousness of the faithful believer.

We know from his biography that between 1941 and 1944 Hitler's devastating regime resulted in a severe hiatus in Baeck's literary activity. Yet, even in the concentration camp of Theresienstadt, where he stayed from 1943 to 1944, Baeck did not stop working. What emerged were two volumes titled *This People: Jewish Existence.*[60] In *This People* he replaced the concept of "essence" with that of "existence." The Jewish religious tradition appears no longer as a mere phenomenon in the history of ideas but as the very expression of the uniqueness of the people. Baeck had previously pointed out the uniqueness of ethical monotheism as some revolutionary force that broke into the world constituting a "revelation." Now, he describes the historical appearance of this people as something quite extraordinary, as *"ein Einmaliges."* A particularistic touch prevails. In Baeck's theology "nation" was a part from the very beginning. In his search for the idea in the long succession of generations, he counters Harnack's emphasis on the Protestant individual as a wanderer toward a relationship with Jesus. Only the Jewish people, Baeck points out, has the peculiar gift of embracing both mystery and commandment. Jews experience the metaphysical as the "commanding mystery" *(das gebietende Geheimnis).* Seen from this perspective, Jewish mysticism has now become a manifestation of Israel's regenerative power rather than a distortion of the regenerative process.[61]

In his criticism of Baeck in *"Apologetisches Denken,"* Franz Rosenzeig sees the basic dogma of Judaism as the election of Israel.[62] In that, he challenges Baeck's position that there are no dogmas at all in Judaism. This dogma, however, has to be experienced rather than pronounced. Rosenzweig would set this closed-off mystery against christological dogmas. One could live within this mystery without systematizing it. Contrasted with Baeck's early position, his new existential approach touches on the ideas his friend Rosenzweig held.

The experience of the Holocaust changed Leo Baeck's position. His work is a true witness of the development of Jewish theology in the twentieth century: from the denial of the uniqueness and essential otherness of the Jew toward a reaffirmation of Jewish uniqueness in metaphysical terms. How the issue shifted from the "essence" to the "existence" of Judaism will have to be investigated.

MODERN JEWISH THEOLOGY AND THE POSSIBILITIES OF INTERFAITH DIALOGUE

Affinity and division had been the striking features in the relation of liberal Protestantism and liberal Judaism on the way toward a democratic and pluralistic society. Both groups sought to reinterpret their religious traditions using reason and scholarly investigation as their criteria. Both clothed their new interpretations in traditional garments, nevertheless, and cited traditional authorities to support their claims.[63] Both liberal Protestants and liberal Jews sought a way to combine tradition with the liberal concept of history as a conscious progression toward ethical perfection and monotheism, which provided both a ritual framework for daily life and a cognitive framework for humanism and rationalism. Both liberal Protestantism and liberal Judaism vehemently repudiated those elements of their respective faiths that they considered irrational. They particularly attacked belief in miracles and what they called paralysis by dogma as well as "primitive" and "unaesthetic" rites. For both groups the central focus of religion was now the human being, either as the "spirit of the nation" *(Volksgeist)* or the "soul or the nation" *(Volksseele)*.[64] What intrinsically divided them were two main issues: the superiority of either Judaism or Christianity as a religion and the question of Jewish attempts to gain equality and emancipation within a Protestant Christian state.

Where are Jewish theologians in their relation to Christianity in general and Protestantism in particular? It is true that the Holocaust has considerably diminished the theological rivalry between the two sisters, Church and Synagogue, in their enlightened emanations and brought them closer in understanding and appreciation. Internationally, this has fostered a development of even closer links between modern Jewish theology and other schools of thought. It is good to remember that so often Jewish as well as Christian thinkers have argued on a common philosophical assumption and will probably continue to do so. We can learn from this example that we combat most fiercely those with whom we have most in common.

Leo Baeck, together with Martin Buber and Franz Rosenzweig, ends a period of search for the essentials of Jewish faith in a Hegelian and Kantian fashion that had enormous influence on Jewish spirituality in our time. Until recently one could be considered a good Jew if one believed in God and led a moral life. Baeck and his contemporaries, however, provided a bridge of deeper understanding between the mystical and the rational elements of Jewish tradition that later generations could use to go back and experience anew what their ancestors had known: an existential possibility of knowing God transcending all the sets and systems that could be developed from the institutional side of faith.

What remains of these Jewish endeavors to exercise enduring influence? It is certainly the ethical approach that placed humanity and its autonomous creativity at the focus of attention. It is also the preservation and reappreciation of the emotional and mystical forces that work in Judaism despite the neglect they had suffered in the Age of Enlightenment. And, moreover, we are reminded again of a tendency within Judaism toward moral universalism, a messianic tendency reaching out to all human beings and to all the world.[65]

The task of Reform Jewish theologians today remains much the same as it was in the nineteenth century: to find a balance of continuity and change that, on the one hand, safeguards the authenticity of Jewish religious life and, on the other hand, takes seriously the perception that God is on a journey with His people that will produce new insight into the relationship between Him and His people.

Notes

1.   Wolfhart Pannenberg, *Systematische Theologie 1* (1988).

2.   See, for example, Walter Homolka, *Der Midrasch der Pessach-Haggada: Untersuchung zur theologischen Wirkungsgeschichte biblischer Texte am Beispiel der jüdischen Sederbelehrung*, Munich University Thesis (unpubl.), 1986.

3.   Eugene. B. Borowitz, *A New Jewish Theology in the Making* (Philadelphia, 1968), p. 72.

4.   See Robert Weltsch, "Die schleichende Krise in der jüdischen Identität," and Pinchas E. Rosenbluth,"Die geistigen und religiösen Strömungen in der deutschen Judenheit," both in *Juden im Wilhelminischen Deutschland: 1890–1914*, Werner E. Mosse, ed., (Tubingen, 1976).

5.   Hans Liebeschütz, "Jewish Thought and its German Background," in *Leo Baeck Institute Year Book* 1 (1956).

6.   See Julius Guttmann, *Die Philosophie des Judentums*, 1st ed. of the reprint (Wiesbaden, 1985), p. 317.

7.   Morris Lazarus, *Ethik des Judentums* 1 (Berlin, 1904): §87: "Every age is justified in disregarding, more, is in duty bound to disregard, the written law whenever reason and conviction demand its nullification." (Also see §52.) Also see Nathan Rotenstreich, *Jewish Philosophy in Modern Times: From Mendelssohn to Rosenzweig* (New York, 1968), p. 45ff.

8.   Kurt Wilhelm, "Zur Einführung in die Wissenschaft des Judentums," and Sinai Ucko, "Geistesgeschichtliche Grundlagen der Wissenschaft des Judentums," both in *Wissenschaft des Judentums im deutschen Sprachbereich*, 2 vols., Kurt Wilhelm (ed.), (Tübingen, 1967).

9.   Frankel is widely respected as the founder of the Conservative Jewish movement. The legacy of his teaching is preserved at the Jewish Theological Seminary, New York.

10.   For many Jews the "entrance ticket" to this world seemed to be baptism, as Heinrich Heine comments on his own decision to convert to Christianity.

11.   Hans Liebeschütz, "Wissenschaft des Judentums und Historismus bei Abraham Geiger," in *Essays Presented to Leo Baeck on the Occasion of his Eightieth Birthday (Festschrift)* (London, 1954).

12.   Emil Fackenheim, *Encounters between Judaism and Modern Philosophy: A Preface to Future Jewish Thought* (Philadelphia, 1973), p. 130.

13.   Which was not at all that complete if one looks at the Hegelian influences within Neokantianism; see Siegfried Marck, "Am Ausgang des jüngeren Neukantianismus," in *Materialien zur Neukantianismus-Diskussion*, Hans-Ludwig Ollig (ed.) (Stuttgart, 1987), p. 19.

14.   For a critique of *Wissenschaft des Judentums*, see Ismar Elbogen, "Neuorientierung unserer Wissenschaft," in *Monatsschrift für Geschichte und Wissenschaft des Judentums* 62: N.S. 26 (1918) and, by the same author, *Ein Jahrundert Wissenschaft des Judentums* (Berlin, 1922).

15.   See Trutz Rendtorff, "Das Verhältnis von liberaler Theologie und Judentum um die Jahrhundertwende," in *Das deutsche Judentum und der Liberalismus (Dokumentation)*, (Sankt Augustin, 1986), pp. 96–112; Max Wiener, *Jüdische Religion im Zeitalter der Emanzipation* (Berlin, 1933); David Bronsen, *Jews and Germans from 1860–1933* (Heidelberg, 1979).

16.   See Karl Kupisch, *Zwischen Idealismus und Massendemokratie: Eine Geschichte der evangelischen Kirche in Deutschland von 1815–1945* (Berlin, 1955).

17.   L. Mueller, "Die Kritik des Protestantismus in der russischen Theologie und Philosophie," in *Hamburger Akademische Rundschau* 3:1 (1948/49), 45ff; Salo W. Baron, *Modern Nationalism and Religion* (New York/Philadelphia, 1960).

18.   Rudolf von Bennigsen, *Der liberale Protestantismus* (Berlin, 1988), p. 1.

19.   *Symposium der Freunde der Christlichen Welt* (Berlin, 1899), pp. 14–18.

20.   See Kurt Nowack, *Schleiermacher und die Emanzipation des Judentums am Ende des 18 Jahrunderts in Preußen* (Berlin, 1984).

21.   Joseph Eschelbacher, "Der konservative Protestantismus und das Judentum," *Verband für Jüdische Geschichte und Literatur (VJGL)* (Berlin, 1898), p. 2.

22.   Martin Phillipson, "Konservative und liberale Protestanten: ein Wort über die Ritschelsche Schule!" *Verband für jüdische Geschichte und Literatur* (Berlin, 1903), p. 4–14.

23.   Adolf von Harnack, *Das Wesen des Christentums* (Leipzig, 1900).

24.   Uriel Tal, "Protestantism and Judaism in Liberal Perspective," in *Christians and Jews in Germany* (Ithaca/London, 1975), p. 221.

25.   Ernst Troeltsch, *Die Bedeutung des Protestantismus für die Weiterentwicklung der modernen Welt* (Munich/Berlin, 1906), p. 32. In 1889 Martin Rade declared, "Through knowledge and understanding of, and belief in, the life of Jesus, and...the first three Gospels, as illuminated by scholarly, philological and historical research,..we will be able to build ethical lives in the spirit of the German nation...." (Martin Rade, *Die "Mission" der Deutsch-Evangelischen Kirche* (Berlin/Leipzig, 1890), p. 1). For an overview of the situation in the Weimar Republic, turn to Kurt Nowack, *Evangelische Kirche und Weimarer Republik: Zum politischen Weg des deutschen Protestantismus weischen 1918 und 1932* (Göttingen/Weimar, 1981).

26.   *Allgemeine Zeitung des Judentums (AZdJ)*, 1872 (23) p. 42.

27.   In contrast to this, the reformed church showed less antagonism toward this part of the legacy of the Hebrew Bible.

28.   See Friedrich-Wilhelm Graf, "Konservatives Kulturluthertum," in *Zeitschrift für Theologie und Kirche* 85 (1988), especially p. 45ff.

29.   To paraphrase Otto Liebmann's famous saying.

30.   In Breslau Joel succeeded Abraham Geiger, by far the most important representative of Protestant influence on Jewish theological ideas.

31.   Manuel Joel, *Religionsphilosophische Zeitfragen in zusammenhängenden Aufsätzen besprochen* (Breslau, 1876), pp. 3ff and 55ff.

32.   Fackenheim, *Encounters*, p. 132f.

33.   Hans Joachim Störig, *Weltgeschichte der Philosophie* (Stuttgart, 1985), p. 543.

34.   Hermann Cohen, *Religion der Vernunft aus den Quellen des Judentums* (Frankfurt/Main, 1919).

35.   Uriel Tal, "Protestantism and Judaism," p. 187.

36.   Martin Rade, *Die "Mission,"* pp. 2–4.

37.   For an overview turn to Walter Jacob, *Christianity through Jewish Eyes* (Cincinnati, 1974).

38.   Uriel Tal, "Liberal Protestantism and the Jews in the Second Reich, 1870–1914," in *Jewish Social Studies* 26 (1964), p. 23.

39.   Karl Jaspers, *Die geistige Situation der Zeit.*

40.   Alexander Altmann, "Theology in Twentieth-Century German Jewry," *Leo Baeck Institute Year Book 1* (1956), pp. 93–216.

41.   See Alexander Altmann, "Zur Auseinandersetzung mit der 'dialektischen Theologie'," in *Monatsschrift für Geschichte und Wissenschaft des Judentums* 79: N.S 43 (1935), pp. 349ff.

42.   In *Bericht der Lehranstalt für die Wissenschaft des Judentums* 49 (1932), pp. 42–54.

43.   Leo Baeck, "Theologie und Geschichte," in *Aus drei Jahrtausenden* (Tübingen, 1958), p. 37. See also the *"Babel und Bibel"* controversy.

44.   Adolf von Harnack, *What Is Christianity?* (Philadelphia, 1986), pp. 207ff.

45.   Leo Baeck, "Besitzt das überlieferte Judentum Dogmen?" in *Monatsschrift für Geschichte und Wissenschaft des Judentums*, Vol. 70, pp. 225–36.

46.   Leo Baeck, "Theologie und Geschichte," p. 39.

47.   See Albert H. Friedlander, *Leo Baeck: Teacher of Theresienstadt* (London, 1973), p. 50.

48.   Borowitz, *New Jewish Theology*, pp. 88ff.

49.   Tal, Protestantism and Judaism, p. 188.

50.   For another example of Jewish-Kantian synthesis, see Friedrich Newöhner, "Isaac Breuer und Kant," in *Neue Zeitschrift für systematische Theologie und Religionsphilosophie* 17 (1975), pp. 142ff and 19 (1977), pp. 172ff.

51.   Immanuel Kant, *Kritik der Urteilskraft*, §29, Allgemeine Anmerkung.

52.   Immanuel Kant, *Grundlegung zur Metaphysik der Sitten* 2 Abschnitt; also *Kritik der praktischen Vernunft*, 1. Teil, 1. Buch, 1. Haupstück, §8, Lehrsatz 4.

53.   Immanuel Kant, *Kritik der reinen Vernunft*, Mehodenlehre, 2. Haupstück, 2. Absatz; also *Kritik der Praktischen Vernunft*, 1. Teil, 1. Buch, 1. Haupstück, §8, Anmerkung 2, and ibid., 1. Teil, 2. Buch, 2. Haupstück, 5; also *Die Religion innerhalb der Grenzen der bloßen Vernunft*, Vorrede zu 1. Aufl., 1. Anmerkung and ibid., 1. Stück, Allgemeine Anmerkungen, 2. Anmerkung, also *Metaphyzik der Sitten*, Einleitung 2.

54.   Immanuel Kant, *Metaphysik der Sitten*, Tugendlehre, Einleitung 12b.

55.   Kant, *Kritik der praktischen Vernunft*, 1. Teil, 1. Buch, 1. Hauptstück, §7, Anmerkung.

56.   Kant, *Kritik der praktischen Vernunft*, 1. Teil, 1. Buch, 1. Hauptstück, §1; also ibid., 1. Teil, Buch., 1. Hauptstück, §7; also *Grundlegung zur Metaphysik*, 1 und 2. Abschnitt.

57.   Leo Baeck, *Das Wesen des Judentums*, 1st Ed. (Berlin, 1905), p. 71: "Der göttlichen Liebe, diesen umfassenden göttlichen Attribute, entspricht im Menschen eine religiöse Grundempfindung als innerster Quell alles Glaubens und aller religiösen Stimmung, aller Empfänglichkeit und Erschlossenheit gegenüber Gott. Es ist die Demut, die nichts anderes ist als das Bewußtsein der unermeßlichen göttlichen Liebe. Wie diese eine Verknüpfung Scheinbarer Gegensätze ist, so auch die Demut. Ganz wie in Gott, der an Liebe unendlich reich ist, es sich eint, daß er der Ehrabendste und doch der Nächste ist, so lebt dem Demütigen in all dem Gefühl, klein, unzulänglich und ohne Verdienst ohne Gott dazustehen, doch auch die fest persönliche Zuversicht, das Kind Gottes zu sein, in ihm den Hort und Fels des Daseins zu haben, auf seine Güte immer wieder hoffen zu können—unsagbar gering vor Gott und doch unsagbar groß durch ihn."

58.   Borowitz, *New Jewish Theology*, p. 79.

59. Baeck, *Wesen des Judentums*, p. 80: "Das ist der große Mangel in Schleiermachers Begriff der Religion, daß er ihr Wesen ausschließlich in dem Gefühl der Abhängigkeit von Gott findet und das ebenso wesentliche Freiheitsmoment in ihr außer Achr läßt...."

60. Leo Baeck, *Dieses Volk: Jüdische Existens,* Vol. 1 (Frankfurt am Main, 1955); Vol. 2 (Frankfurt am Main, 1957).

61. Leo Baeck, *The Essence of Judaism,* 1st ed.

62. Franz Rosenzweig, "Apologetisches Denken," in *Kleinere Schriften* (Berlin, 1937).

63. With regard to Baeck, see Borowitz, *A New Jewish Theology,* p. 86.

64. It was Herder that coined these terms.

65. Leo Baeck, "World Religion and National Religion," in Mordecai Kaplan, *Jubilee Volume* (New York, 1953).

RESPONSE TO DR. WALTER HOMOLKA

Debra Pine

I am honored to respond to Dr. Homolka's fine paper. I share Walter Homolka's reverence for our teacher Walter Jacob. Dr. Homolka wrote, "Jewish theology has always been determined by the distinctive social environment in which it develops its particular character." This is what is most exciting about Jewish theology. At every stage in our history, great Jewish thinkers have wrestled with the ideas of the time. We have attempted to create an understanding of God that fits with our world and with Judaism. I would like to explain some of the wonderful ideas that Dr. Homolka taught us.

German thought focused on idealism. Our own definition of idealism is quite different from the German idealism that Dr. Homolka discussed. When we think of an idealist, we think of Dr. Walter Jacob, someone who lives up to his highest moral ideals and perhaps ignores pragmatics.

Dr. Homolka addressed a different understanding of idealism. In Germany at that time, idealism was a way of understanding what was real in the world. This is the central question in philosophy. How do we know what is real? Other Jews, like the Israelites in the Bible, based everything on their senses. They knew what was real by what they saw and heard. The Israelites saw the Red Sea part; they knew that God's presence was real. For these German thinkers reality could be rationalized. They could understand the world with their rational capabilities. Judaism had to make sense of the rationalism of that time. These thinkers strove to understand God, based not on what they saw and heard in the world, but on what they could deduce from their logical and rational capabilities.

Dr. Homolka introduced us to a number of wonderful German idealist thinkers. The two that I want to talk about briefly are Hermann Cohen and Leo Baeck, who understood God in very different ways. To me, this is the kernel of Jewish theology. We find different thinkers with unique ways of understanding God. Consistent with idealistic thought, Hermann Cohen emphasized that, as Jews, we should have a rationalist approach to God. He spoke of ethical monotheism—not just that we believe in one God, but that God is truly unique. Judaism is based on universal ethical existence. We are correlated with God through our understanding of ethics. The God-idea, a very phrase from the Pittsburgh Platform, brings about a world view within us. To Hermann Cohen, observances simply empower us to be ethical. As Dr. Homolka said, "Ethical duty is paramount, whereas nonethical activities might be valuable or useful but not permanently or absolutely obligatory." For Hermann Cohen universal ethics are at the center of Judaism. Rationality leads us to ethical behavior, an idea that we find central in Reform Judaism today.

For Leo Baeck, the rationalism of Hermann Cohen was not quite enough. He modified that rationalist interpretation to bring us one step further in our understanding of God and German idealist thought. To Leo Baeck, Hermann Cohen's God was logical but too abstract to elicit real piety. The gap between this lofty idea and what we are supposed to do with our everyday lives as Jews was too big. To Leo Baeck, religious experience testifies to what lies beyond the ethical. Baeck took Cohen's understanding of rationalism and added a mystery about God, a mystery of religious consciousness. He created a certain tension with the ethical. Baeck taught that revelation was not just for Jews but for everyone. Our goal as Jews is simply to be human, to live up to ethical commandments. Dr. Homolka discussed how both thinkers addressed Christianity. They found some similarities between the two faiths and pinpointed the differences between them.

Dr. Homolka concludes his paper by saying, "God is on a journey with his people that will produce new insights into the relationship between Him and His people." This journey continues. Reform Jewish theology from the very beginning of our philosophic history is open. Different Jews throughout our history have understood God in very different ways. Just as these post-Enlightenment German thinkers wrestled with the questions and the ideas of their time, it is up to us to struggle with the theological and the philosophical questions that confront us in our own age. Walter Homolka helps us understand how German idealism truly shaped, and continues to shape, Reform Judaism today. Through a very different idealism, Dr. Jacob is bringing liberal Reform Judaism back to Germany. I am very grateful for both idealisms and, truly, for both Walters.

PAPYRUS—ITS HISTORY AND USES

Irene Jacob

Mention the word papyrus and immediately paper comes to mind. Although it was mainly used in ancient times to write on, papyrus was also used to build boats. What better plant to choose to celebrate Walter Jacob's retirement? It is the retirement of a scholar, a plant lover and a traveler. Meeting Walter at the office or relaxing with him at home, it is immediately apparent that he is a papyromaniac and a papyrophogiac.

How else can one connect Walter to the papyrus plant? Let's look at the word Bible. It derives from the major ancient Phoenician port, Byblos, through which papyrus is assumed to have reached Greece from Egypt. The Greeks used papyrus to write books, including "the Book," the Bible. In modern European languages the word Bible has generated a series of words including bibliography, bibliophile, and bibliomania. Surely, this plant is important to a rabbi who has served Rodef Shalom in Pittsburgh, Pennsylvania, for forty-two years. There he has written, studied, and taught Bible, influenced by his grandfather, Benno Jacob, one of the foremost Biblical scholars of the twentieth century.

But the pleasures of life for Walter lie not only in study. What better use of time is there than to "fill up" with new ideas through travel (even if never on a papyrus boat) and through nature. His knowledge of plants goes back to his college summers working for the Forest Service in Montana and as a nature counselor in Georgia. Married to a wife who is a "plant nut," he was the co-creator of the Rodef Shalom Biblical Garden. Unlike most people, he can recognize not only temperate plants, but also tropicals—like the papyrus.

Now, let us turn to the papyrus. It is hard for us to imagine the excitement that must have been stirred by the world's first paper made from papyrus, replacing as it did such bulky writing materials as bone, stone, clay tablets. These were heavy and difficult to transport and store. Writing on them could become expensive because they did not lend themselves to reuse. This meant that they were limited to documents deemed absolutely necessary. Literary forms were restricted to religious texts, royal decrees, or triumphal statements. Commercial use consisted of inventories, bills of sale, and important legal documents—all restricted by the high cost of production and storage. Papyrus changed that drastically.

We will divide this essay into sections on the plant itself, its nonpaper uses, the ancient production of papyrus products, papyrus commerce in ancient and medieval times, and the competition between papyrus and parchment. We will conclude with a summary of the modern papyrus industry.

THE PAPYRUS PLANT

The writing material we call papyrus is made from the white pith contained in the tall stem of the freshwater reed *Cyperus papyrus (Cyperaceae)*, a native of Egypt. It also grew in Israel's upper Jordan Valley, where we find a narrow belt of tropical and semitropical plants.

Its broad root grows horizontally under the mud. Strong, triangular stalks grow to a height of fifteen feet and have a diameter of two to three inches at the base. A tough green rind covers the white pith. At its tip, the stalk splits into an umbel inflorescence with many brown flowers. In the Nile Delta marshlands it often grows in dense thickets. Samples can be found in America in various gardens. Our

Biblical Botanical Garden has some lovely plants, but they are limited in size because we must bring them inside each winter.

The origin of the word "papyrus" is unknown, but it may derive from a late-Egyptian phrase *pa-en-peraa*, material of Pharaoh, perhaps because trade in the writing material was under royal control in the third century B.C.E.[1]

DAILY PEASANT USE OF PAPYRUS

In ancient times the papyrus plant was important in everyday life. Its stalks were used to build huts.[2] It had many practical uses in garments much like ponchos, sandals, and tunic fasteners.[3]

As we can see in pharaonic monuments, in the household papyrus fibers were made into sieves and used for chairs and pillows; they were used as wrapping paper, mummy wrappings, and boxes like those found in King Tut's tomb.[4] Baskets, mats, and coverlets were woven from the fiber.[5] The stalks burned with a pleasant odor and were used as perfume and as incense. They were also used as fuel. They burned fast, however, so they were most frequently used as wicks of lamps.[6] The flowers were used as garlands on statues.

The lower stalk and root, particularly, were a valuable food that could be boiled or baked and served as a good source of starch.[7] The juice of the plant provided a tasty drink, and the reeds could be chewed.

Papyrus was also used as an ingredient in a variety of medicinal recipes and performed well as a bandage.[8]

PAPYRUS BOATS

The prophet Isaiah mentioned that the Ethiopian ambassadors came north "by the sea even in vessels of bulrush upon the waters." This demonstrates that as late as 700 B.C.E. officials made the sea passage of about 100 miles from Pelusium to Gaza in papyrus boats.[9] We also have the biblical passage about Moses and the bulrushes; for both verses biblical commentators consider that the word "papyrus" and not "bulrush" should have been used for the Hebrew word *gomeh*.[10]

Papyrus boats were very buoyant, owing to the internal structure of the pith, which is a network of loose cells that form myriad tiny air pockets. When immersed in water these become flooded only very gradually.[11] Boats comprised three tightly bound bundles of papyrus stems; they had the advantage of being watertight and light. They could be ten meters long[12] and were especially useful for fishing and hunting, as they sailed very quietly. We find them used also as passenger, cargo, and funerary vessels. Tackholm and Drar indicated that they could carry as many as sixteen passengers. The boats could be left in water for only two weeks, however; then they would become waterlogged.[13]

Thor Heyerdahl, the Norwegian ethnologist and author, won fame through his experiments in 1969 and 1970 testing his theory that papyrus boats could sail long distances. He sailed his papyrus boats, the RA 1 and RA 2, twelve-ton oceangoing vessels, across the Atlantic. Obviously, when properly prepared, the boats would last longer.[14]

Nautical use of papyrus must have begun early; it included rope, sails, and caulking as well as the hull.[15] Papyrus stems were used to caulk the seams of wooden ships.[16]

PAPYRUS IN EGYPTIAN ARCHITECTURE

Papyrus was of enormous significance to the Egyptians as we can see from its use in plant motifs. The lotus, water lily *(Nymphaea lotus* and *N. caerulea),* and papyrus were the plants shown most often.[17] The lotus represents Upper Egypt and the papyrus, Lower Egypt. By the first dynasty, the union of the two countries was symbolized by the intertwined stalks of these two plants.

Papyrus columns, bundles of papyrus, are a frequent theme in architecture throughout Egyptian history. The temple of Zoser, which dates back five thousand years, has papyrus columns. Other papyrus columns can be seen in reliefs or wall paintings; such columns usually had a papyrus umbel as the capital.[18]

Papyrus was also a favorite ornament in ancient Egyptian art and can be seen in fans, household furniture, and handles for mirrors.[19] Tutankhamen's scepter was made of wood carved in the form of a papyrus flower head. A papyrus clump can be seen on his furniture, appearing on the gold-plated foot panel of a folding bedstead and on the back of a throne.

HARVESTING

The collection of the papyrus plant was a cottage industry and employed a large number of both men and women through the millennia. Since not all the reeds were suitable for paper production, some were used for other purposes, such as basketry.

Although we have no written description of the papyrus gatherers, we can see them at work in various wall paintings. The perennial plant grew wild, and, initially, for propagation, the collectors relied on the shoots, which regenerated each season. Later, plants were tended specifically for this crop. The harvest itself was carried out between June and September, although it was possible to harvest the plant at any time during the year when farmers were not busy growing other food plants.

The stems, twelve to fifteen feet high, were cut with knives at water level. This allowed regrowth from the rhizome. Harvesters worked from shallow boats or simply waded in the mud. The bundles were then carefully transported to the landing area so as not to bruise them in any way, for this would cause brown spots. They were then tied into sheaves and carried to fabrication areas that lay along the river.[20]

To obtain the pith, after the flower head had been removed the outer green rind was peeled or sliced off. The pith was sliced longitudinally and the strips soaked in water. The slices were laid side by side, with a second layer laid on top at a right angle. This double layer was then gently beaten and pressed together, the two layers sticking together to form a sheet of paper. In his *Natural History,* Pliny the Elder claimed that the muddy properties of the Nile created the bonding agent, but we have since discovered that natural substances within the plant itself provided the adhesive necessary to bind the pressed strips into a single sheet of paper.[21] The surface was then rubbed with a special smoothing instrument and the sheets trimmed to the desired size.

It is rather surprising that the Egyptians have left us no information or paintings that deal with the production of paper or the paper industry. We know that paper was consumed in enormous quantities—millions of rolls annually—especially in the Hellenistic and Roman periods. It has long been assumed that papyrus manufacture was a pharaonic monopoly, since later it was controlled by the Ptolemies,[22] and this may account for the lack of technical information from ancient Egyptian sources. Our sole description comes from Pliny the Elder, who described the process, though as we have seen, not always correctly.

PAPYRUS FACTORIES

We have no direct evidence about papyrus factories; we can only speculate that they must have been situated at various places along the river banks, with Alexandria believed to be the headquarters of the industry. We don't know whether these factories were large or small, or to what extent the state owned them or merely supervised them.

Once it is removed from the water, papyrus must be used quickly, because the pith shrivels and dries in forty-eight hours, especially in Egypt's sunny climate. After that it is useless,[23] so factories had to receive fresh supplies almost daily.

THE INVENTION OF PAPYRUS PAPER

The most inventive use of papyrus, of course, was as writing material. We can only speculate about the date and the manner of the invention of papyrus paper. It probably occurred through the use of papyrus in basketry or the weaving of mats. Strips laid together and then dried presented a good surface for writing, but, of course, that assumed someone literate was at hand. Many of the world's greatest inventions—for example, the leavening of bread—were discovered by just such an accident.

PAPYRUS—ITS HISTORY AND USES

The earliest papyrus paper samples date from a tomb built in 3000 B.C.E. This is rather near the time in which the Upper and Lower Kingdoms united to form Egypt. The need for such a readily available and constantly renewable writing material becomes clear when we think of the administrative problems that faced this new, very large kingdom, which extended over almost two thousand miles from north to south. The administrative tasks were made infinitely easier by the availability of a good, cheap writing material.

We know that the Egyptians had developed a system of writing that was in regular use before the introduction of the first calendar in 4241 B.C.E. Writing probably became widespread somewhat earlier. The methods of papyrus production remained essentially the same for 4,000 years until paper, which originated in China, replaced papyrus in the Arab world after 800 C.E.

QUALITIES OF PAPYRUS

The finest papyrus was made of the heart of the stalk, where the papyrus strips are the longest and widest, to produce a thin, white, smooth, and flexible sheet. It was then possible to write on it without causing any feathering.[24] The Egyptians named this quality of papyrus "hieratica," or sacred, as it was used for holy books and funerary texts as well as for important official documents.

Since we have no classification of paper from ancient Egypt, we have to look to Roman Egypt, which provided ten gradations, some of which permitted writing on both sides.

The cheaper, coarser grades were used for ordinary business transactions and were available to the merchant. The most common form of papyrus paper was used for accounts, schoolboys' exercises, or scrap; the still coarser types were used to wrap parcels. The paper could be reused by sponging off the writing.

The paper industry was probably the largest employer in Roman Egypt, along with food and textile production designed for export. In the Hellenistic and Roman periods, the cost of a blank roll of paper matched or exceeded an ordinary worker's average daily wage. Since the common laborer would not have purchased papyrus in any case, it did not matter if he could afford it.[25]

The original color of freshly prepared papyrus paper was usually depicted in Egyptian paintings as ivory white. Classical authors refer to its whiteness as a valuable quality in fine sheets (hence the care noted earlier not to bruise the bundles during harvesting). The material darkens with age to a yellow-brown. The whiteness was probably obtained by bleaching the sheets in the sun. In storage, a roll could grow mould or rot; when buried, it could be eaten by rodents and insects, particularly white ants. These problems were all present in antiquity.

THE SCRIBE

We have to learn only 26 letters; an Egyptian scribe had to learn 700 hieroglyphics![26] Scribes are usually shown squatting or cross-legged with papyrus in their laps. Statues of scribes were often placed in tombs, along with other images, to care for the deceased. Scribes held high rank in ancient Egypt, a society that valued literacy greatly. Only individuals able to write could serve the nation as administrators. (In Egyptian literature the word for scribe and administrator were the same.) Schools for scribes dated to the period of the Middle Kingdom. One school text read: "Be a scribe. Man decays, his corpse is dust, all his kin perish, but a book makes him remembered through the mouth of its reciter."

Egyptian scribes liked to have themselves depicted with the god of writing, Thoth, usually in his baboon form. Unlike Mesopotamia, where scribes usually came from wealthy families, in Egypt the scribe could come from any class. There was a certain hierarchy among the scribes: at the lowest level were those who dealt with the cattle and grain merchants, but even such people were part of an elite. At the top were the administrators of government, who can be compared with our ministers and high officials. Only the king held higher rank.

Ezra the Scribe was the Jewish spiritual leader of his time. Later Jewish scribes had the status of scholar. The Hebrew term *sofer,* usually used to mean scribe, also means author.

When the New Kingdom was established it brought much more contact with the outside world and thus broadened the intellectual horizon of the Egyptian empire. Many Egyptian scribes became bilingual, especially in the Amarna period, when Akkadian was the diplomatic language.[27] We know almost no details of scribal life—for example, was paper allotted to the scribe or did the person who needed the records or the state purchase it for him?[28]

The scribe wrote with pens made of rush or reed, and always had several pens in reserve, often held behind his ear, usually one for black ink and one for red. The black ink was composed of carbon soot scraped from cooking utensils, and the red ink, of red ocher mixed with gum and water. The inks were ground into cakes with a mortar and pestle and carried in a small bag. As we can see in wall paintings, the scribe held his pens with two fingers, rather than the three fingers we use. Some portraits depict the scribe's tools slung over his shoulder.

The thin reeds were stored in palettes made of wood, ivory, or gold. The palette always had two circular depressions to hold the small cakes of.[29] A tassel or rag was attached to the palette for erasing mistakes, and a small jar of water was kept nearby to dissolve the ink as needed. The scribe had to dip his brush-pen quite often: he could write only from five to nine hieroglyphic characters with each dip of the pen.[30]

PREPARATION OF PAPYRUS BOOKS

The papyrus manufacturer glued the sheets with a natural starch paste into rolls of twenty sheets. Joints generally were glued right over left, which suited the usual direction of writing, since the pen would not be obstructed by the extra overlapping layers of the next sheet.[31] The average length of a sheet during the Middle Kingdom was fifteen to sixteen inches.

The scribe may have received the roll ready to use, or he may have had an apprentice to help him with this task. In a Nineteenth-Dynasty letter a scribe told his apprentice to work hard at his profession rather than share the lot of the soldier, who is "laid out, beaten like a papyrus roll, and violently thrashed."[32]

The preparation of a roll would have involved vigorous action. Sheets could be added or cut off to adjust to the length of the roll; they would then be wound on a stick. The Egyptians did not provide wooden handles for their scrolls, Jews usually did so, and Romans, occasionally.[33] The text was written in a column or a series of columns called *paginae* in Latin, which is the source of our word *page*.

The title of the book and a summary of its contents were sometimes, written on the outside of the scrolls, beginning with the name of the author.[34] Scrolls were stored in ceramic jars, wicker baskets, or wooden boxes and chests. Some Egyptian scroll cases had cords by which they could be carried.

SOME FAMOUS PAPYRI

The modern interest in papyri was a result of the unearthing from the ashes of Herculaneum, Italy, a library of over a thousand papyri. Serious collecting of Egyptian papyri began with the French occupation of Egypt under Napoleon Bonaparte (1798– 1801). A little later, in 1827, two rolls on a mummy at Thebes were bought for Tsar Alexander II of Russia and remain in the Hermitage in St. Petersburg. Such manuscripts were unreadable until 1810, when Thomas Young deciphered demotic, and 1822, when Jean Francois Champollion deciphered hieroglyphic writing.[35]

Very few papyri from the Greek and Roman period are complete; most are small fragments excavated from rubbish heaps. Several Pharaonic rolls have survived intact, however, because they rested in dry cemeteries.[36] Unrolling even perfectly preserved manuscripts that had been undisturbed for millennia naturally presented problems. One technique calls for wrapping them in damp cloth for several hours and then unrolling them in stages. The moisture has to be controlled so as not to affect the ink or any pigment.[37]

The oldest surviving papyrus is a blank roll found in a box in the tomb of Hermaka, an official of the First dynasty. The manufacturing process had already been perfected by this early date, and there is no evidence of any experimentation.[38]

Among papyri of interest for the history of writing is the "Report of Wenamon," which told of the author's mission to purchase timber in the Phoenician port of Byblos during the reign of Ramses XI (ca. 1090–1080 B.C.E). From this report, a typical administrative document, we learn that Egypt exported papyrus. Many papyri deal with the afterlife, and some—like a "Harper's Song" from the New Kingdom—reflect the writer's doubts about any afterlife and recommend making the best of life here on earth.[39]

Other works preserved are astronomical and astrological texts, calendars, magic spells and medical lore. The best-known Egyptian literary work, however, is *The Book of the Dead*. Copies were commissioned by high court officials, temple priests, and wives or daughters of priests who led the temple choir. Later, common folk were able to acquire it, and scribes made stock copies with blank spaces left for the purchaser's name.[40]

Copies of *The Book of the Dead* vary. The Papyrus of Ani, now in the British Museum and dating from the Eighteenth or Nineteenth Dynasty, is beautifully illustrated but full of scribal errors; one chapter was even written twice.

What is the content of these texts? Some describe ceremonies that preceded burial; others contain prayers, spells, confessions, and proclamations of innocence. Some portray the purchaser in his or her existence in the next world alongside the trials and dangers of the world beyond. Instructions are given on how to proceed in the netherworld.[41]

Papyrus scrolls are frequently decorated. Papyrus Ani, for example, obtained in 1888 by E.A.W. Budge, is fifteen inches wide and dates from the Eighteenth Dynasty (1570–1350 B.C.E.). Its writing is enclosed in a double border of two lines of color, the inner one brick red, the outer, dull yellow. It is adorned at intervals with brightly colored pictures illustrating the passage of the deceased and his wife. Thus, we have Ani, the royal scribe and overseer of granaries at Thebes, and his wife, along with representations of many strange gods.[42]

Magical prescriptions are preserved in Papyrus Ebers, which measures nearly sixty-seven feet and dates from the early Eighteenth Dynasty. It was bought in Luxor in 1873 by G. Ebers, after whom it was named. This "medical" or "surgical" papyrus represents a mixture of science, superstition, and magic. The Edwin Smith Surgical Papyrus provides treatments for a fractured skull that include an ostrich egg ground and applied to the fracture, along with some good medical advice.[43]

Other papyri are of a literary nature. One of the best examples of literature of the New Kingdom is the Anastasi Papyrus, now in the British Museum. It dates from the late Nineteenth Dynasty (end of 1300 B.C.E.) and is a sarcastic epistle sent by a high official to a royal scribe. The Papyrus Prisee was compiled in 2650 B.C.E. and presents a collection of Egyptian moral and religious teachings.[44]

A large number of papyri are practical, like the following letter from the mayor of Thebes to his estate agent, Baki (1439– 1413 B.C.E.) This letter was bought in Egypt in 1935 and was in the same condition as when the mayor sent it, with its seal still intact. Obviously, Baki never received it:

> Someone brings you this message to inform you that I will arrive as soon as I have landed [he traveled by boat] in Husechem, in approximately three days. Let me not find fault with your

administration, but let everything be in best order. Besides this, pick for me many plants, lotus flowers and flowers, and also cut 5000 boards [?], and 200 [not clear]. The ship, with which I will arrive, will get them, because you have not hewn any wood this year. You better be careful and not be lazy. If one does not allow you to cut the wood, go to the mayor User from Hu. Also get a shepherd from Kus and Kuhhirten, who are under my control, to cut the wood, together with your people. See to it that the shepherds have milk ready for me in new containers when I arrive. Pay attention, and don't relax. Because I know that you are a lazy one and would even prefer to eat lying down.[45]

JEWISH PAPYRI

Paper is not mentioned in the Bible, since, as we shall see, it became known outside China only at a later date, but the papyrus plant, Hebrew *gomeh,* was mentioned in Exodus 2:3 and Isaiah 18:2. The most ancient Jewish papyri consist of a hundred official and private documents from 450 B.C.E., written in Aramaic in a Jewish military colony on the island of Elephantine in the Nile River. Papyri dating from the Roman occupation have also been found in Dura Europus. A small number of Egyptian Aramaic papyri belong to the late Ptolemaic or early Roman period, but very few Hebrew papyri are in existence. The Nash Papyrus, which contains the Hebrew Decalogue and *shema,* and a Hebrew papyrus codex are now in the Cambridge University Library.

PAPYRUS IN THE ANCIENT WORLD OUTSIDE EGYPT

Papyrus was exported from Egypt to Arcadia in 1600 B.C.E., to Phoenicia before 1100 B.C.E., and to Assyria and Palestine by 800 B.C.E. The Greeks were writing on papyrus paper by the sixth century, when they ruled Egypt. As schooled Greeks colonized many Egyptian regions, papyrus production increased greatly. Papyrus, of course, had to compete with parchment for a major part of this period. Parchment could be manufactured anywhere, since its raw material was less geographically restricted than the papyrus plant and so had an advantage, but in many areas it was more difficult to procure and to prepare.

THE HELLENISTIC AND ROMAN EMPIRES

Papyrus continued to be produced in Egypt throughout the Greek period, which began in 332 B.C.E. In classical and late antiquity, Egypt supplied the entire Mediterranean area with papyrus. Hellenistic and Roman Egypt consumed millions of rolls each year. When the Romans conquered Egypt they carried papyrus into other Mediterranean regions and made it the principal writing material of the area. It was used not only for books, but commonly for domestic purposes and legal documents, as well, as mentioned earlier.

FROM SCROLL TO CODEX

The employment of the codex, which is the modern form of the book, can be traced to 100 B.C.E. By the time of Constantius II (337–361 C.E.), this was the common form of written documents, so Constantius instructed the scribes of the Pergamon library to copy the texts that were preserved on papyrus rolls onto parchment codices.[46] Papyrus scrolls continued to be used in Byzantium until 1100 C.E.[47] The scroll was less convenient than the book, especially when used for biblical references. It was not necessary to unroll a long document, and, furthermore, the codex was easier to store. The earliest Christian Bible codices, which came from Egypt, were written on papyrus.

A codex was generally made of a series of papyrus or parchment sheets folded in the middle, producing a sort of pamphlet, much like the modern book. Papyrus codices were prepared with their quires gathered first for binding, then written on. The sizes varied from fifty-six sheets to as many as one hundred twelve, but the usual number was ten to twelve. There was usually one column per page, much like a modern book. Papyrus was less suitable than parchment for a bound codex because of its brittleness when sewn and folded, and many old paper codices had to be reinforced at the spine with parchment.

Papyrus sheets in book or codex form were found mainly later, in the Hellenistic period. For many centuries scrolls and books coexisted. The growth of the codex came about primarily through the growth of Christianity: the church preferred it. Papyrus did not disappear altogether from the European continent, however. A few works were written on it in the sixth century, and it was still used for official documents by the Merovingian kings of France. The last Papal bull written on papyrus was in 1057.[48]

PAPYRUS IN THE MEDIEVAL PERIOD

By 641 C.E. the Arabs had conquered Egypt, and papyrus was exported to central France, Italy, Turkey, and Spain until the

end of 1100 C.E. Then the use of papyrus for paper almost ceased, to be replaced by parchment and rag paper. By 800 C.E. paper made of linen thread had already been introduced into Egypt. The manufacture of paper was presumed to have been discovered by Ta'ai Loun in China circa 105 C.E.; in 751 C.E. the Arabs in Samarkand forced Chinese war prisoners to explain the method of preparing paper from rags and cotton. Linen paper dominated the industry until the middle of the nineteenth century, when it was replaced by cellulose.

PAPYRUS TODAY

In the late nineteenth century the growing of papyrus in Egypt was revived, but because the plant needs much fresh water, which was in limited supply in the densely populated Delta, the attempt was short-lived. Today, two institutions produce papyri for the tourist trade and export: The Papyrus Institute and Museum of H. Ragab in Alexandria, Egypt, and the Corrado Basile Museum in Syracuse, Sicily.[49] Purchasers should be wary, as some papyrus is imitation and is actually made of banana leaves, which is less smooth; sheets are often available from artist supply houses.

Notes

1.   Richard Parkinson and Stephen Quirke, *Papyrus* (London: British Museum Press, 1995), p. 11.

2.   Naphtali Lewis, *Papyrus in Classical Antiquity* (Oxford: Clarendon Press, 1974), p. 31.

3.   Ibid., p. 28.

4.   Ibid., pp. 27, 29.

5.   Ibid., p. 25.

6.   Ibid., p. 20.

7.   Ibid., p. 22.

8.   Ibid., p. 26.

9.   Isaiah 18:2; Vivi Tackholm and Mohammed Drar, *Flora of Egypt* (Koenigstein: Otto Koeltz, 1973), pp. 114–115.

10.   Exodus 11:3.

11.   F. Nigel Heppner, *Pharaoh's Flowers* (London: HMSO Publication, 1990), p. 30.

12.   Tackholm and Drar, p. 116.

13.   Ibid., p. 117.

14.   Thor Heyerdahl, *The Tigris Expedition* (London: Unwin, 1982), Introduction.

15.   Lewis, p. 28.

16.   Tackholm and Drar, p. 117.

17.   Heppner, p. 11.

18.   Tackholm and Drar, p. 111.

19.   Ibid., p. 112.

20.   Lewis, p. 112.

21.   Pliny the Elder, *Natural History* (Boston: Harvard University Press, 1924), Book 13, Chap. 23, v. 77; Lewis, pp. 47–49.

22.   Leila Avrin, *Scribes, Script, and Books* (Chicago: American Library Association, 1991), p. 87.

23.   Lewis, p. 115.

24.   David Diringer, *The Book before Printing* (New York: Dover Publications, 1982), p. 134.

25.   Avrin, p. 87.

26.   Ibid., p. 91.

27. Ibid., p. 93.

28. Parkinson and Quirke, p. 19.

29. Avrin, p. 89.

30. Ibid., p. 90.

31. Parkinson and Quirke, p. 15.

32. Ibid.

33. Avrin, p. 86.

34. Ibid., p. 91.

35. Parkinson and Quirke, p. 73.

36. Ibid., p. 76.

37. Ibid., p. 77.

38. Ibid., p. 17.

39. Avrin, p. 93.

40. Ibid., p. 94.

41. Ibid., p. 94.

42. Diringer, p. 146.

43. Ibid., p. 121.

44. Ibid., p. 144.

45. A. Schlott, *Schrift und Schreiber im Alten Ägypten* (Munich: C.H. Beck, 1989), p. 72.

46. Parkinson, p. 72.

47. Ibid.

48. Avrin, p. 174.

49. Parkinson and Quirke, p. 83.

PROPHETIC JUDAISM WITHOUT PROPHETS

W. Gunther Plaut

The long association that my dear friend and colleague Rabbi Dr. Walter Jacob has had with Rodef Shalom encouraged me to begin my contribution to today's symposium by touching on some aspects of the Temple's history. Let me start with a lighter comment.

The name *Rodef Shalom* clearly denotes that the synagogue was most likely the result of a split in the original congregation. In most communities the name *Shalom* or Temple *Shalom* is usually attached to the congregation that splits away, and I understand that such was the case with this Rodef Shalom as well. I further conclude that the quarrel must have been bitter, for the secessionist party saw itself as a veritable *rodef shalom,* chasing after peace.

No wonder, therefore, that one of the early functionaries of the congregation, back in 1854, was a Rev. Armhold, whose name was an interesting wrestling term. Anyone called "Armhold" could doubtless keep his pugnacious members under control and was probably just the right kind of man for his multifarious responsibilities, for he had to act as *hazan, shochet, melammed,* and *mohel.* Such combination was the custom in those days, and Holy Blossom Temple in Toronto (founded at about the same time as Rodef Shalom) also had as one of its first ministers a gentleman whose duties were exactly the same as those of Rev. Armhold. His name was Goldberg, and he came from Buffalo.

Although the early minutes of Rodef Shalom are missing, and the historian cannot find out the reason why Mr. Armhold left his employ, the minutes of Holy Blossom are in good shape and show that Mr. Goldberg had become the target of complaints launched against him because of his circumcisions. The Temple struck a committee to see how well or poorly he performed these delicate operations, and the minutes say the following about the findings of the committee: "Rev. Goldberg, when he performs circumcisions, is more like a *shochet.*" The report, not surprisingly, led to the discontinuance of Mr. Goldberg's services. Let me speculate that Rev. Armhold left Rodef Shalom for more ordinary reasons.

In any case, the Pittsburgh temple went on to play a leading role in the history of Reform Judaism, as did the city; and I now turn to certain aspects of Reform development during the years since the Pittsburgh Platform was fashioned one hundred twelve years ago. Incidentally, the representative of the congregation, who played the host at the time, was Rabbi Lippmann Mayer, who can be said to have assisted his colleagues in the metaphoric circumcision of the *Halakhah,* the body of rules for Jewish life that the assembled committee of fifteen rabbis considered contrary to the modern spirit. In its place the creators of the Pittsburgh Platform put what was then and later on called "Prophetic Judaism." In their view the real future of Judaism lay with the religious ideals of the prophets of yore. They often quoted Isaiah, Jeremiah, Amos, Hosea, Micah, Zechariah, and their colleagues to buttress the Reformers' concern for social justice. They loved Isaiah when he said in God's name:

> Is this the fast I have chosen? A day of self-infliction?
> Bowing your head like a reed, And covering yourself with sackcloth and ashes?
> Is this what you call a fast? A day acceptable to the Eternal?
> Is not *this the fast* that I have chosen: to unlock the shackles of injustice....[1]

They cited Amos as an advocate of racial equality: "Aren't you [Israelites] like the Ethiopians unto Me?[2] The prophet went on to expound his theme that although God had a special love for Israel, this

100

did not give it the right to feel safe and superior. Human equality before God was the core of Prophetic Judaism.

Or take the saying of Zechariah, "Not by might, nor by power, but by My spirit, says the God of Heaven's hosts."[3] It isn't the physiological exercise of power, but rather spiritual strength, that makes for true religiosity. That was the spirit that underlay the Pittsburgh Platform of 1885, and with it went regular references to the prophets of Judaism.

I have looked for a summary expression of Judaism that conveys this vision. The person who wrote and spoke about it most insistently was Emil G. Hirsch, Rabbi of Temple Sinai of Chicago, whose love for social justice expressed itself in vigorous public action. He was the founder of some of the great social institutions of the city of Chicago that have survived to this day. It is worth noting what he wrote nearly a hundred years ago:

> Sacrifices, the phylacteries or talismans, in fact all that Oriental pomp and circumstance which of late days has been urged as a very life air of Judaism cannot show credentials to this distinction when examined before the forum of comparative ethnography....
>
> In what was Judaism original?...[It] was the contribution made to humanity by the prophets. Not sacrifices, not ritual, not holy convocation as such are religious. They are inconsequential, and if urged as final and essential, cease to be religious and sufferable. In the stead of the religion that operates with sacrifices and rites, the Prophets taught a religious view of life and world in which the Holy God could only be revered by holiness on the part of men. And this divine-like holiness of men consists in doing justly, loving mercy, and so forth.[4]

No other religion, says Hirsch, had known of this interpretation. From Israel's seers the larger world learned a revolutionary philosophy, and ethical monotheism was the original and essential content of our faith. Similarly, British liberal Claude G. Montefiore found more to affirm in the prophetic literature than in the Torah.[5]

Social action is still a major preoccupation of our movement, and I am happy to acknowledge this. But I am sad to say, at the same time, that nowadays most social action efforts in our movement are bereft of the prophetic presence. We still call it Prophetic Judaism, but the prophets have left the presence of those who sail under their banner. In part this is the result of the pervasive secularism of the North American cultural scene, which has produced what is often called "America's civil religion." Its reference is the U.S. Constitution, but not God.

This detour, unfortunately, has infected our movement. Where formerly our love affair with social action was grounded in Prophetic Judaism in the literal sense—that is to say, in the knowledge of prophets that invoked the presence of God and proclaimed, "Thus says the Eternal, and God spoke to me saying..." —our modern-day reformers base themselves on other sources. Ask the average member of a Reform congregation in North America about prophets and he/she will more likely think of profits. Prophecy is something that has to do, so it appears, with palm-reading and astrology but not with, "Thus says the Eternal One."

There is a remarkable aspect to this development. The prophets were formerly ever-present on Shabbat morning, because after the Torah reading came the haftarah, and the haftarah was largely prophetic teaching. Today, all too many of our congregations omit the haftarah or no longer have a Shabbat morning service unless they have a Bar/Bat Mitzvah celebration, and consequently—aside from our depletion of worshippers—most members of our congregations never listen to a haftarah save on the High Holy Days. If they hear of Prophetic Judaism they are probably not sure what that term betokens.

Even the social action pronouncements of the Central Conference of American Rabbis during the last fifty or sixty years made few references to the Bible. Instead, their prime inspiration was the American Civil Liberties Union, and it was its authority that was quoted, not that of the biblical prophets. This was one of the reasons I was moved to write a commentary on the haftarot, to let my colleagues and the public know that there is a readily available source book that will undergird the social activism to which we have subscribed and that remains a chief endeavor of our movement. Reform Jews once dwelt proudly in a God-oriented spiritual Garden of Eden, but they have left it, and an angel with a flaming sword stands at the gate and says, "You cannot enter here, you belong elsewhere. You have subscribed to a civil religion that has left God's prophets behind. This Garden is no longer for you."

Does that really matter? It does, indeed, for what the prophets have to say is often incompatible with what North American culture says to us. That culture is highly individualistic, whereas Prophetic Judaism was highly collectivist. North American culture allows each person to determine what is right and wrong, because right and wrong are considered relative. *I* determine what is moral and immoral, which is an attitude that stands in direct opposition to the teachings of the prophets. It is safe to assume that Dr. Solomon Freehof would never have bothered to write his commentaries on Isaiah, Jeremiah, and Ezekiel if he had not been convinced that they were a counterweight to American civil religion. He wrote these books to make it clear to his readers that for the prophets, as for God, there is a right and a wrong, as there is an authentic Judaism. All true religion must in the end be countercultural if need be, and rabbis are there to lead their flocks.

The rediscovery of prophecy, therefore, is for us a religious must. I should like to think that the kind of service that the rabbis of Rodef Shalom have rendered to our movement is an ideal held out before all of us. It has been the seminal teaching of Rabbis Freehof and Jacob that Jewish idealism must have a religious basis and that at the same time there must be boundaries to our behavior, Jewish boundaries, which we call *Halakhah*. That is why both Rabbi Freehof and, following him, Rabbi Jacob—whom we have come to honor this weekend—combined their study of our religious tradition and prophecy with a study of *Halakhah*. They have taught us prescriptions for Jewish living, and this combination of prophecy and *Halakhah* represents to me the acme of Reform Judaism. It is Prophetic Judaism at its best. The prophets railed against inauthentic sacrifice but not against sacrifice, against inauthentic prayer but not against prayer.

Your rabbinic service, Walter, has been devoted to the pursuit of such ideals. It is a heritage worth honoring and, I might stress, worth recovering, because we need the dual recovery of spiritual ideals and Jewish living. Unbounded ideals together with guides for Jewish living have been the core of your ministry and thereby mark the essence as well as the future of Reform Judaism.

Notes

1.   Isaiah 58:5–6.

2.   Amos 9:7.

3.   Zechariah 4:6.

4.   See W.G. Plaut, *The Growth of Reform Judaism* (New York: World Union for Progressive Judaism, 1965), p. 229.

5.   Michael A. Meyer, *Response to Modernity* (Oxford: Oxford University Press, 1988), p. 215; see also Kaufmann Kohler, *Jewish Theology* (New York: Macmillan, 1918), p. 330.

RESPONSE TO RABBI GUNTHER W. PLAUT*

Andrew Busch

It is a great honor not just to speak in tribute. Walter Jacob, but also to respond to Dr. Gunther Plaut. In Dr. Plaut's writings he mentions that he was inspired by the writings of Benno Jacob, Dr. Jacob's grandfather, who was a very prominent and important biblical commentator. Rabbi Plaut's commentary on the Torah was published in 1981. As we began serious study, either before Bar Mitzvah or after, my generation of Reform Jewish rabbis learned to read Torah through the eyes of Rabbi Plaut and through the broad range of views he brought into his commentary.

Allow me just a few words of response to Rabbi Plaut's concern about the lack of knowledge and inspiration from the prophets in contemporary Reform Judaism. He is accurate in talking about issues of secularization and Americanization. Let me suggest one other aspect that, certainly to my generation and to the generation we are now educating in our religious schools, is a very relevant aspect of the distance between Jews today and the books of our prophets. Let me do it by asking two questions: How many of you, when you were going to school, had to memorize a poem? How many of you had to memorize more than ten poems? My father constantly, every year of my schooling, would remind me of the poems he needed to memorize. Memorizing doesn't necessarily mean one learns to relate to something, but it was a step. It was a step that showed the importance of poetry in the educational system in this country in earlier generations. It is something that was absent when I was going to school. America of my generation,

---

*Rabbi Busch's response is to the paper originally prepared by Gunther Plaut, not that submitted for publication.

and of the next generation, is largely distant from poetry, be it our own poetry or be it the poetry of the Bible. When we teach and study about the Torah a lot of material relates well to our congregants and to ourselves. A difficulty arises when we try to reach into the prophets, into sections written largely in poetic form. The distance comes not only from secularization, but also from education, a distance arising from the very form in which those important prophetic messages are written, a largely poetic form.

This became very clear to me during my first year at Hebrew Union College in Jerusalem. T. Carmi, an important Israeli poet, taught the rabbinic students Israeli poetry. It was actually through that experience of Israeli poetry that poetry began to come alive for me. It made it all the easier to approach the books of the prophets themselves. We need to think about that, as we reach out to American Jewry and try to reintroduce them to the works of the prophets. We need to think about reintroducing them to the joys of poetry in general. I hope they will hear the message imbedded in our classical prophets because they will all the better understand and love the form. We might do this through the study of haftarah, or through the study of prophetic passages before we engage in social action projects. Both are possible. One of the aspects we need to consider are the structural blockades in our way. Only then can we step forward to the important challenge that Dr. Plaut has laid before us.

DESTABILIZING THE TALE OF JUDAS ISCARIOT:
A Vehicle for Enhancing Christian-Jewish Understanding

Michael J. Cook[*]

INTRODUCTION

Although not maintaining an especially high profile in Christianity, Judas Iscariot has nonetheless remained conspicuous throughout *Jewish* history. As the disciple of Jesus who presumably betrayed him, Judas has been readily exploited by those wishing to stereotype Jews as traitors, money-grubbers,[1] even agents of Satan.[2] No doubt, the assonance of "Judas" and "Jew" (not to mention their virtually identical spelling in Greek as well as in Hebrew[3]) has aided such endeavor, even suggesting that some equation of the two may have been intended by the Gospel writers themselves.

Anti-Semitic appropriation of Judas's image over the centuries is a subject with which Christians, not just Jews, should be made conversant. A promising opportunity arises each spring, when churches invite Jewish communities to demonstrate the Passover Seder, so commonly misconstrued as the setting of Jesus' Last Supper.[4] Since Matthew presumes Jesus' last meal to have been *Judas*'s also, a presentation of the Seder could readily incorporate some discussion of Judas as well. Christians might thus learn not only about Passover as Jews have come to observe it, but also about the abiding and noxious impact of Judas's image on Christian-Jewish relations even in the current day.

---

[*]I express my appreciation to colleagues Susan Einbinder and David Turner, who were kind enough to comment upon, and improve, this essay. Any error in my argumentation of course remains my responsibility alone.

DESTABILIZING THE TALE OF JUDAS ISCARIOT

THE STORY LINE

Although Paul never mentions him, Judas appears prominently later on, in each of the four Gospels as well as in the opening chapter of Acts. Treatment of him in Mark, the earliest of these accounts, is sparse. Here Judas offers to assist Jewish authorities bent on arresting Jesus. They gladly promise him money in return. During the Last Supper, Jesus predicts that he will be betrayed by one of those present and warns of the traitor's fate. All adjourn thereafter to the Garden of Gethsemane. As Jesus prays, an armed party arrives with Judas at its head (although Judas is nowhere said to have left the disciples' company). Judas kisses Jesus to identify him for the captors. As Jesus is arrested, the other disciples flee. Of Judas's aftermath we learn nothing from Mark.

Lacunae in Mark's account are glaring: What is Judas's motive in betraying Jesus? Of precisely what does the betrayal consist? Why identify Jesus by a kiss rather than simply by pointing him out? What is the meaning of Judas's surname, *Iscariot?*[5]

Not surprisingly, in embellishing Mark, the other Synoptists try plugging some of these gaps. Matthew, guessing avarice as Judas's motive, has Judas ask the authorities up front what his services are worth to them (26:15ff.). But Matthew's surmise is itself problematic: Why so diabolical a deed for a paltry thirty pieces of silver, and why so greedy a man in a company so poor to start with? Admittedly, such puzzlements recede somewhat once Luke (4:13; 22:3) and John (6:70; 13:2,27; 17:12) have *Satan* enter Judas: a person possessed by the Devil now needs less by way of psychological motivation!

Is Judas ever paid as promised or punished as predicted? Matthew tells us that, overwhelmed by remorse, Judas returns the money he received and then hangs himself (27:3ff.). Acts, likewise, reports Judas's death (1:18ff.), but here it is not by suicide; instead, he ruptures himself in a fall[6] (or swells up) and bursts asunder, and his bowels gush out. This disparity—two such incompatible modes of death[7]—has naturally invited desperate conflation: for instance, that as Judas was attempting his hanging the rope snapped, plummeting him to the ground where he exploded upon impact![8] More plausibly, Judas's deed was deemed so dastardly that hanging (as in Matthew) appeared simply too good for him—so worse fates had to be devised. The suggestion in Acts that Judas burst apart, although a seeming "improvement," was still unsatisfying, at least to Papias,[9] for whom Judas's flesh became

> so swollen that where a wagon could pass with ease he was unable to..., not even...his head.... After many torments..., he died on his own property, which...remained...deserted because of the stench, and not even to the present day can one walk by...without holding fast his nose..., so great had been the efflux from [Judas's] flesh upon the ground.[10]

DETERMINING THE BETRAYAL'S HISTORICITY

Embellishments aside, what of the story's nucleus? Is a betrayal of Jesus by Judas authentic history? In the Synoptic Gospels, at least, certain anomalies must detain us, especially the unnatural *passivity* of the other disciples. In Mark (14:19ff.) and Matthew (26:22ff.), when Jesus announces that one of their company will betray him, why do the disciples fail to interfere, seriously investigate, or even say anything of consequence? In Luke (22:23ff.), their behavior

111

seems all the more astounding; here not only do they essentially skirt the issue, but they also embark upon foolish wrangling over who among them will be greatest in the coming kingdom! Jesus himself, for that matter, also behaves oddly: he is relatively mute in Gethsemane as Judas approaches to kiss him (Mark 14:45; Matthew 26:50; Luke 22:48).[11]

Is the story, then, only fiction introduced without sufficient forethought of how to have the cast respond? Or did Christian tradition know an actual betrayal by Judas but just not how Jesus or his disciples dealt with it? Mystery as to Judas's motivation invites similar reflection: does the absence of any stated motive undermine the credibility of the story—or is it just that Judas's act alone was remembered but not his reason for committing it?[12]

Although none of these matters, however vexing, disqualifies Judas's betrayal as authentic history, another consideration is more compelling: the remarkable parallels (in number and substance) between the Judas story and motifs from Jewish Scripture— correspondences so uncanny as to fuel suspicion by some readers that the *entire* episode may be fabricated (i.e., *derived* from these texts).[13] Many correlations echo the story line of King David—as if to suggest that whatever King David experienced transpired thereafter also with Jesus (likewise referred to as David's "son"; cf. Mark 10:47f.; 11:10; 12:35ff. [and parallels]). Thus,

—David's betrayal by a trusted advisor, Ahithophel, who hangs himself (2 Samuel 17:23),[14] could have engendered not only Judas's supposed suicide by hanging (in Matthew) but even the very *nucleus* of the Judas story, especially when considered in conjunction with

112

—(David's) Psalm 41:9, revealing how "even *my bosom friend* [= Ahithophel] in whom I trusted, who *ate of my bread,* has lifted his heel against me" (cf. John 13:18),[15] as well as

—(David's) Psalm 55:12–14, averring that "it is not an enemy who taunts me—then I could bear it.... But it is you... my *companion,* my *familiar friend.*"

—Joab, about to assassinate Amasa (David's preferred general), treacherously takes hold of him as if to *kiss* him (2 Samuel 20:9), even as

—David's son, Solomon (paralleled by Jesus, also "son of David"), informs us (in Proverbs 27:6) concerning "the *kisses* of an *enemy.*"[16]

Correlations of Matthew 27:3–5 with Zechariah 11 seem equally sobering:[17] in the latter,

> —the wages of the shepherd king of Israel (v. 12) are thirty pieces of silver (matching the sum of Judas's blood money),
> —which are (v. 13) hurled into the (temple) treasury (as with Judas's payment in Matthew 27:3ff.).

Of course, we could just as well imagine that an *actual* betrayal by Judas was *subsequently* embellished by recourse to these Jewish scriptural motifs. But the parallels noted remain striking —especially since 2 Samuel 15 (where Ahithophel appears [v. 30]) and the last chapter of Zechariah (14:4) have as their setting the Mount of Olives, site of Jesus' Passion! More determinative, still, could have been the seeming correlation between Judas, one of the twelve, selling his

113

master for silver, and *Judah*—also "one of twelve"—urging the sale of *Joseph* for silver (Genesis 37:26–28; in the Septuagint, of course, Judah is called *Judas*).[18]

ASSESSING FACTORS FAVORING HISTORICITY

Two arguments seem to reassure us that Judas's betrayal of Jesus was factual. Both, however, break down under scrutiny:

(1) Paul's Last Supper Testimony: In the mid-50s C.E., Paul introduces his sole reference to the Last Supper with words commonly translated as "the Lord Jesus on the night when he was *betrayed* took bread..." (1 Corinthians 11:23b). This suggests that Paul is not only familiar with, but also accepting of, the betrayal story. But the ambiguous Greek verb, *paradidonai,* is here virtually always misrepresented. Paul means not that Jesus was "betrayed" but rather that he was "delivered up" or "handed over,"[19] consistent with Paul's regular use of the same verb elsewhere.[20] In all likelihood, the *presumption* that Paul has the betrayal in mind *predetermines* the mistranslation. In this respect, *The New English Bible* is correct in rendering the passage as "the night of [Jesus'] arrest."[21] Should Paul have been thinking of any transferral (of Jesus) at all, he would probably have meant that Jesus was "delivered up" by the arresting party to the High Priest, not by Judas to Jesus' captors!

Another rendering, however, is more compelling still. In Romans 4:25, Paul says that Jesus "was delivered *to death* for our misdeeds,"[22] and arguably this is precisely Paul's intent here, also, in his Last Supper reference: that Jesus took bread on the night when he was delivered to *death* (not delivered by any one party to another).

114

This interpretation seems confirmed by Paul's culminating remark (in 11:26): "for as often as you eat this bread and drink this cup, you proclaim the Lord's *death* until he comes."

To defend the historicity of Judas's betrayal by appeal to Paul's sole Last Supper reference is thus hardly persuasive. Neither here nor elsewhere does Paul make any mention of the betrayal, or even of Judas for that matter.

(2) Embarrassment for the Church: Some defend the historicity of the betrayal by arguing that Christian tradition would not invent a story so damaging to Jesus' image. Around 200 C.E., for example, the pagan Celsus (Origen, *Contra Celsum* 2.11) ridicules the presumably all-knowing Lord of Christianity for having a traitor among his close followers. The Fourth Gospel had struggled valiantly on this score to shore up presumptions of Jesus' omniscience[23] or foreknowledge:[24] John shows Jesus (1) (purposely?) choosing Judas, already knowing well his evil character (6:64–70f.);[25] (2) exposing Judas *in particular* at the Last Supper (13:26);[26] and even (3) stage-cuing Judas as to when to begin his invidious deed (13:27).[27] All along, we are reassured that Jesus "know[s]...all that was to befall him" (John 18:4).

Yet the argument from embarrassment is not compelling, particularly when we consider the earliest Gospel. Why should we zero in here on Judas alone when the behaviors of *other* Marcan disciples also entail levels of betrayal? Haplessly opaque and "hardened of heart,"[28] neither discerning the obvious nor learning from experience, *all* of Jesus' companions coalesce in a most undependable lot. On guard in Gethsemane, Peter, James, and John imperil not only Jesus' life but also their own by falling asleep (and not once but thrice)! Insisting that though the others deny Jesus *he* never will, Peter denies him nonetheless (here, again, not once but three times). It is also Peter (not Judas) whom Jesus calls "Satan" (8:33), and (unlike the case with Judas) *Peter's* cowardly treachery is never requited. The disciples *as a whole* forsake Jesus in Gethsemane, and not one of them shows up to succor him during his agony on the cross.

The primary question thus becomes not how a foreknowing Jesus could have appointed *Judas,* but how he could have appointed *any* of this motley crew! The disappointment in Judas is thus merely *akin* to that in the others, different in degree but not necessarily in kind. If we accept as compelling the arguments of many scholars that *all* these denigrations of the disciples are Marcan inventions[29]—and therefore untrue to history—the embarrassment Judas causes in particular could actually *weaken* the case for the historicity of the betrayal!

TELL-TALE CLUES OF LATE INVENTION

At least three other factors may heighten our skepticism:

(1) How many disciples saw the resurrected Jesus—twelve or only eleven? The earliest New Testament tradition, the kerygma Paul quotes in 1 Corinthians 15:3b–7, affirms that, following resurrection, Jesus "appeared to Cephas, then to the *twelve.* "[30] But surely we are not meant to infer that the "twelve" still included Judas? Had a betrayal actually occurred, how could Christians even have imagined

116

Judas continuing in association with his eleven colleagues, let alone being rewarded along with them by a manifestation of the resurrected Christ? Would it not be more likely that, once Judas left the close fellowship of the followers of Jesus, he simply never returned? For the early tradition to insist on a postresurrection appearance to the *twelve* suggests that a betrayal episode was not yet known.

We may seek refuge, of course, in the tradition from Acts that, at Peter's initiative, Judas was immediately replaced by Matthias. Yet we hear nothing of this Matthias until Acts 1:23–26 (in a work written probably no earlier than the 90s C.E.). Might he be pure fantasy contrived by the author of Acts to allow *continued* reference to Jesus' inner circle as "twelve," only with Judas now no longer among them? Why, moreover, this pretense that the number twelve had to be maintained? Was this the case when any other disciple died or was martyred—why then this procedure in the case of a *betrayer?* Indeed, why record the death of Judas but not that of any other disciple? Since the ranks of the inner circle had been established solely through appointment by the Lord Jesus himself, whence the notion that one could now gain entry by merely *human election,*[31] and how are we to tolerate the scenario of "the traitor Peter arranging for a substitute for the traitor Judas...a monstrosity beyond imagination"?[32]

We could, of course, suppose the mention in the kerygma of "twelve" to be simply *formulaic,* referring to *whatever* number of worthy disciples remained to witness the resurrected Jesus— whether or not, in point of fact, they still numbered exactly twelve. Yet surely this was not the Synoptists' understanding! Indeed, it is precisely because they took "twelve" literally that in all post-resurrection settings they insisted on paring the witnesses down to "eleven" (Table

1). This "careful insistence [especially in Luke, Acts[33]]...that the resurrected Jesus appeared to only eleven disciples suggests...a *contrary* tradition...that needed to be undermined...the earlier tradition which Paul received and handed on" that Jesus had appeared to the *twelve!*[34]

It looks very much, then, as if a fictional betrayal story developed in the *interim* between Paul in the 50s C.E. (who still accepts, unquestioningly, the resurrected Jesus' appearance to the *twelve*) and the Synoptists after 70 C.E. who, in postresurrection settings, overlook no chance to scale the number of witnessing disciples down to eleven so as to prevent us from ever imagining that Judas had rejoined them.

TABLE 1

Mark   16:14 — "Afterward he appeared to the *eleven* themselves as they sat at table; and he upbraided them...because they had not believed those who saw him after he had risen...."

Matthew 28:16 — "Now the *eleven* disciples went to Galilee, to the mountain to which Jesus had directed them. And when they saw him, they worshiped him...."

Luke   24:9 — "And returning from the tomb they told all this to the *eleven*...."

24:33 — "And they found the *eleven* gathered together and those who were with them, who said, 'The Lord has risen indeed, and has appeared to Simon!'"

Acts   1:13 — "They went up to the upper room, where they were staying, [1] Peter and [2] John and [3] James and [4] Andrew, [5] Philip and [6] Thomas, [7] Bartholomew and [8] Matthew, [9] James the son of Alphaeus and [10] Simon the Zealot and [11] Judas the son of James."[35]

1:26 — "And the lot fell on Matthias; and he was enrolled with the *eleven* apostles."

(2) Jesus' contradictory intentions for Judas's future: Mark and Matthew cast Jesus as predicting, during the Last Supper, the direst future for his betrayer ("it would have been better for that man if he had not been born" [Mark 14:21; Matthew 26:24]). Yet, elsewhere in Matthew, Jesus also informs *all twelve* disciples: "In the new world, when the Son of man shall sit on his glorious throne, you who have followed me will also sit on *twelve* thrones judging the *twelve* tribes of Israel" (19:28). By envisioning *each* of the twelve disciples as such a judge over Israel (with the judges, in number, matching the tribes), Jesus here appears to be reserving one judgeship for Judas as well![36]

Which of these conflicting destinies, then, awaits this traitor: torment or honor? Inheriting this dilemma,[37] Luke moves to confront it. He can hardly pare *twelve* thrones down to *eleven,* for this would leave a bothersome asymmetry: *eleven* disciples on *eleven* thrones judging *twelve* tribes! So Luke simply omits the *number* of thrones altogether (Table 2).

119

TABLE 2

Matthew 19	Luke 22
[28]...in the new world... *you* who have	
	[28]*You* are those who have
followed me	continued with me...;[29]
	...I appoint for you,[30]
will...	that *you* may...in my kingdom....
sit on *twelve* thrones, judging	sit on___thrones judging
the *twelve* tribes of Israel....	the *twelve* tribes of Israel.

Luke's removal of the numeral, however, resolves nothing. Three times Jesus employs the plural "you" (in vv. 28–30) as the referent for who will be judges, and each time he must be including Judas; for but a few passages earlier (v. 21), Judas is obviously present when Jesus announces that "the hand of him who betrays me is with me on the table"; and Judas *remains* present when Jesus now promises judgeships (in v. 30). Whereas in Matthew the offices are promised (19:28) *before* Jesus reveals the betrayal (26:21), in Luke matters are reversed: Jesus reveals the betrayal (22:21) and then by implication offers a judgeship to Judas anyway (22:30)!

It is hard to explain how the *twelve*-judgeship saying could have been preserved to begin with in the face of a historically *genuine* betrayal. Whether this saying is authentic to Jesus' ministry[38] or developed only later, it could have become current only in an environment *as yet* unaware of a betrayal story—i.e., "penned before the stultifying story of the treason of Judas" had come into being.[39] In this respect as well, then, the Judas story appears fictional.

(3) Judas's apparent failure to take leave of the disciples: In the Last Supper scene in Mark, the traitor is not mentioned by name or said to depart the company of Jesus and the other disciples (either during or after the meal). Accordingly, when Jesus adjourns the supper, it appears that everyone, including the betrayer, accompanies him to Gethsemane. How, then, does Judas manage to arrive in Gethsemane at the head of an arresting party whom he has guided *from* wherever they have been in waiting? John alone directly handles the problem—by casting Jesus as stage-directing Judas's departure during the Last Supper itself (13:27–30).

Mark, of course, may simply intend us to assume that, sometime during or after the meal, Judas quietly managed to slip away to rendezvous with the captors and then to lead them to where Jesus was in Gethsemane. Another conjecture, however, is intriguing and plausible: that it is precisely within the Gethsemane scene itself that a betrayal story became interpolated (in its *entirety*) into an earlier body of tradition knowing no such incident! Thereafter, so as to lay the groundwork for what was coming, Mark manufactured the *preparatory* episodes of Judas conferring with the chief priests and of Jesus "predicting" the betrayal at the Last Supper.[40] On this basis, Mark's failure to specify Judas's departure, either during that meal or later, stands exposed as an editorial oversight—also a tell-tale clue of how the story was expanded under Mark!

Interesting in this regard is the fact that the clause (in 14:18) introducing the betrayal in Mark's Last Supper scene (*"and as they were...eating* [Jesus announced the betrayal]") is echoed almost identically, with no narrative need, but four verses later (*"and as they were eating* [Jesus took bread]"). This undue repetition may point to a still visible seam where new material has been spliced into already received tradition, "a double use of the catchword, which reveals the process of interpolation deliberately gone about."[41] The "first" item, Jesus' prediction of the betrayal, now appears secondary, intruded into an *already established* Last Supper narrative[42] initially knowing no betrayal announcement! When Matthew splices an obviously later Judas element (27:3–10) into earlier material, a similar dynamic of repetition (by v. 11 of v. 2[43]) comes about.

This series of conjectures may also explain why, as "late" as Gethsemane, Mark is still identifying Judas as "one of the twelve" (v. 43). Does Mark presume we are forgetful? Why restate what we ostensibly heard as recently as 14:10 and 20 (not to mention as early as 3:19)? "One of the twelve," admittedly, could simply be a formulaic refrain, repeated perhaps to emphasize how close the perpetrator was to Jesus—i.e., a traitor among Jesus' own chosen—and thus how outrageous was his defection. Alternatively, however, is it not possible that a *rudimentary* betrayal story, in circulation by Mark's day, had *introduced* the culprit in Gethsemane? At this stage the Gethsemane episode would thereby have become the *first* time the betrayer had been mentioned—hence the need to identify him as "one of the twelve"! If so, all anticipatory references to the felon (3:19; 14:10f.,18; 14:20f.[44]) could constitute only Mark's editorial readying of his readers for what would transpire in Gethsemane rather than anything firmly imbedded in early strata of the tradition. Some have suspected that originally the entire passion narration *began* with the arrest in Gethsemane.[45] I would add, in any event, that the Gethsemane episode itself had started out as a far simpler report devoid of any betrayal story whatsoever (the latter being only a later embellishment).

This reconstruction would thus account for four anomalies in Mark: (1) the curious and undue repetition of 14:18 by 14:22; (2) Mark's neglecting to mention the traitor's departure from the meal; (3) the ostensibly unnecessary *re*introduction of the betrayer as "one of the twelve" in 14:43; and, we may now add, (4) Mark's failure to explain how Judas even knew that Jesus was going to Gethsemane (since we are given no hint that Jesus had ever been there before or that he had announced his intent to go there now). The conclusion seems inescapable: fundamental aspects of the Judas story simply do not sit comfortably in their current contexts (the Last Supper and Gethsemane scenes). The significant editorial activity evident in these pericopes points to a *belated* introduction of Judas material. Such a consideration further undermines confidence that the betrayal episode as we have it genuinely derives from *early* Christian tradition.

Should all the aforementioned arguments, especially in combination, persuade us that the historicity of our story is suspect, what then might we surmise brought the tale into being? What purposes did its incorporation serve? Why was the traitor imagined as "one of the twelve"—and why "Judas" in particular?

BETRAYAL BY "ONE OF THE TWELVE":
ORIGINS AND INCORPORATION OF THE STORY

The insistence of Christianity that Jesus' death was *necessary* became one way of coping with an otherwise crushing disappointment. *Because* Jesus was executed, it became helpful to consider whether his death may not have been *required*. Once this conjecture congealed into conviction, predictions of Jesus' fate (Mark 8:31f.; 9:31; 10:32f.[46]) came to be retrojected to him personally, constructions after the fact now reconfiguring his execution as having been anticipated rather than unexpected.[47]

Remaining especially incongruous, however, would have been the Gethsemane scene where, gauged from a later vantage point, the ostensibly powerful Christ and Son of God had anomalously fallen prey to mere mortals! The insistence of the Gospels that Jesus foreknew all that befell him probably belies an altogether different and potentially disconcerting reality: that his capture in Gethsemane had constituted an incomprehensible, not to mention dispiriting, surprise.[48]

The Evangelists are certainly hard pressed to clarify this mystery. Matthew is particularly energetic (in 26:51ff.), insisting that although Jesus could have thwarted arrest by summoning divine assistance (appealing to his Father for more than twelve legions of angels), instead he had deliberately *chosen* not to do so;[49] and that Jesus *had* to undergo arrest, for otherwise "how...should the scriptures be fulfilled, that [Jesus' fate] must be so?" Luke[50] and John[51] similarly try their hands at resolving the essentially irreconcilable.[52]

Since this gnawing enigma evidently so plagued Matthew, Luke, and John, it probably stymied as well not only Mark but also Christians before him. It is reasonable to suspect that at least one theory, possibly among others, would inevitably have occurred to some: if the priestly emissaries had located Jesus so readily and opportunely and arrested him without incident, *surely they could have had some inside help—someone near to Jesus (even "one of the twelve") might have disclosed some needed information!* In other words, the notion of a traitor *could* quite easily have been sparked by mere guesswork alone, by reasoned or at least reasonable surmise, a function of developing Christianity's need to explain *the sheer incongruity of Jesus' capture!* Such a tale—however it arose and became assimilated with the Gethsemane tradition—would most likely have begun to catch on no earlier than during the 50s C.E.[53] Mark thereafter introduced his own preparatory notices both before[54] and during[55] the Last Supper scene, for he saw that the story could readily lend itself not only to explaining the ease of Jesus' arrest but also to addressing a host of additional Marcan concerns.

124

One need was to help Christians cope with Roman persecution, recently initiated. Nero is said to have scapegoated Christians in particular for a fire in Rome in 64 C.E. (Tacitus, *Annals* xv. 44) and to have inflicted upon them "grievous torments" (Suetonius, *Life of Nero* 16). Whether or not Mark wrote in the Roman capital itself,[56] his Gospel certainly reflects wariness of this localized occurrence. It suggests, moreover, that apprehension over *betrayal* to Rome was running rampant in at least some Christian circles— with the informants drawn not only from one's enemies but also from one's erstwhile friends, even relatives! At least so we gauge when Mark has Jesus predict that "they will deliver you up to councils.... And when they bring you to trial and deliver you up, do not be anxious.... *Brother* will deliver up brother to death, and the *father* his child..." (13:9).[57] Against the backdrop of "delivery up" even by siblings or parents, surely a story that Jesus himself likewise had been betrayed by one of *his* closest companions would have proved instructive, even comforting, to Christians fearing such treachery—whether during the mid-60s C.E. (before Mark wrote) or in Mark's own day (ca. 70 C.E.). Here we must reckon as well with the virtual interchangeability of "deliver up" and "betray" (both from *paradidonai*). We have already noted how Paul's Corinthian reference to "the night when [the Lord Jesus] was delivered up [to death]" has been so routinely misrendered as "the night when he was *betrayed*." Any inkling that a *traitor* might have facilitated Jesus' arrest would surely have been immediately fueled by this ambiguity![58] Moreover, against a setting of persecution in Mark's day, how naturally the term "delivery up" could have become retrojected to the ministry of Jesus as well, now *historicized* to mean literal acts of bodily delivering up Jesus from one party to another. We can see such historicization worked through in five major episodes of Jesus' Passion in Mark (Figure 1).

| JUDAS "delivers up" Jesus to the ARRESTING PARTY (14:18, 43f.) | ARRESTING PARTY "delivers up" Jesus to the CHIEF PRIESTS (14:53) | CHIEF PRIESTS "deliver up" Jesus to PONTIUS PILATE (15:1, 10) | PONTIUS PILATE "delivers up" Jesus to the ROMAN SOLDIERS (15:15) | ROMAN SOLDIERS "deliver up" Jesus to DEATH (15:15ff.) |

<----------- < ----------Backworking----------- < ----------- <
Least likely   Most likely

FIGURE 1

The most historically certain of these deliveries would be the *last:* the soldiers' delivery up of Jesus to death. The probability of historical authenticity decreases as we move *backward* in the story line, suggesting the direction and process by which the events occasioning Jesus' death came to develop or be reconstructed. The least likely segment in this chain would, in any event, have been the opening link, the delivery up of Jesus by a traitor—especially since this supposition may have arisen only to explain the extraordinary *ease* by which Jesus' capture had been achieved.

In terms of circumstances in Mark's own day, this story could be usefully directed not simply toward the *victims* of betrayal but also toward the *informants* themselves. Woe to them (as to Jesus' own betrayer). It would have been better for them, too, had they never been born (cf. 14:21)! Moreover, lest loyal Christians, overly confident, imagine themselves immune from betraying tendencies, *they* should know that Jesus' own deceiver had himself been one of the twelve, at the very core of the Church. Let all Christians, therefore, imagine themselves sitting at the Last Supper when the betrayal was announced; and let the query of Jesus' original disciples—"surely not I?" (Mark 14:19)—be a question on the lips of later Christians as well.

Above and beyond fears of persecution or betrayal, disillusionment over delay in the Second Coming must likewise have prompted Christians in Mark's day to fall away or to deny Jesus. "Mark's portrait of Judas warns his community that as Jesus and his...disciples could not protect themselves from the defection of Judas, neither can the church protect itself from defectors."[59] Consider how progressively *alone* Jesus was left by an ever diminishing circle of adherents—by the Jewish masses who had originally welcomed him on Palm Sunday; by the disciples in general who had all along been opaque to his teachings and his identity and were soon to abandon him; by three disciples in particular (Peter, James, and John) who fell asleep on him; by one of the twelve (Peter) who *denied* him; and *now* by another of those twelve (Judas) who *betrayed* him!

In all these cases Mark has a propensity for enlisting the disciples as object lessons. He dramatizes the folly of defections by having *all* the disciples abandon Jesus; foreshadows denials of Christianity by having *Peter* disavow Jesus; and addresses betrayal by incorporating the treachery of another one of the twelve, *Judas*.[60] In the face of all these calamities, the common exhortation throughout becomes: "he who endures to the end will be saved" (13:13).

WHY *JUDAS* IN PARTICULAR?

When the betrayal story first arose, the traitor was not yet designated by name—instead, he was simply an unspecified "one of the twelve." How, then, would he have become identified with Judas in particular—and was this identification pre-Marcan, or was Mark himself responsible? In my view, Mark himself determined the name, influenced perhaps by the story in Genesis 37:25—where Judah (LXX *Judas*), "one of twelve" sons of Jacob, suggested the *selling* of Joseph for *pieces of silver*.[61] Mark (3:16ff.) lists the twelve disciples as: Peter, James, John, Andrew, Philip, Bartholomew, Matthew, Thomas, James, Thaddaeus, Simon, and Judas. Of these, only the last two, *Simon* and *Judas,* corresponded to names (Simeon and Judah) among the Genesis group (Figure 2).

128

Reuben Simeon Levi Judah Zebulun Issachar Dan Gad Asher Naphtali Joseph Benjamin

Peter James John Andrew Philip Bartholomew Matthew Thomas James Thaddaeus Simon Judas

FIGURE 2

Whereas the affinity of *Simeon* with *Simon* is unlikely to have conjured up any special associations, the correlation of the one Judas with the other may have seemed significantly more promising—especially when considered against the backdrop of Mark's basically anti-Jewish disposition. For Judah/Judas bore the name of that tribe of Israel from whom the name "Jew" derived; "Judas" thus echoed the Jewish people whom Mark wished to present not only as opposing the Jesus movement but as responsible for Jesus' death. The name was reminiscent as well of Judea, home of the Sanhedrin by which Jesus had been falsely tried and condemned. In Mark's own day Judea was likewise where the Jews just quashed by Rome were based and where their Temple (run by "chief priests"—recalling Jesus' own enemies) had just been burned.

Thus would a fictionally altered Judas have made it easier for Mark to affix the blame for Jesus' death onto the Jewish nation whose name Judas bore, as if to say that not only *Judas the Jew,* but *Judas = the Jews,* betrayed Jesus! Admittedly, nowhere do the Gospels explicitly cast Judas as representing the Jewish people as a whole. Yet, there is "an extraordinary thematic echo between the story of individual betrayal by a close disciple and the story of communal betrayal of Jesus' blood-relatives the Jews.[62] The question is often asked: *if* "the Jews" were determinative in his execution, why *blame* those so instrumental in effecting humanity's salvation? Soberingly, a parallel question could be posed in regard to Judas: why vilify Judas if it was his betrayal of Jesus that had set into motion Jesus' saving death?[63] Thus does Jesus' response to Judas at the Last Supper become so uncannily applicable to the Jews as well: "the Son of man goes as it is written of him, but woe to that man [= the Jews] by whom the Son of man is betrayed."[64]

SUMMARY AND CONCLUSION

All the foregoing observations should be enough at least "to destabilize the traditional Christian assumption" that the betrayal narrative is "a simple literal description of actual events." Virtually everywhere in the Judas story we have discovered lacunae and puzzlements, inconsistencies and irregularities, "exactly what occurs when a late-developing tradition has been read back into the ancient story where it did not originally exist."[65] In this light the *twelve*-judgeship saying (Matthew 19:28; Luke 22:30) proves particularly instructive, since it would probably have become current and been preserved only in an environment as yet unaware of a betrayal story. In postresurrection settings, meanwhile, we have seen how the Synoptists invariably scale the number of witnessing disciples down to *eleven,* thereby undermining the earlier tradition (handed on by Paul) that Jesus had appeared to the *twelve!* It thus looks very much as if a fictional story of a traitor developed in the interim between Paul in the 50s C.E. and the Synoptists beginning with Mark, around 70 C.E.—sparked perhaps by the need to explain how the powerful Son of God could have fallen prey to mere human captors.

As we have also noted, Paul himself never mentions Judas or a betrayal. We should be mindful that in many analogous cases Paul's lack of awareness of a major Gospel theme has suggested the *lateness* of origin of that motif;[66] the same could be the case here as well[67] Yet, even so, in this instance Paul may have himself unwittingly contributed to the development of the story, given the misreading to which his Last Supper reference has usually been subjected.

However the suspicion of a traitor first developed, it would hardly have taken much to substantiate it,[68] merely recourse to the

131

Psalms and stories of King David. Did not these speak of the righteous man as ruthlessly abused by his own familiar friend (Psalms 41:9 and 55:12–14) and reveal that David personally had been deceived by a trusted advisor (2 Samuel 15:30ff.; 16:15, 20ff.; 17:1ff., 23)—texts more than sufficient to flesh out speculation not only that Jesus likewise had been betrayed, but that the perpetrator of this indignity was, also in the case of Jesus, a faithful—actually faith*less*—friend?

When the rudimentary myth of a traitor first began to catch on in the 50s C.E. or later, the villain was still an unspecified "one of the twelve." In according him a name, Mark may have been influenced by the apparent correlation between Judas, one of the twelve, selling his master for silver, and the *Judah* (LXX *Judas*) of Genesis—another "one of twelve," and the one who suggested the selling of Joseph.

After incorporating the primal betrayal story, in its *entirety,* into the Gethsemane scene—where the betrayer thus now *appeared for the first time*—Mark constructed for his readers two preparatory episodes. In one, he may have been further influenced by the Genesis story: since the plan to sell Joseph was broached *during a meal* (37:25ff.), Mark now had Judas's intention to betray Jesus exposed during the Last Supper. Thereby what was originally the *first* mention of the traitor was now moved back from Gethsemane to this earlier setting. Additional back-revising created the episode of Judas negotiating with the authorities and also adjusted the list of disciples (in 3:19) so that Judas was now specified as the one who was to betray Jesus. All such adjustments were consistent with Mark's general "penchant for preparing the reader for what follows."[69]

The incorporation of the story served a variety of Marcan interests: consoling Christians fearful of betrayal to Rome, admonishing informants, and urging the faithful to beware their own betraying tendencies; counteracting fallings-away, defections, and denials; and dramatizing Jesus' ever-increasing aloneness. (In some of these regards, Mark's denigration of Judas is akin to his sweeping disparagement of the disciples as a group.) More potently still, the story of Judas in particular supported Mark's anti-Jewish stance in general, rendering it inevitable that later Christian commentators[70] would see in correspondences between "Judas" and the "Jews" divine hints of the Judas-role *of* the Jews. Now Judas became the quintessential Jew, "the eponymous representative of the Jewish people as a whole."[71] This later led to the exploitation of Judas in both anti-Jewish art and drama, which accorded him grossly exaggerated "Semitic" features (hooked nose in profile, pointed hat, horns, yellow garmentry, and money bag).[72]

What, however, about the *real* Judas? Present in early listings of the twelve, *he* was no fiction—only the traitorous role later foisted upon him! Such a transformation would, of course, have been profoundly unfair to the reputation of the actual Judas who we have no genuine reason to doubt had been as faithful to Jesus as the eleven other disciples. Hence the early (in my view, reliable) tradition that Jesus included Judas among the twelve he destined to judge the tribes of Israel (Matthew 19:28; Luke 22:30). Judas, too, would have mourned Jesus' death, and, as late as the 50s, would still have been assumed to have shared in the witnessing of the resurrected Christ by the "twelve" (1 Corinthians 15:5b). Only thereafter did the fiction of a traitor among the twelve gain currency, with Mark himself the one who, later still, designated him as "Judas" in particular.

One may naturally wonder how Mark got away with sullying Judas's good name without anyone who knew the true figure protesting! Among a variety of possible responses are the following:

(1) Was anyone who had known the true figure still alive and present in Mark's vicinity? Mark wrote forty years after Jesus' ministry and, I would argue, most likely in Rome itself. Chronology makes it likely that the real Judas was long dead, and the geographical distance alone would diminish prospects that some acquaintance of Judas was present to protest Mark's portrait of him.

(2) More important, however, we should not presume that Mark saw himself as a faithful writer or transmitter of *history,* nor that the environment in which he functioned would even have expected that of him. Rather, he was penning *theology,* and the introduction of Judas as the betrayer was consistent with Mark's other (and far more substantial) adjustments of his story line with theological purpose in mind. Thus, in my view, Mark altered the Last Supper from an ordinary meal into a Passover observance; related a full-fledged Sanhedrin trial whose proceedings never transpired; substituted "blasphemy" for sedition as the alleged offense for which Jesus was consigned to the cross; developed a Barabbas story to establish the pacifism of the crucified Jesus and to shift responsibility for his execution from Pilate to the Jews; advanced a previously unknown empty tomb story to silence Jewish denials of the resurrection; and so forth. Compared to any of *these* editorial transformations, naming the betrayer Judas would appear a relatively minor adjustment, especially since I have
not proposed Mark himself as responsible for the myth of a traitor in Jesus' midst— *that,* I believe, he inherited. With the tale already current, it remained for Mark merely to identify the betraying disciple as Judas in particular.

(3) To ask how Mark could get away with sullying the image of Judas is to beg the larger question: how he could have tainted the reputation of *all twelve* disciples (as we have repeatedly noted) without anyone

134

protesting? His motive in doing so was probably tied up with Claudius's expulsion of Jews from the capital city back in 49 C.E.,[73] and with ensuing developments. Ousted along with Jews were Jewish-Christians,[74] founding and leading elements of Rome's Christian community. By default, dominance in Roman Christianity now passed to *Gentile*-Christians (who had not been forced to leave). The latter probably interpreted the banishment of Jewish-Christians as God's judgment concerning who was fit to run the Roman church and encouraged feelings that God's overall purpose had now moved on from the Jews and that a status-reversal had set in (with Jews, rather than Gentiles—and Jewish-Christians rather than Gentile-Christians—now the fringe element). With Claudius's death (in 54 C.E.), however, his edict expired, and Jewish exiles—Jewish-Christians among them—began trickling back into Rome. Gentile-Christian elements would now have required some defense of their recently established dominance.[75] I see Mark as attempting to justify and solidify this dominance by discrediting the *forerunners* of the Jewish-Christian wing of the Roman Church in favor of Gentile-Christianity. It was as a function of this agenda that Mark in essence says that no Jewish-Christians (not Jesus' disciples [especially Peter, James, and John],[76] or even Jesus' family) could figure out who Jesus was or behave in an appropriately impressive manner. What right, therefore, do *Jewish*-Christians have to leadership in the church? This explains why the only person Mark presents as immediately discerning Jesus' identity (as "son of God") is a *Gentile* (the centurion in 15:39, who presumably has never even seen Jesus before)! Mark's identification of the betrayer as Judas, one of the twelve, is therefore altogether consistent with this wider orientation of discrediting *all* the disciples. Since Mark got away with sullying the good names of Peter, James, and John,[77] as well as of the other disciples in general, the question of how he got away with tainting the image of Judas in particular loses considerable force!

DESTABILIZING THE TALE OF JUDAS ISCARIOT

The nagging conjecture remains, of course: "Had Iscariot been named Jacob, David, or Jonathan instead of Judas, a name that too easily could become universalized to become a symbolic figure for all Jews,...how many could have been spared a martyr's death?"[78] Given the later synonymity of his name with *shame,* how ironic are these sentiments from Genesis: that the name suggests a reason "to praise the Lord" (29:35) and that Judah is himself deserving of praise (49:8). All the more incentive, therefore, for us today to redress this grievance on his behalf so as to return veneration to the Jewish people who still proudly practice and maintain their Juda[h]ism!

Notes

1.   "The money of which every Jew is regarded as desirous is...the thirty pieces of silver...the price of Judas's treachery. In...[medieval] Passion Plays...Judas bargained with the Jewish elders for his blood money, each trying to outdo the other in avarice....[Here] the image of the Jewish miser was indelibly forged" (Hyam Maccoby, *Judas Iscariot and the Myth of Jewish Evil* [New York: Macmillan, 1992], p. 6).

2.   See Joshua Trachtenberg's treatment of Judas in *The Devil and the Jews* (New Haven: Yale University Press, 1943), passim.

3.   In Greek *Ioudas* ("Judas") and *Ioudaios* ("Jew"); in Hebrew, *Yehûdâ* and *Yehûdi.* Jewish parents might well name a son Judah, Jehuda, or Yehudah, but never Judas. A German law forbids "the name Judas (along with Satan) for the good of the child...a...dilemma for Jewish parents in Germany who wish to name their son Yehudah" (William Klassen, *Judas: Betrayer or Friend of Jesus?* [Minneapolis: Fortress, 1996], p. 5).

4.   The Seder is an outgrowth of developments from the end of the first century C.E. in response to the Temple's fall (in 70 C.E.) and to the problem of Roman oppression, as well as in reaction to the Gospel appropriation of Passover motifs. Jesus himself could not have celebrated a Seder, since it did not exist in his day, nor was his Last Supper likely to have been a Passover meal of *any* sort! In Mark, the earliest Gospel, mention of *matzah* (cf. also 1 Cor. 11:23) and lamb (the main article of food) was absent, as was mention of the exodus from Egypt. Moreover, all Passover imagery in connection with the Last Supper is here concentrated within a single pericope (14:12–16), strongly suggesting that the paragraph was interpolated into earlier tradition that had set the Last Supper *before* Passover (cf. vv. 1–2). This explains why the story line reads *better* when this pericope is *deleted;* (1) We no longer have to wonder what went awry with the plan to arrest Jesus *before* Passover because, without vv. 12–16, the plan *succeeded!* (2) Mark's mathematical error (in v. 17) now disappears; having sent two disciples from Bethany to Jerusalem to prepare the Passover meal, Jesus cannot then come with "the twelve" but only with *ten*—yet without vv. 12–16 he still has twelve. The

136

telescoping of Passover with the Feast of Unleavened Bread (v. 12) betrays a post-70-C.E. perspective when, after the fall of the Temple, sacrifice of Passover lambs ceased. Such tell-tale clues suggest that it was *Mark* who turned the Last Supper into a Passover meal (probably for theological reasons: Passover, the festival of freedom, now becomes correlated with and incorporated into Jesus' death, held to bring *freedom* for humanity).

5.   The Synoptists' lists of the names of Jesus' inner circle are thought to derive from early apostolic times. Judas Iscariot is mentioned in each (Mark 3:19; Matt. 10:4; and Luke 6:16 [John has no list]). Did the Evangelists themselves find "Iscariot" unintelligible, or, if we assume its meaning was known, feel it needed no explanation? Did Judas himself use or at least know the term, or did it emerge only later on to distinguish him from Judas the son of James (as in Luke 6:16: "Judas the son of James, and Judas Iscariot, who became a traitor" [cf. also Acts 1:13]; and also as in John 14:22: "Judas [not Iscariot]"). Some interpret "Iscariot" as the Hebrew *'îš Qêrîyôt* = "a man of [the village of] *Qêrîyôt*" (making Judas the only disciple from Judea [cf. Josh. 15:25] rather than Galilee); others connect Iscariot with *Sicarii* (dagger-wielding activists against Rome), or claim that the reference was to a character defect (as in *'îš šĕqārîm* = "a man of lies") or to the nature of Judas's deed (as in *sikkartî* [in Isa. 19:4] = "I will deliver up" [suggesting Judas "who delivered up"; cf. Mark 3:19: "Judas Iscariot...who gave him over"]). If he already bore the surname Iscariot, the most likely explanation becomes that it was simply a place name (rather than a reference to any facet of his behavior or character).

6.   On property he purchased with the blood money.

7.   Klassen details the many contrasts (*Judas*, pp. 169ff.).

8.   Yet even so, incongruities will remain: e.g., a penitent's attempted suicide (Matthew) versus an unrepentant scoundrel's heaven-imposed death (Acts); see Maccoby, *Myth*, p. 3.

9.   Second-century Bishop of Hierapolis (*Hist. Eccl.* 3.36.2). The following account of what Papias recorded in his fourth book of the now lost *Logiōn kyriakōn exegeseis* (first half of the second century) is attested to by Apollinaris of Laodicea (fourth century); cf. Cramer's *Catena ad Acta S.S. Apostolorum*, pp. 12–13, and other sources listed in Gebhardt, Harnack, and Zahn, *Patrum Apostolicorum Opera* (Oxford: 1844), p. 73; cf. Morton S. Enslin, "How the Story Grew: Judas in Fact and Fiction," *Festschrift to Honor F. Wilbur Gingrich*, Eugene H. Barth and Ronald E. Cocroft, eds. (Leiden: Brill, 1972), p. 128; Raymond E. Brown, *Death of the Messiah* (New York: Doubleday, 1994), pp. 1408ff.

10.   Papias could well have taken his cue from the demise of other evil persons such as Alcimus (1 Macc. 9:55); Antiochus IV Epiphanes (2 Macc. 9:5ff.); the traitor Nadan (*Tale of Ahiqar* 8:41); Herod the Great (*Antiquities* 17:168–77); Herod Agrippa (*Antiquities* 19:344–52; cf. Acts 12:23); even the suspected adulteress whose belly swells up (Num. 5:21ff.).

11.   This ordinarily might reflect the motif of the sheep dumb before the shearer (Isa. 53:7; Acts 8:32), except that Matthew, Luke, and John, in varying ways, try backing away from it. This suggests that they found Mark's account troubling simply as a story line.

137

12. Not surprisingly, mystery concerning motive has rendered Judas the disciple most ripe for character development by novelist and dramatist alike.

13. Already at the Last Supper we hear: "the Son of man goes as it is *written* of him [i.e., in Jewish Scripture]" (Mark 14:21; Matt. 25:24) or "as...*determined*" (Luke 22:22); earlier, Paul proclaimed more generally still (1 Cor. 15:3f.): "Christ died...*in accordance with the scriptures*" and "was raised *in accordance with the scriptures.*" (Emphases here are added—so also in all other biblical quotations in this essay.)

14. Though not from remorse, but rather because his plans have miscarried; having "forfeited his right to be the trusted counselor of the king...he cannot bear to live with that shame" (Klassen, *Judas*, p. 170).

15. The next verse (Ps. 41:10) asks that God *"raise* me up, that I may requite them" so that "my enemy has not triumphed over me," understandable as Jesus' ultimate triumph over his enemy *by resurrection.*

16. Jewish tradition considers Proverbs to have been written by Solomon.

17. Zechariah could actually provide the framework for the *entirety* of Jesus' last days: from 9:9ff. (a basis for Jesus' entry to Jerusalem on an ass during Palm Sunday) through 14:16ff. (a basis for Acts 2, where peoples assemble in Jerusalem to receive the gift of the spirit under the symbol of water). Zechariah 12:10 relates that Jerusalem will "look on him whom they have pierced,...mourn for him as...for *an only child,* and weep...as one weeps over a *first born* [i.e., *of God,* in some Christian interpretation]." See John S. Spong, "Did Christians Invent Judas?" The *Fourth R* 7 No.2 (March/April 1994), p. 8.

18. True, the accounts differ: twenty pieces of silver (for Joseph) versus thirty (for Jesus). But the latter sum could well have been influenced by the thirty sheqalim one had to pay if one's ox gored a slave. Cf., as well, the wages of Zechariah's shepherd king, also thirty pieces. That the *gematria* (Hebrew numerical) value of the basic letters of Yehudah is thirty (10 + 5 + 6 + 4 + 5) may be only incidental, or coincidental, and not relevant.

19. "What emerges is that the term 'deliver over' acquires nuances in the New Testament not found anywhere else.... The meaning 'betray'...has no basis in the original meaning of the word. Yet it appears in all standard Bible translations and in most commentaries" (Klassen, *Judas,* p. 54; see also Brown, *Death,* pp. 211–13).

20. In Romans 4:25 Jesus was *"delivered* to death for our misdeeds"; in 8:32 God *"gave up* [His own Son] for us all." In Galatians 2:20 Paul says that Christ *"gave himself* [to death] for me." The Gospels often use the term with no necessary (or even possible) reference to *betrayal;* the chief priests *delivered* Jesus up to Pilate (Mark 15: 1, 10; Matt. 27:2, 18; Luke 24:20; John 18:30, 35); Pilate *"delivered* Jesus to be crucified" (Mark 15:15; Matt. 27:26; Luke 23:25; John 19:16). In Mark 1:14 John the Baptist also was *"delivered up."* Certainly there is no betrayal in any of these.

21. *The New English Bible* (New York: Oxford University Press, 1976); cf. Maccoby, *Myth,* p. 24.

22. Perhaps with an eye here to the Suffering Servant (of Second Isaiah) who "bore the sins of many, and was *delivered* because of their iniquities" (LXX Isaiah 53:12).

23. Admittedly, the notion that the Gospels themselves insist on an omniscient Jesus requires nuance. Jesus, for example, is not presented as aware that a fig tree is barren until he inspects it (Mark 11:13; Matt. 21:19), and he declares that he does not know the day he will return to earth (Mark 13:32; Matt. 24:36). Yet, the presence of Judas among Jesus' inner circle is a disconcerting problem of consequence: "This choice in some way reflects upon Jesus, with respect either to his lack of insight into the person of Judas or to his inability to reform Judas once he became a follower, to exorcise the demons that allegedly possessed him" (Klassen, *Judas,* p. 3).

24. All Matthew (26:50) and Luke (22:48) seem able to do (vis-à-vis Mark 14:45f.) is to strengthen Jesus' assertiveness.

25. "'Did I not choose you, the twelve, and one of you is a devil?' He spoke of Judas the son of Simon Iscariot, for he, one of the twelve, was to betray him.... 'But there are some of you [disciples] that do not believe.' For Jesus *knew from the first* who those were that did not believe, and who it was that should betray him."

26. "Jesus answered, '[The traitor] is he to whom I...give this morsel of bread....'...[Then] he...gave it to *Judas.* "

27. "What you are going to do, do quickly."

28. Cf. Mark 6:52; 8:17. This expression is applied more than a dozen times to the archetypal villain, Pharaoh (Exod. 7–14, passim; cf. Isa. 63:17).

29. Cf., e.g., Ernest Best, "Discipleship in Mark...," *Scottish Journal of Theology* 23 (1970): 323–37; John R. Donahue, *Are You the Christ?...* (Society of Biblical Literature Dissertation Series, 10. Missoula: SBL, 1973), pp. 11ff., 43ff.; Seán Freyne, "At Cross Purposes: Jesus and the Disciples in Mark," *Furrow* 33 (1982): 331–39; David J. Hawkin, "Incomprehension of the Disciples in the Marcan Redaction," *Journal of Biblical Literature* (1972): 491–500; Werner Kelber, "Mark 14:32–42: Gethsemane, Passion Christology and Discipleship Failure," *Zeitschrift für die neutestamentliche Wissenschaft* 62 (1971): 166–87; Elizabeth S. Malbon, "Fallible Followers: Women and Men in the Gospel of Mark," *Semeia* 28 (1983): 29–48; Joseph Tyson, "The Blindness of the Disciples in Mark," *JBL* 80 (1961): 261–68; C. Weber, "Jesus' Opponents in the Gospel of Mark," *Journal of the Bible and Religion* 34 (1966): 214–22; Theodore Weeden, "The Heresy That Necessitated Mark's Gospel," *ZNW* 59 (1968): 145–56. On Peter in particular, see the summation of scholarship in Robert W. Herron, Jr., *Mark's Account of Peter's Denial of Jesus: A History of Its Interpretation* (Lanham: University Press of America, 1991).

30. I contend that "the twelve" go back to Jesus' ministry itself; cf. especially Robert Meye, *Jesus and the Twelve* (Grand Rapids: Eerdmans, 1968).

31. The reasoning and proof texts offered in Acts 1:15–20 reflect Luke's rationalization for this transparently *improvised* (not to mention imagined) practice.

32. J. M. Robertson, *Jesus and Judas: A Textual and Historical Investigation* (London: Watts & Co., 1927), p. 40. Robertson's conclusion that the Matthias story of Acts was therefore earlier than the tradition of Peter's denial is unwarranted. Luke has already sufficiently rehabilitated Peter for the fiction of Peter's choosing Matthias now to be at least tolerable.

33. Our only New Testament source for Matthias.

34. Maccoby, *Myth*, p. 25 (emphasis added). Also p. 180, n. 10: "The original expression 'the twelve disciples' does not show...concern for numbering, since this was a conventional epithet, like 'the twelve tribes,' used sometimes for poetical effect as an alternative to the prosaic 'disciples' or 'tribes.' But to specify 'eleven' is to show an anxiety to state the right number...best explained not by the narrative context but by the exigencies of editing."

35. This Judas is different from Judas Iscariot.

36. It will not do to argue, on the basis of "you who have followed me," that Judas was *excluded* once he ceased to follow Jesus. The tradition that Jesus specified *twelve* thrones implies he has *all twelve* disciples in mind. Luke has Jesus render this clearer still: "You [in context = all twelve] are those who...."

37. Whether from Q or directly from Matthew.

38. So E. P. Sanders, *Jesus and Judaism* (Philadelphia: Fortress, 1985), pp. 98ff.; idem, *The Historical Figure of Jesus* (London: Penguin, 1993), pp. 120ff.

39. Robertson, *Judas*, p. 33.

40. Another prefatory touch was the specification of Judas as the disciple "who betrayed him" (3:19). Such anticipatory editing is characteristic in Mark: e.g., his mention of "blasphemy" in 2:7 lays the groundwork for charging Jesus with blasphemy in the Sanhedrin (14:64); and the young man is introduced in Gethsemane (14:51) so that he can reappear in the tomb (16:5)—a device to reassure readers that the women went to the *correct* tomb (not a *different* tomb that happened to be empty).

41. Robertson, *Judas,* p. 32. A similar dynamic appears in 15:1–5. The beginning of verse 2 ("and Pilate asked him") is echoed in verse 4 ("and Pilate again asked him"), suggesting that verse 2, "again" in verse 4, and "further" in verse 5, are all Marcan editing.

42. The Lord's Supper (Eucharist), Mark 14:22–25, already in Mark's *received* tradition, may itself have previously been added to a still earlier story line (a function of Pauline influence [cf., 1 Cor. 11:24–25]?).

43. "And they bound him and led him away *and delivered him to Pilate the governor* (Matt. 27:2); repeated by *"Now Jesus stood before the governor,* and the governor asked him...." (27:11). See Robertson, *Judas,* p. 32.

44. That 14:18-21 is editorial may be confirmed by the appearance of "Son of man" in v. 21 (cf. also v. 41). Thirteen of fourteen references to "Son of man" in Mark are due, I believe, to Marcan redaction (the one exception, that in 13:26, being originally embedded within a Jewish apocalypse that Mark inherited and here revised). The thirteen references (including 14:21) appear in passages that I have determined on independent grounds to reflect Marcan editorial interests (see *Mark's Treatment of the Jewish Leaders* [Leiden: Brill, 1978], Chap. 4-5).

45. Cf. G. Schneider, "Die Verhaftung Jesu. Traditionsgeschichte von Mk 14:43-52," *ZNW* 63 (1972): 196; K.G. Kuhn, "Jesus in Gethsemane," *Evangelische Theologie* (n.s.) 12 (1952-53): 261.

46. Mark 9:12b adds to these the consideration that Jesus had to die in order to *fulfill Jewish scripture.*

47. Since a presumably foreknowing Jesus would have anticipated any harm slated to befall his own person, any calamity—provided that it was both believed to have been prophesied by Jesus *and* that it actually transpired—could then serve to *corroborate* Christian faith instead of to undermine it!

48. Jesus is said to ask why they came out against him in Gethsemane rather than in the temple (where he taught daily); this query could suggest unexpectedness. So also might the tradition that the disciples fled the garden.

49. Even to the point of reprimanding a zealous follower to "put your sword back into its place; for all who take the sword will perish by the sword" (v. 52).

50. Luke 22:50ff. displays a Jesus so powerful that he could undo the effect of violence (restoring, healed and whole, the ear severed from the high priest's slave)!

51. John 18:4ff. dramatizes Jesus' power: the arresting party actually wilts before its "captive"!

52. Sociologists Leon Festinger, Henry Riecken, and Stanley Schachter explored such compensatory devices in their classic study of cognitive dissonance, *When Prophecy Fails* (New York: Harper & Row, 1964).

53. Given, as explained, the tradition of early Christianity to include Judas among the twelve destined to judge the tribes of Israel, as well as among the twelve who witnessed the resurrected Christ.

54. In listing Judas as he "who betrayed him" (3:19) and casting him as bargaining with the chief priests (14:10f.).

55. Such editorial activity is also consistent here with Mark's transformation of the Last Supper into a Passover meal (by interpolation of a single pericope, 14:12–16).

56. See my supportive argumentation in *Mark's Treatment,* pp. 10ff.; cf. Brown, *Death,* p. 9, n. 8.

57. This may be the only context in Mark that permits an understanding of actual "betrayal" (cf. Klassen, *Judas,* p. 56). Striking is M.A. Tolbert's phraseology (albeit in a different context): "Jesus is to be delivered up to death by his 'brother' in the family of God" *(Sowing the Gospel: Mark's World in Literary-Historical Perspective* [Minneapolis: Fortress, 1989], p. 274f.).

58. Notable is Mark's "first" mention of Judas the traitor (3:19), where either of two translations seems possible: Judas as the one "who *delivered up* Jesus" or the one "who *betrayed* Jesus." Observe the juxtaposition in Matthew 27:2 and 3: "and they bound him and led him away and *delivered* him to Pilate the governor. When Judas, his *betrayer,* saw..." (did "delivered" suggest "betrayer"?).

59. Klassen, *Judas,* p. 90.

60. To diminish any impression that Jesus was a victim, Mark ascribed to Jesus *predictions* of each unsavory development: of the disciples' defection (14:27); of Peter's denial (14:30); of Judas's betrayal (14:18).

61. The analogy is imperfect: the object of the sale, Joseph, is *himself* one of the twelve, not outside them; yet typological exegesis often takes its cue from the elements that correlate, irrespective of others that may not.

62. Maccoby, *Myth,* p. 5.

63. An imagined response could well be that Jesus had to die, but woe to *heinous* Judas who need not himself have opted to betray him (he was, in other words, not a blind instrument of fate). This *same* answer could then be applied to the Jews: Jesus had to die, but woe to those *heinous* Jews who need not themselves have opted to condemn him! Yes, what happened to *Jesus* was divinely ordained, but the crime that Jews *of their own accord* chose to commit was entirely without Divine sanction. Thus, the Jews remain a truly *guilty* party.

64. In Matthew, ironically, Jews suffer not only from their *correspondence* with Judas, but even from their *divergence* from him; for Matthew depicts Judas as repenting his misdeed (27:3), yet presents the Jews as manifesting *no* remorse for theirs (27:25: "His blood be on us and on our children".

65. These quotations are from Spong, "Invent Judas?" pp. 4, 9.

66. Paul knows nothing of the *disciples' falling away* or of *Peter's denial of Jesus*—themes that, had they been authentic and known, he could well have used in shoring up his own credentials vis-à-vis those of his Jerusalem Church opponents (cf., e.g., Galatians 1 and 2). He also seems unaware of the *virgin birth* and the *empty tomb* traditions (the latter would have been extraordinarily helpful in defending Jesus' bodily resurrection to recalcitrant Greeks who associated afterlife with escape from the body).

67. Admittedly, arguments from silence are hard to weigh since the reason for the silence may elude us. This does not mean, however, that they should not be considered.

68. I.e., the conjecture of a betrayal arose first and only thereafter looked to scripture for confirmation and embellishment.

69. Donahue, *Christ*, p. 206f.

70. Especially St. Jerome (340–420) and St. John Chrysostom (345–407). See treatment by Maccoby, *Myth*, pp. 101ff., 182, nn. 1–3, and the Appendix, pp. 193ff., relative to (1) Jerome, In Ps. 108 (*PL*, 26, 1224), commented thereon by M. Simon ("St. Jerome, for whom Judas is the image of Judaism...." [*Verus Israel: A Study of the Relations between Christians and Jews in the Roman Empire (135–425)*, (Oxford: Oxford University Press, 1986); translated from 1964 French edition)]); and to (2) Chrysostom, whose Homily III on the Acts of the Apostles 1:15–22 declares that "we may with propriety apply this same [i.e., Jesus' prophecy of woe against Judas] to the Jews likewise...," and that the desolation characterizing the "field of blood" (Aceldama) that Judas purchased "was the prelude to that of the Jews" (Maccoby explains: "the punishment of Judas...prefigures that of the Jews, for...'the field of blood'..., where Judas died, prefigures the destruction of Jerusalem, where the Jews suffered their national defeat in punishment for killing Jesus").

71. Maccoby, *Myth*, p. 296f.

72. See Ruth Mellinkoff, *Outcasts: Signs of Otherness in Northern European Art of the Late Middle Ages* (Berkeley: University of California Press, 1993) 1:134ff.; Maccoby, *Myth*, pp. 112ff.; cf. Trachtenberg, *Devil*, p. 193.

73. Suetonius, *Lives of the Twelve Caesars*, Claudius §25.4; on the dating, see the Roman historian Orosius, *Hist.* 7, 6, 15.

74. Acts 18:2 plausibly reports that Paul "found [in Corinth] a Jew named Aquila, a native of Pontus, lately come from Italy with his wife, Priscilla, because Claudius had commanded all the Jews to leave Rome." They must *already* have been (Jewish-)Christians since they immediately entered into relationship with Paul with no suggestion that Paul "converted" them.

75. Cf. Paul's epistle to the Romans, which arrived in Rome after the return of Jewish-Christian believers commenced. Paul undoubtedly had heard from contacts in Rome that Gentile-Christians were now precipitating trouble by treating returnees with arrogance. This is why chapters 9–11 are replete with warnings to Gentile-Christians against judgmentalism, animosity, condescension, and

overestimation of self.

76. E.g., 9:2–8 (the confusion of Peter, James, and John over the Transfiguration); 14:33–42 (their failure to stay awake on guard in Gethsemane); 14:29–31, 54, 66–72 (Peter's denial of Jesus); etc. Paul opposes the same triumvirate of names ("James and Cephas [= Peter] and John, who were reputed to be pillars") in Galatians 2:9. Although it is a *different* James, of course, might Mark have deliberately enlisted the same three *names* (whom Paul attacks) as part of his own disqualification of Jewish-Christians as fit leaders?

77. As noted earlier (n. 66), in defending his own credentials vis-à-vis the "pillars" of the Jerusalem Church, Paul never mentions (or even seems aware of) traditions that would compromise their claims to leadership. This is consistent with the suggestion that Mark's later reportage about the disciples is distortive.

78. Pinchas Lapide, *Wer war Schuld an Jesu Tod?* (Gütersloh: Mohn, 1987), p. 15.

RESPONSE TO MICHAEL COOK
ON JUDAS ISCARIOT

H. Eberhard von Waldow

I should like to begin with a personal word to Walter Jacob: Walter, my participation in this symposium gives me the opportunity to thank you. I want to thank you for many years of personal friendship; and for your teaching of theology, for you have been a great colleague. Whenever I needed your help or cooperation, you were always there. Thank you, Walter.

And now my reaction to Dr. Cook's paper. This paper critically examines the historicity of the Judas tradition in the New Testament. Michael Cook asks, What really did happen? Or, What is the historical background that led to the New Testament image of the disciple Judas, who betrayed Jesus in exchange for money?

The result of this very careful inquiry is that the image of Judas the betrayer is fiction. There may have been a historical disciple Judas, but he was probably as faithful to Jesus as the other eleven. Only later was he turned into the one disciple who became the traitor.

I find the evidence for these conclusions convincing, and as a Christian theologian, basically, I can only wholeheartedly agree. In my response, therefore, I do not criticize; rather, I want to underscore the importance of this paper by placing it in a larger context. And this is our hermeneutical approach to biblical stories, both in the New Testament and in the Old Testament.

Because of the special character of the story material in the Bible, what Dr. Cook is doing here with a little piece of the New Testament, the Judas tradition, must actually be done with all biblical stories. The issue here is the historicity of all biblical accounts. With this I mean the general question: How dependable is the Bible as a history book? This question has preoccupied Christian theologians for about 200 years, and it is still debated today. When I was a young student, the answer was given by my teacher in Old Testament studies, Professor Gerhard von Rad, who again and again pointed to the—as he called it—wide gap between the history reflected by the Bible and the history that really happened. He called this the most difficult problem to confront all interpreters of the Bible, and I would add today, Jewish and Christian interpreters alike. Michael Cook with his focus on the Judas story has just demonstrated this.

The gap between biblical history and actual history is indeed wide, but the gap between biblical scholarship and the people in our pews is also wide. Those in the pews—as we can often hear them say—tend to take the Bible literally or what they think to be literally, and this includes the picture of history as given by the Bible. This is—unfortunately—reinforced today by Hollywood and its spectacular Bible films and by the videos *Reader's Digest* puts out. The results can lead to serious implications when, for example, the fictional disciple Judas is turned into the prototype of a money-grubbing Jew or—to take the almost classical example of the Old Testament—the creation story, which led to the unnecessary controversy between creationism and evolution.

In his example Michael Cook asks the right question: What is the true historical background of the New Testament Judas tradition? His answer is, a disciple Judas who was probably not different from his fellow disciples. In general terms, some biblical stories have no historical kernel whatsoever (for example, Genesis 1–4). But most have a historical base; in some instances it is very weak, in others it is stronger. As far as the Old Testament is concerned, in stories dealing with events prior to David's founding of a state, the actual historical

146

facts are unclear; but in stories belonging to the period after David, the gap between true and contrived history narrows considerably.

This observation leads to the inevitable question: Why were the actual historical events changed in the biblical stories about them? Why was the actual Judas tradition changed to what we read now in the New Testament? One answer is—I am phrasing this for those who live here in Pittsburgh—that the biblical story tellers did not report for Channel 4 Action News claiming "to be everywhere," or for Eye Witness News "with the hometown advantage." Rather, they are using historical figures or incidents to give testimony to what they or others have experienced in the real world as a religious or theological truth. What shaped their stories was not the historical incident as such, but rather a theological or religious point that they intended to communicate. When we read these stories the question to be raised is not, What happened? It is, rather, Why did the author tell us that it happened this or that way? The question is not, What did Abraham or David really say? People tend to forget that no tape recorder was running. When we read these stories the question to be asked is, Why did the author make them say this or that? This applies also to the Gospels of the New Testament. The four Gospels cannot be used as a basis for a biography of Jesus.

To articulate their beliefs the biblical authors used stories. They were Jews, and Jews were always great story tellers. But there is more to it. What these stories intended to communicate as truth was experienced in the real world, in daily life. These story tellers were not dealing with abstractions; their truth was not acquired in an ecstatic state of mind or in a mystical experience where the human mind leaves the realm of reality; no, this is experienced truth. A fundamental biblical truth is that God is the Lord of history; and the best way to give testimony to that is to tell stories. But to make the theological point, the actual event of the story can be changed so that it serves the theological purpose.

In the case of the Judas story, Dr. Cook points to the precarious situation of the new Christian church in the Roman empire. Here the betrayer becomes a warning, under pressure or in view of repercussions, not to fall away from Jesus Christ. The details of the developing story are taken from the biblical tradition. Judas is chosen because of his reprehensible deed in Genesis 37:25ff., and the thirty shekels come from Zechariah 11:12. Here, I am in basic agreement with Dr. Cook. But now, as a Christian exegete, I would interpret differently. My focus would not be on the fact that the negative example, Judas, is a Jew. This can indeed give rise to Christian anti-Semitism. I would rather see the disciple Judas as a member of the chosen people of Israel, the partner of God's covenant. Of course he was a Jew; what else could he be? Christian post-Holocaust theology maintains that after Jesus Christ this covenant includes now Jews and Gentiles, Christians and Jews. In this sense the betrayer Judas becomes a warning to Christians not to betray their faith in Jesus Christ for any form of material goods or for any other reason. When the New Testament Judas tradition is used with the focus on the Jew for the promotion of anti-Semitism, the reason is not necessarily this tradition as such; rather, it is the anti-Semitism in the mind of the interpreter, who reads it into the Bible and then turns around and tells us this is the word of God in the Bible.

RESPONSA AND THE ART OF WRITING*

Three Examples from the *Teshuvot* Of Rabbi Moshe Feinstein

Mark Washofsky

BY WAY OF INTRODUCTION:
IS THERE SUCH A THING AS *HALAKHAH*?

What do we mean when we use the term "the halakhic process"? What kind of intellectual practice do we signify with those words? And what manner of individual is the *posek,* the scholar whose rulings serve to define the *Halakhah,* authoritative Jewish legal teaching, for those who turn to him[1] for guidance? What scholarly commitments, what habits of mind does he bring to his work, thereby shaping his activity and his very image, in his own eyes as well as in the eyes of his community?

One noted contemporary Orthodox legal scholar, Rabbi J. David Bleich, describes the process of halakhic thinking as one of rigorous, rational analysis.[2] The *posek,* he writes, never allows "subjective considerations or volitional inclinations" to influence his scholarly opinion. Decisions are to be reached "in as detached and dispassionate a manner as is humanly possible." To be sure, since the interpretation of the sources of Jewish law is "no longer in Heaven,"[3] it is "conceivable that two different individuals of equal intelligence and erudition, both possessed of equal sincerity and objectivity, may reach antithetical conclusions." As long as both these conclusions "are

---

*To Dr. Walter Jacob, the very model of the scholarly rabbi, in appreciation for his leadership, creativity, and accomplishment in the writing of Reform responsa and in advancing the cause of liberal *Halakhah*. He is in the deepest sense *rabi umori*, my teacher, to whom I owe a profound intellectual and professional debt of gratitude.

derived from accepted premises and both are defended by cogent halakhic argumentation," both are legitimate statements of *Halakhah* (provided, "it goes without saying," that each individual is a person of unquestioned piety and religious probity). With all this room for dispute and disagreement, however, the methodology of *Halakhah* is "not a matter of arbitrary choice"; the rules by which some opinions are accepted and others excluded must themselves "be applied in an objective manner." The decisor may not "arbitrarily" rule in accordance with an individual opinion *(da'at yachid)* in the law against the weight of halakhic precedent or consensus. "He most certainly may not be swayed by the consideration that the resultant decision be popular or expedient or simply by the fact that it appeals to his own personal predilection." The law must rather "be determined on its own merits and let the chips fall where they may." In short, the halakhic process is one of thoroughgoing rationality, a mental operation in which intellectual detachment and impartial analysis overpower whatever desire the *posek* may have to place his own subjective and individual stamp upon the *Halakhah*. The law is not whatever he would like it to be or even what he most fervently believes it ought to be; the law is what it in fact *is,* derived through the objective reading of the texts and sources.

There is another possible understanding of the process of halakhic decision making, however, one that emphasizes the more subjective side of the intellectual coin. This portrait of the *posek* is drawn for us by Rabbi Louis Jacobs,[4] who rejects the image of the halakhist as "an academic lawyer who, when he sits down to investigate his sources dispassionately and with complete objectivity, never knows beforehand what his conclusions will be." Although "the Halakhist obeys the rules and plays the game according to them," using all the "acceptable legal ploys" to arrive at his decisions, these rules and ploys do not in reality determine those decisions. Even when he begins his investigation the halakhic scholar knows full well that he can reach only one correct conclusion, "not because the sources he is about to examine will inevitably lead to that conclusion but because his general approach to Judaism compels him to come up with a conclusion that must not be at variance with Jewish ideas and ideals as he and his contemporaries or his 'school' sees them." Thus, says Jacobs, one cannot draw a firm distinction between *Halakhah* and *Agadah,* the law and lore of Judaism, for "behind the most austere Halakhist there sits the passionate, easily moved, poetic Agadist."

We should not portray the contrast between these two scholars as stark and total. Bleich, as we have seen, does make room in his description of the halakhic process for the "human" factors of uncertainty and disagreement. Jacobs, for his part, would probably concede that there are any number of "easy questions" in Jewish law that the halakhist would decide on purely formal, technical halakhic grounds without need of recourse to a general religious approach or to "ideas and ideals" of Judaism. And, despite his assertion that rabbis tailor their legal reasoning to justify whatever decisions their hearts tell them to reach, he does admit to some intractable halakhic problems that even the most creative legal thinker and "poetic Agadist" cannot solve.[5] Yet, the general tenor of each writer's position is clear enough, and the difference between them is nothing less than the difference between reality and the appearance of reality, between substance and illusion. Bleich presents *Halakhah* as an autonomous intellectual discipline that operates by its own immanent procedures, that is independent of alternative ways of thinking and cannot be reduced to any of them. This means that the rules and principles of Jewish law act as real constraints upon the *posek*'s freedom by dictating the correct answer to any Jewish legal question.

151

That "correct" answer is emphatically *not* left to the whim, the discretion, or even the moral conscience of the individual rabbi, even should he be a "poetic Agadist" at heart. *Halakhah* differs from *Agadah* in the same way that law differs from morality: "legal integrity often prevents a lawyer from finding in the law what he wishes were there."[6] Jacobs, meanwhile, suggests that halakhic thought and language are but a mask disguising the rabbi's "real" religious and ethical predilections, that the rabbinic decision is in fact determined by other thought processes—philosophy, theology, psychology, and so on— than those we usually identify as "halakhic." The "immanent rules and procedures" of the *Halakhah* do not constrain the *posek*'s choice but are resources that he can manipulate to create a post facto justification of the ruling that his general sense of religious propriety demands that he render. Jacobs's portrait of *Halakhah* is therefore at once liberating and skeptical: liberating, in that it allows the decisor to arrive at that decision that in his heart of hearts he thinks is right and just; skeptical, in that *Halakhah* as a matter of law has little real existence apart from the religious and ideological predilections of the rabbis who speak in its name.

At stake in our choice between these two descriptions is our measurement of the power and significance of the halakhic process itself, a process long identified as the central activity of the rabbinic mind: is it a set of substantive rules, principles, and teachings that exist in reality—that is, autonomously, independent of the will and the subjective preferences of the rabbis? Or is it simply a linguistic convention, an inherited and habitual practice by which the rabbis translate their sincerely felt and eminently nonhalakhic religious beliefs into the "acceptable legal ploys" demanded by a traditional vernacular?

As liberals, I suspect most of us would find Louis Jacobs's theory a persuasive one. We do so, first of all, because we would like to think that Jewish law possesses much more flexibility and creativity than most Orthodox rabbis attribute to it. Jewish law, we affirm, demands that we uphold the highest and most humane religious values; we believe that the *poskim* could issue decisions that reflect the spirit of these values if they so chose; and we are convinced that if they do *not* so choose, this is not because the *Halakhah* itself constrains them from making that choice but because their own illiberal religious values lead them in a very different direction. Moreover, trained as we are in the habits and outlooks of critical academic scholarship, we understand Judaism as a historical phenomenon whose institutions have undergone myriad changes in response to the social, political, economic, and cultural circumstances the Jews have faced. To claim, as Bleich seems to do, that *Halakhah* "works by its own rules" in isolation from these powerful historical trends is to contend that Jewish law possesses a cultural immunity from which no other Jewish intellectual activity—philosophy, mysticism, Bible commentary, belles-lettres— can be said to benefit. This assertion, to us, is counterintuitive, and it is conclusively refuted by the work of Jacobs and other researchers who have documented the changing content of Jewish law from age to age.[7] The upshot is that we find it difficult if not impossible to speak of *Halakhah* as a process governed by reason alone, or even by reason chiefly. We comprehend Jewish law rather as a tool in the hands of the rabbis, the record of numerous, discrete acts of legislation by which rabbinic authorities make the necessary adjustments—sometimes lenient, sometimes stringent—to the received legal corpus so as to enable the community to prosper, to survive, to respond successfully to the needs of the times.

Indeed, the fact that contemporary Orthodox halakhic decision *(pesak)* is almost uniformly stringent and "right wing" is itself testimony to the permanence of change in *Halakhah*. As academic scholars, we know that Jewish law was not always rejectionist, that in former times it displayed ample ability to confront the challenges of the age and adapt itself positively to them. The emergence of a self-consciously "orthodox" Judaism in the early nineteenth century produced a trend toward *pesak* that either sanctified the religious status quo or granted preference to the most stringent legal alternatives. We explain this "charedization" of *Halakhah* in various ways: as a defensive posture against secularism and religious reform;[8] as a reaction to the loss of Jewish political and juridical autonomy;[9] as a result of the transformation of the halakhic "audience" from the entire Jewish community into a more rigidly defined sect comprising the rabbis and the relatively small circle of their unconditionally observant followers.[10] Orthodox observers, too, account for the changing direction and substance of *pesak* by pointing to fundamental transformations in the sociology of their own community.[11] The most significant of these is the tendency in contemporary Orthodoxy to recognize the *gedoley hador,* the great "Torah sages," as possessing supreme halakhic authority. The rise of the *gedolim,* who are usually the heads of leading *yeshivot,* has been accompanied by the parallel decline in the status of the community rabbinate as the ultimate authority over questions of Jewish law.[12] The contrast between these two types of rabbinic leadership could hardly be more striking. The traditional rabbi was appointed by the community's secular leadership and functioned in a "judicial" fashion, as the head of the local *beit din* and as the interpreter of the legal texts and precedents that governed the public and religious lives of his people. The *gedolim,* on the other hand, are generally described as uncommonly saintly men who occupy an almost superhuman plane. They are not elected to their office; rather, they are

> selected by a sure and subtle process which knows its leaders and places them in the forefront of a generation. Call it mystical, call it non-rational: it is both. But somehow the genius of *K'lall Yisroel* has been able to distinguish between a true *Gadol B'Yisroel* and an ordinary scholar. The *Gadol* not only knows Torah: his life is Torah, his every word, even his ordinary conversation, is Torah, so that he is in a very real sense the repository of Torah on earth... [endowed with the] capacity for the intuitive flash of insight which discovers reality not as it appears to be but as it is: reality in the light of Torah.[13]

If one can declare that *"Gedolei Yisrael* possess a special endowment or capacity to penetrate objective reality" and that "this endowment is a form of *ruah ha-kodesh* as it were, bordering, if only remotely, on the periphery of prophecy," it but stands to reason that *"Gedolei Yisrael* inherently ought to be the final and sole arbiters of all aspects of Jewish communal policy and questions of *hashkafah*...even knowledgeable rabbis who may differ with the *gedolim* on a particular issue must submit to the superior wisdom of the *gedolim.*"[14] The submission of the Orthodox community to the judgment of these sages on "all aspects of Jewish communal policy" lies at the heart of the institution of *da'at torah*, the authoritative pronouncement of "the Torah position" on a wide array of social, cultural, and political questions that lie outside the boundaries of *Halakhah* as these are usually conceived. The origins of *da'at torah* as a contemporary Orthodox religious practice are a matter of debate among historians.[15] Similarly, although some Orthodox scholars note this transformation in the style of rabbinic leadership with regret,[16] others view it in a much more positive light.[17] What no one denies, however, is that the power to declare the *Halakhah* for Orthodox

Jewry rests today with a small group of charismatic leaders, products of a very particular kind of environment, who have issued a very particular kind of *pesak,* one that tends almost exclusively in the direction of *chumra,* religious stringency, and away from the more lenient alternatives that exist in the legal sources.

All this evidence, of course, supports Louis Jacobs's portrayal of the halakhic process. If *Halakhah* has exhibited substantial change and development over the centuries, one can hardly contend that Jewish law is a static reality, a collection of preexisting and eternally stable truths waiting to be uncovered through the operation of dispassionate reason. And if the direction of *pesak* is set by the social and cultural context in which the *poskim* operate, we cannot describe Jewish law as possessing a fixed and determinate content. To put it in more specifically legal terminology, there is no "one right answer" to interesting halakhic questions.[18] If rabbis could decide the *Halakhah* differently, the decisions they do render would result from choices they make between available alternatives and not from constraints imposed on them by the iron logic of the law. By "choice," I do not mean individual whim. Halakhic choice is a communal matter, sculpted and shaped by the social context in which the *gedolim* have grown to adulthood, studied Torah, developed their self-image, and exercise their intellectual and spiritual leadership. The point is that the factors that control halakhic choice are not specifically halakhic factors but rather this very social context, the forces of history and culture, the "ideas and ideals" of Judaism as viewed by the "school" to which the *posek* belongs.

Yet, if we liberals find ourselves sympathetic to the position of Louis Jacobs, we cannot simply dispense with David Bleich. For if Bleich's view of *pesak* does not comport with the "big picture" history

156

and sociology provide, it is nonetheless reinforced by arguments both practical and theoretical. The practical argument stems quite literally from the *practice* of rabbinic decision making. Whereas Jacobs asserts that halakhic decision is unconstrained by purely halakhic rules, those who engage in this activity, who issue rulings and write codes and responsa, say otherwise. That is to say, when they speak of their work they report that although they considered alternatives to their ultimate decision, they were constrained *by reasons of Halakhah* from choosing those alternatives. They tell us that they are engaged in legal thought, a process possessing its own inherent integrity and governed by particularly *legal* rules, rather than an exercise in philosophy, theology, or ethics. As halakhists, these scholars must be presumed to recognize a legal process when they see one, and their descriptions of it are by all appearances sincere. Thus, unless we wish to dismiss these estimable rabbis as being either naive or duplicitous, there is no reason why we should not take them at their word and accept as valid their own account of their own experience.

The theoretical argument has to do with the dominant role of law, of *Halakhah,* in Judaism. We know that we cannot explain the phenomenon called Judaism without placing *Halakhah* and halakhic thinking at its center. The Jewish legal tradition has comprised the bulk of the literary output and intellectual activity of the Jewish mind for nearly twenty centuries. *Halakhah,* in other words, is basically what the rabbis have been doing since talmudic times; it is the very language of Jewish religion, that aspect of Jewish religion that is the most *particularly* Jewish, the constitutive rhetoric by which Jews have conducted their most basic arguments and constructed their religious universe. To draw the radically skeptical conclusion that the rabbis have "in fact" been doing something else, that the law that emerges from all these books and rulings has no autonomous existence, that what really determines halakhic decision is not law at all but rather ideology and "religious values" is to declare that what we know to be the central Jewish literary and religious experience is nothing but a snare and a delusion.

I doubt that we really believe in such a declaration. The very point of *Halakhah* has always been the conviction that when rabbis say "this is the law," they are referring to a reality that is not of their own creation, to a tradition of text and practice that stretches far back beyond their own place and time. When rabbis issue halakhic rulings, therefore, they are making a claim for *legitimacy:* that is, that this ruling is a correct interpretation of the sources that the halakhic community accepts as authoritative. The halakhic decision, in other words, must be constrained by the halakhic sources, and its validity must be measured and tested against them. To say that *Halakhah* is nothing more than the will of the rabbis is to give up on the concept of legal legitimacy. If rabbis may decide according to *any* factors they find relevant, if the *Halakhah* is by definition whatever the rabbis say it is, the legal sources no longer serve as a constraint on legal decision. The rabbi becomes the legislator, the creator of new legal norms, rather than the judge, the interpreter of those norms that already exist. Yet this is not what Jews mean when they say that a decision is or must be made "according to *Halakhah,* " which implies that a ruling is not the source of its own legitimacy and that such legitimacy must be judged against a legal standard to which both *posek* and community are bound.

We liberals, for our part, also believe in the concept of halakhic legitimacy. For if we accept the notion that halakhic decision is nothing more than the subjective value preferences of the rabbis, disguised in legal language, we must admit that liberal *Halakhah,* too, is nothing more than *our* value choices, our own subjectivities masked in the same deceptive way. But when we engage in our halakhic thinking, we do not imagine that we are performing some manner of intellectual sleight of hand. It seems to us, rather, that the halakhic process *is* a process, a practice possessing a unique substance that distinguishes it from other kinds of thought, a substance made up of rules and principles that can be interpreted in many different ways but that are not infinitely manipulable. *Halakhah* is a distinct subject matter, worthy of study in its own right and not merely as a subset of religious thought in general. At the same time, we know too much to accept at face value the claim that halakhic decision is but the end result of the operation of legal logic and rational objectivity. I think we believe that somehow each of these descriptions, that of Bleich as well as that of Jacobs, is both accurate and incomplete, that each captures in large part the nature of *pesak* but that neither in and of itself offers a sufficient explanation. A proper theory of *Halakhah*, one intended to account for the Jewish legal process as it really is, must therefore do justice to both points of view.

BY WAY OF COMPARISON: IS THERE SUCH A THING AS "LAW"?

A debate similar to the one I have described is carried on today in the fields of Anglo-American jurisprudence and legal theory. There, as in *Halakhah*, scholars question whether and to what extent law is an autonomous intellectual discipline, whether questions of law can be said to have correct legal answers or whether those answers are in fact determined by the political and social predilections of judges and other legal officials. As is the case with *Halakhah*, it may not matter to most citizens of a political community that the law of their regime is either "autonomous" or not "autonomous"; the law is the law, which they are required to obey regardless of how the theoretical question is answered. But as is also the case with *Halakhah,* issues of theory are of central importance to the community's understanding of itself and of the nature of the process by which it determines the norms of social behavior and communal life.

On one side of the debate in legal theory stand those thinkers and scholars devoted to the concept of *the rule of law,* which affirms that law enjoys a real and independent existence and that the answers to legal questions are derivable and must be derived through the operation of a specifically legal method. Law, in this view, is a self-sufficient discourse that yields its own conclusions and that is independent of any other form of thought or theorizing. As one observer puts it:

> The law wishes to have a formal existence. That means, first of all, that the law does not wish to be absorbed by, or declared subordinate to, some other—nonlegal— structure of concern; the law wishes, in a word, to be distinct, not something else.[19]

If law is a distinct manner of discourse, it resists any attempt to explain legal issues and concepts by means of other manners of discourse, such as politics or morality. It accomplishes its task through a process often called *formalism,* the statement of a question in the proper legal form: that is to say, once any question is translated into correct and appropriate legal language, its answer will be more or less automatically generated by the formal procedure of the legal system "free of all ethical-political value judgments."[20] Therefore, "formalism reflects the law's most abiding aspiration: to be an immanently intelligible normative practice."[21] Not all Rule-of-Law theorists state their case so unequivocally. Although some do seem to define law as a kind of transcendental entity, governed by conceptual thought and

160

procedures and unaffected by its social and economic context, others concede that legal factors are not immune to the workings of the outside world and that law cannot be reduced to the pure logic of the syllogism. Yet all Rule-of-Law theorists are united in seeing law as an inherently *rational* enterprise that "elaborates itself from within."[22] Legal meaning resides in legal text and is not to be imposed upon the text from without. The judge enjoys no discretion to rule according to conscience, considerations of public policy, political conviction, or any other "outside" agenda. Rather, judicial decision (and legal truth in general) is determined by the formal process of legal reasoning, which sets limits on the judge's freedom to act as he or she sees fit. This process, if not identical to mathematics and formal logic, is nonetheless objective. Legal reasoning is that set of rules and procedures that the legal community applies in the act of decision making as the means of discerning *legal* correctness.[23] The decision of a judge or another legal actor is legitimate, therefore, because it is an objectively *legal* conclusion, disciplined by specifically legal rules.[24]

The Rule-of-Law approach has historically based itself on the philosophical heritage of the Enlightenment, particularly its belief in the capacity of reason itself to discover fundamental truth. This belief does not mean that all judges will agree on all legal questions, since they obviously do not and never have. It does imply, however, that jurists hold that a single "right answer" does exist to every legal question and that this answer can be derived through rational means. Disagreements over the right answer can be attributed to judicial error or to inevitable differences in perspective. Judges must interpret the law, after all, to fill its lacunae, to answer those legal questions that the texts themselves do not explicitly address. But legal interpretation is a species of *legal* thought, disciplined by the law's systemic rules and directed toward the discovery of those meanings inherent in the texts. Judges adjudicate; they do not legislate. Unlike legislators, who create law to address some particular purpose or social or political policy, judges derive their answers through the application of "neutral principles"[25] of analysis that transcend the particular decision and ensure the coherence of law as a whole, that each of its components "fits" within the overall structure of its rationality.

The other side of this debate is taken by scholars who deny the objective existence of legal rules and principles and are accordingly skeptical of the formalist notion that correct legal decisions can be derived through logical means. In this view, the "legal" arguments by which jurists explain and justify their actions are but a cover for judgments that are primarily political and social. In the United States the origin of this sort of "rule skepticism" is generally traced to the influence of the noted Supreme Court Justice Oliver Wendell Holmes, Jr. In his scholarly writings and judicial decisions Holmes put forth the view that "the life of the law is not logic but experience,"[26] that "general principles do not decide concrete cases,"[27] and that "the prophecies of what the courts will do in fact, and nothing more pretentious, are what I mean by law."[28] In other words, in legal reality, decisions are generated by the social context in which jurists work, by considerations of public policy, by history, and by the accumulated experience of the legal community. The behavior of legal officials is in fact all that the law is. Logic is of but secondary importance, and it does not succeed in turning law into a formal and rational science.

> The felt necessities of the time, the prevalent moral and political theories, institutions of public policy, avowed or unconscious, even the prejudices that judges share with their fellow men, have had a good deal more to do than the syllogism in determining the rules by which men should be governed.[29]

These pragmatic sentiments[30] became a rallying cry for the academic movement known as Legal Realism, which flourished in elite American law schools during the early decades of the twentieth century.[31] Although the Realists disputed each other on a number of issues, they were united in the view that legal decision cannot be understood apart from the political and other value judgments of legal actors and that "law" properly conceived should be studied according to the methodologies of social science. Attention should be turned away from formal logic and doctrine and toward an investigation of those "real" factors that determine "the rules."

To assume a "realistic" posture is to suggest that the ideal of the Rule of Law is largely a myth. The "rules" and "principles" on which legal meaning is constructed are based ultimately on political, ideological, or social value judgments.[32] Law is therefore indeterminate: legal reasoning cannot *on its own* arrive at uncontroversial answers to legal questions, because as an essentially social practice, governed by a founding ideology, the roots of the law lie deeply embedded in extralegal soil. This theme was disturbing to those legal scholars dedicated to the proposition that law is a self-sufficient discipline, controlled by rules that could produce authentically *legal* truth and meaning. And for a time, "realism" was eclipsed in jurisprudential circles by theories that defined law, again, as a reasoned discipline, whose immanent rules and procedures constrain legal decision, rather than as a pale reflection of politics or sociology. Yet "realism" returned with a vengeance in the 1970s and 1980s, as movements such as Critical Legal Studies[33] and Law and Economics made their presence felt in law schools. For all the differences between them, the adherents of these approaches agree that law does not exist as an "autonomous discipline,"[34] one that operates according to and can be sufficiently explained by internal

163

legal criteria. Rather, "there is never a 'correct legal solution' that is other than the correct ethical or political solution to that legal problem."[35] The decisions of judges and other legal actors are choices that are political or economic and are then rationalized in legal language designed to make these choices appear natural, value neutral, and inevitable. Since legal doctrine is indeterminate—that is, since any given set of legal principles can be used to yield competing or contradictory results—it is useless to inquire as to the "legitimacy" of a judicial decision. Law, the texts and doctrines in the books, does not constrain judicial discretion. Rather, the judge determines the "law" according to the operative nonlegal factor and then massages the texts and doctrines so as to claim legal legitimacy for what is, in fact, his or her subjective choice.[36] As one critical scholar phrased the matter: "lawyers, judges, and scholars make highly controversial political choices, but use the ideology of legal reasoning to make our institutions appear natural and our rules appear neutral."[37]

The foregoing description, a necessarily brief and insufficient one, indicates something of the fragmentation of current legal thought. This breakdown of consensus is perhaps only natural, given that the rise of "postmodernism"[38] and the collapse of "foundationalism"[39] have seriously undermined the faith in our ability to discover firm truths and to impose a rational order on experience. This intellectual climate affects philosophy and many other fields of inquiry. In jurisprudence it expresses itself as a seemingly unbridgeable chasm between those who believe in law as a rationally comprehensible phenomenon and those who identify it with politics, ideology, or some other form of social thought. The former condemn the latter as "nihilists"[40] and speak darkly of the end of their discipline,[41] for if the skeptics should manage to convince the public that there is indeed no authentically *legal* content to the law, the law as a distinct discourse will surely disappear. The "skeptics," for their part, have long since done away with the "noble dream" of law's self-sufficiency and objectivity and are committed to speaking the truth as they see it.

TOWARD A LITERARY SOLUTION

The extreme positions in halakhic thought represented by Bleich and Jacobs are therefore mirrored in the legal academy as well. In both venues, the controversy consists of two sides— "formalists" versus "rule skeptics"—and the stakes are also the same. Either *Halakhah*/law is a practice based on the "rule of law," a set of immanent procedures capable of yielding demonstrably correct legal answers by which the legitimacy of decisions is tested; or *Halakhah*/law is the collection of "acceptable legal ploys" by which the decisor expresses a decision that is in fact not "legal" at all, which therefore cannot be "legitimate," and whose authority is established solely by his or her political or social power to issue it. As is the case with *Halakhah*, the conflict in law is not easy to resolve, since both the formalist and the skeptical positions are plausible and have much to recommend them.

It is thus not surprising that much recent jurisprudential writing has been devoted to the attempt to resolve or at least to minimize this conflict. Legal positivists, for example, seek to compromise between the extremes by asserting that legal rules and concepts possess both a "core" of settled, determinate meaning and a "penumbra" or "open texture," a range of uncertainty at the edges of the concepts as to how they should be applied to concrete cases. Judges enjoy discretion only on issues falling within this range. This, of course, means that in "hard cases," those for which settled answers do not yet exist, the law is in fact indeterminate until such time as the

165

judges create those answers. Positivists concede that judicial discretion amounts to legislation but that, since most legal questions are "easy cases," the amount of indeterminacy in the legal system is moderate and does not threaten the system's legitimacy.[42]

Ronald Dworkin, in a series of powerful if much-debated writings, argues that legal indeterminacy and "strong" judicial discretion do not exist. There is "one right answer" to every legal question, a *legal* answer, and the judge is obliged to search it out. Judges solve "hard cases" through the application of principles of political morality that are inherent in the law and that the judge constructs into a theory that gives the data of the law—the cases and statutes that might be interpreted in several different directions—their best and most coherent explanation. Since theories of political morality differ from critic to critic and from judge to judge, there will always be differences over which answer is "right." The point, though, is that the standards of judgment used are internal to the practice. Thus, judicial decision is a process of adjudication and interpretation whereby the judge endeavors to present the existing law in its fullness and integrity; it is not legislation, the imposition of policy choices by a judge turned legislator.[43]

One of the intellectual trends that holds the most promise for legal theory is the recent "turn to interpretation" in many fields of inquiry. By "interpretation" I mean the contemporary version of that process of knowing. Under the influence of such thinkers as Gadamer[44] in philosophy and Kuhn[45] in physical science, theorists have begun to question the old epistemological distinction between "explanation," that is, objective, verifiable scientific findings, and "interpretation," which signified the more impressionistic type of understanding associated with the human sciences.[46] That distinction, these theorists suggest, is untenable, for no knowledge is "neutral," objective, or context-free. All knowledge is hermeneutical and contextual; one can know a thing only from the perspective he or she occupies and against the backdrop of his or her experience. Every act of inquiry is perforce an exercise in interpretation, the construction of knowledge by an interpreter who stands in the shadow of his or her interpretive "horizon," the theoretical frameworks and preconceptions within which we all operate and without which no understanding can take place. The significance of the "interpretive turn" for legal theory is that it affords an explanation for judicial decision that avoids the pitfalls of either the formalist or the skeptical position. The legal decision is neither the result of a purely deductive process carried out by a detached observer nor of the manipulation of data in accordance with the decisor's subjective value judgments. Rather, like all knowledge, the legal decision is an attempt at understanding, the product of a dialogical meeting between a situated observer, who of necessity perceives the world from the context of a particular horizon or perspective, and the legal text, whose concrete existence limits but does not dictate the outcome of the decision.

If law could be viewed as an interpretive process, it was only natural that legal scholars would perceive that a fruitful connection might be drawn from literature to law. The study of literature is the original hermeneutical activity, and if the domain of "hermeneutics" was once restricted primarily to the explication of religious text—Hermes, after all, was the messenger of the gods— legal scholars soon grasped the obvious connections between the canons of religious knowledge and those used in interpreting legal materials.[47] Literary theory, particularly in the 1970s through the 1990s, was heavily preoccupied with the same interpretive issues that engaged lawyers.[48] Given that the law is an activity bound tightly to

167

engagement with the written word, the creation of new legal texts and the application of existing ones, and given the view in critical circles that the act of interpretation is ubiquitous—no text, even the most deceptively simple, can be understood apart from the activity by which the interpreter constructs meaning out of it[49]—it was thought that a literary approach to law might help explain how judges construct meaning from legal sources.

The growing interest in interpretive theory went hand in hand with the rise of two other "literary" approaches to legal studies. The first of these is "narrative jurisprudence," which focuses on both the narrative elements in the law (the way in which legal actors and the law itself construct the raw materials of human experience into a story that lends them meaning) and the origins of the law and its particular institutions within the matrix of the larger narratives by which a community gives meaning to its own existence.

The second is "rhetoric," which in this context is not defined, as is often the case, as the art of eloquence, of speaking well. Rhetoric in the sense I mean it here denotes the entire realm of argumentation, the means by which a speaker or writer attempts to persuade an audience, to elicit its adherence to the correctness of a particular point of view.[50] Since law is an activity consisting in large part of argumentation, a rhetorical study of law, of the techniques by which lawyers and judges frame their persuasive efforts, could offer useful insights into the nature of legal thought. The confluence of these three components, the theories of interpretation, narrative, and rhetoric as applied to jurisprudence, places us within the domain of the academic movement known as Law and Literature.

Unlike other such jurisprudential "movements" or schools, Law and Literature boasts no single organizing platform or agenda. Those scholars associated with Law and Literature occupy various points of the professional and political spectra, disagreeing with each other on numerous fundamental issues. What unites them ultimately is the conviction that the practice of law can be better understood through the application of techniques of literary study, theory, and criticism. This implies a strong affinity between the disciplines. In the words of a "founding father" of the movement:

> The lawyer and the literary critic are both readers of texts, and as such they face difficulties, and enjoy opportunities, that are far more alike than may seem at first to be the case.... Law is in a full sense a language, for it is a way of reading and writing and speaking, and, in doing these things, it is a way of maintaining a culture, largely a culture of argument, that has a character of its own. [In this way] the law can more properly be seen not as a set of commands and rules...but as the culture of argument and interpretation through the operations of which the rules acquire their life and ultimate meaning.[51]

To conceive of law as a literary activity means to understand legal texts as acts of literary creation and performance. Thus, it is not surprising that Law and Literature scholars pay especially close attention to the judicial opinion, for it is here, in the ruling on the specific case, that judges display their literary power in full. It is here that the judge becomes the author, the creator of a textual universe through the use and manipulation of words, the translator who gives life to old texts by rereading them and placing them in new relations, the writer who in his choice of phrase and shaping of language evokes an "ideal reader" and calls upon him to share in a particular experience of community. All this is the province of literature, rather than economics, politics, sociology, or any other "science." A judge's decision may be affected by all these factors, but it is not reducible to them. The opinion is rather a composition that, though it makes use of the data of "real life," presses those facts into a framework of created meaning, a discourse marked by a formal and technical style that invites its partners to share in the author's particular understanding of the legal traditions of the community. The power and effect of an opinion is therefore largely a result of its form, the judge's preformative success according to the canons of his or her "culture of argument." Thus,

> Rhetoric...does not assist an argument to march to its conclusion; rhetoric *is* the argument, and the perceived rightness or wrongness of the conclusion may be as much based on the style and the form of the argument as on the extrinsic application to it of the observer's notion of what the law of the case "should have been."[52]

One need not accept the extreme version of this theory, which posits that there is little or no real difference between the "form" and the "substance" of a judicial opinion[53] or, for that matter, between the disciplines of "law" and "literature" in general.[54] Yet as long as judges issue their rulings in the form of a text containing supporting argumentation, it is difficult to deny that a judge's opinion is a deeply literary and rhetorical exercise, the work of an author seeking to persuade the members of a professional community of the rightness of the decision in terms that the community finds acceptable and compelling.

The literary method suggests one way in which to resolve the formalist/skeptic dispute over the nature of the judicial decision. The theory would hold that the legitimacy of the decision, its "correctness," is a function of the judge's adherence to the literary demands of the craft. The judge's freedom is constrained by the texts with which he or she must support the decision and by the requirement that the ruling be structured within the linguistic framework deemed necessary and sufficient by the intended audience of the opinion. The judge operates according to the rules of a discourse that might be characterized, in terms borrowed from Wittgenstein, as a literary "practice," that is, an internally defined activity carried on by individuals committed to a particular interpretive strategy that applies rules and norms in light of a commonly held conception of the purposes they serve.[55] But if the judicial decision is shaped by these literary requirements, it remains in the end the product of its author(s), an act of writing involving the interpretation and combination of existing texts in a way that is not dictated in advance and that perforce is unique to the mind of its creator(s). If a judge can be free to exercise "subjective preferences" within the parameters of a defined discipline, this is the freedom that he or she can and must enjoy.

ON RESPONSA AS LITERATURE

Would such a literary method be helpful in resolving or elucidating the very similar dispute in halakhic theory, the disagreement highlighted by the positions of David Bleich and Louis Jacobs? Literary theory has lately become a popular academic tool for the study of rabbinic thought. The rabbis, we are now accustomed to say, were not only philosophers, theologians, lawyers, and mystics; they were also writers, who, by presenting their teachings through the vehicle of text, placed an indelible literary stamp on them. Put differently, it is difficult if not impossible to detach the rabbinic message from its medium; the reality of text as *the* form of rabbinic study and conversation is inextricably entwined with the substance of rabbinic Judaism. And, particularly relevant to the subject under discussion here, some preliminary efforts have been made to apply literary analysis to rabbinic responsa *(she'elot uteshuvot),* the "questions and answers" that, containing the legal decisions of rabbis and their supporting argumentation, are the closest analog in traditional rabbinic writing to the judicial opinion.[56]

It seems to me that the kind of analysis described in Law and Literature writings might indeed be useful toward understanding the intellectual activity called *pesak.* To this end, I want to consider three responsa of Rabbi Moshe Feinstein, the acclaimed halakhist, *rosh yeshivah,* and communal leader who died in New York in 1986. Known as a formidable talmudist in his native Russia, in 1937 Feinstein emigrated to the United States, where he achieved renown as one of the outstanding Orthodox *poskim* in the world. His responsa, the *Igerot Moshe,* are widely read for the authoritative halakhic guidance they provide to observant Jews. They have yet, however, to be studied as *literature,* as examples of the art of writing. I want to pursue that study here, if only in brief, as a sample and demonstration of all we might learn from a literary approach to rabbinic legal decision and the *she'elot uteshuvot.*

1. The Wedding in the Reform Temple. The first example is taken from a pair of *teshuvot* in which Rabbi Feinstein allows wives to remarry by declaring their existing marriages null and void.[57] In each case the marriage has ended for all practical purposes and divorces have been secured in the civil courts, but neither husband will agree to grant his wife a divorce in Jewish law *(get piturin).* The stakes are clear: if no halakhic remedy can be found, the women will be *agunot,* "chained" to their husbands and forbidden under *Halakhah* to remarry. Feinstein provides this remedy by annulling the women's marriages on the grounds that their weddings took place in Reform synagogues where Reform rabbis acted as officiants.

He begins his analysis with a paragraph describing Reform Jews as thoroughly alienated from normative Judaism:

> Concerning the woman married by a Reform "rabbi,"[58] in a setting where all those who attended the wedding were non-observant [literally, "evil," *resha'im*] libertines who violate the Sabbath and transgress every commandment of the Torah, and where everyone ate a meal consisting of non-kosher meat....

The fact that the wedding was held in a Reform "temple"[59] allows us to presume that no valid witnesses (i.e., halakhically observant Jewish males) were present at the wedding, and in the absence of valid witnesses, a constitutive component of the Jewish wedding, no valid act of betrothal *(kiddushin)* has taken place. Feinstein, however, must deal with a difficulty posed by a famous responsum of R. Moshe Sofer, who ruled that an act of *kiddushin* may indeed be binding in the absence of valid witnesses.[60] Sofer dealt with a case in which a rabbi mistakenly appointed two relatives as witnesses to a wedding, a technicality that disqualifies their testimony. Nonetheless, he held the wedding valid because, since qualified witnesses outside the synagogue observed "from a distance" that a couple entered the place for a wedding, their testimony can serve to establish that a proper act of *kiddushin* took place even if they did not attend the actual ceremony. Here, too, Feinstein must contend with the possibility that valid witnesses saw the couple "enter the 'temple' in order to marry or saw them leave from there as a 'married' couple." The decision of a great authority such as Sofer is a powerful precedent. But, like any skillful judge, Feinstein is able to distinguish the precedent and to declare that it has nothing whatsoever to do with the case at hand.

Sofer's decision, he writes, applies only when the "distant witnesses," who know that a wedding took place, can presume[61] that the wedding was properly conducted. However,

> with respect to one of these non-observant ["evil"] Reformers who conducts a wedding, it is obvious that we cannot presume that the act of *kiddushin* was conducted properly, with the transmission of an object of value from groom to bride along with the proper declaration of intent. For every "Reform rabbi" simply invents some ritual and calls it *"kiddushin"*....

That is, "distant" witnesses can testify to a legally valid wedding on the basis of appearances only when that "apparent" wedding was conducted by a rabbi who is *presumed* to be observant and knowledgeable of Jewish law. That presumption does not hold in our case. "Clearly," Feinstein concludes, witnesses who were not present at a wedding in a Reform synagogue cannot testify that a valid ceremony occurred, even if they know that the "rabbi" performed "an act which he called *'kiddushin'"* and even if by some chance it turns out that in this particular wedding the "rabbi" did manage to include the necessary halakhic requirements.

By establishing that no proper act of *kiddushin* can be proved or presumed to have taken place, Feinstein is able to dispense with another ground on which this marriage might be valid:
the suggestion that, inasmuch as "no man makes his intercourse an act of licentiousness,"[62] the husband subsequently performed the act of marital intercourse *leshem kiddushin,* "in order to effect a valid betrothal."[63] The reasoning is as follows: the marital intercourse effects *kiddushin* only if the husband intends it as such; but he would only intend it as such if he thought that the original act of *kiddushin* (i.e., the wedding in the Reform temple) was itself of no legal force; and since "those who go to 'Reform rabbis' think, erroneously, that

their wedding was halakhically valid, they perform their marital intercourse on that false assumption," that is, thinking they are already married. Moreover, the presumption that "no man makes his intercourse an act of licentiousness" probably does not apply to "those libertines who violate all the prohibitions of the Torah": why would we say that such persons are not perfectly happy with licentious behavior?

The argument rests, therefore, on the finding that Reform Jews and their clergy are presumed to be nonobservant of Jewish law in general and of the ritual requirements of *kiddushin* in particular. Rabbi Feinstein declares this to be the case in the manner of sweeping generalization: "It is known that" Reform Jews are nonobservant; "it is obvious that" a Reform rabbi "creates" a wedding ceremony that he calls *kiddushin*. Yet nowhere does Feinstein cite any proof for these assertions. Has he observed Reform weddings? Does he have evidence that such ceremonies do not usually contain the necessary halakhic elements for valid *kiddushin?* Does he know for a fact that halakhically observant Jews do not attend Reform weddings? These assertions may be correct, but their correctness is a matter of observable fact, to be established by empirical evidence that Feinstein neither cites nor mentions. This, the assuming of facts not in evidence, would seem to be an egregious error of legal method.[64]

Rabbi Joel Roth levels this very criticism against Rabbi Feinstein, addressing himself to a decision in which Feinstein holds that because Conservative Jews are heretics *(koferim* or *apikorsim),* a "fit" Jew should not accept a teaching position in their community.[65] Again, Feinstein simply declares this to be the case, offering no proof for the heresy of Conservative Jews. And although he enjoys the judicial discretion to make this decision, says Roth, the systemic rules

175

of the halakhic process require that he support it with evidence. Following the theory of legal positivism, Roth notes that Feinstein has confused the boundaries between "questions of law" and "questions of fact."[66] A question of law is one whose answer is derived through interpretation of the legal sources. The definition of heresy, a topic discussed in the texts, is such a question.[67]

A question of fact, on the other hand, must be answered by an examination of the circumstances of the particular case. The determination that Conservative Jews are "heretics" is a question of fact: do Conservative Jews *in fact* ascribe to doctrines to which the legal sources point as indices of heresy? The question must be answered by means of factual evidence. Yet Feinstein never adduces such evidence, even though "such a characterization of Conservative Jews is, at best, a *machloket,* and conceivably a matter of opinion."[68] It may be true, in other words, that Conservative Jews meet the legal definition of *apikorsim,* and if a *posek* can prove this point to his own satisfaction, his decision is a legitimate one. Feinstein's responsum is a failure, however, because his decision rests on facts not in evidence, on a mere assumption rather than the required standard of proof.

Roth makes a good point, especially if one accepts the formalist notion that a legal answer be "legitimate," that it measure up to rational, even "scientific" standards of correctness and proof. The point, however, is totally irrelevant to Feinstein and to the context in which he operates. As an Orthodox *posek* writing for Orthodox Jews, Feinstein does not have to "prove" that Conservative Jews are heretics. Although a readership of Conservative Jews might indeed contest this conclusion, Feinstein is not addressing himself to them. He is speaking to an Orthodox audience, inviting them to share in a particular view of the Jewish religious world and of their place in it.

He creates a community by this linguistic act, this use of words. Feinstein in effect tells his readers: "I want you to join with me in a common Jewish enterprise, one in which we, the Orthodox Jews, are the sole representatives of Jewish religious authenticity." For those readers who accept this invitation, no "proof" of the heresy of Conservative Jews is necessary; that heresy is rather a self-evident fact, an essential element of those readers' self-identification as Jews. The *posek* might not subject the truth of this "fact" to formal demonstration, but it is no less "true" for that. It is a *literary* and *rhetorical* truth, because it meets the test of persuasiveness. In the eyes of the particular halakhic community that Feinstein both creates and addresses through his *teshuvah*, the heresy of Conservative Jews and Judaism is accepted as a convincing interpretation of Jewish law and as proper grounds for legal decision. As such, the *posek* has met the only standard of "proof" that really counts.

In our case, too, Feinstein uses words to create a *rhetorical* and *literary* truth, a truth measured not by its correspondence to some objective standard of correctness but by the quality of its performance, its effect on an intended legal audience. Again, he does not demonstrate through empirical evidence that Reform Jews are nonobservant and that Reform rabbis are halakhically ignorant. And again, this fact is irrelevant. What is relevant, and crucial, is that Feinstein's intended audience is persuaded of the truth of these statements, to the point that no "proof" is necessary for them. Feinstein addresses an ideal reader who cannot imagine that Reform Jewish religious practice could possibly meet the minimum criteria of halakhic acceptability. This reader is the one whom Feinstein addresses and invites to share his own perception of the world of Torah and *Halakhah*. Once again, an audience of Reform Jews and other Jews might object that Feinstein's blithe assertions about

Reform Jews and rabbis are a "matter of opinion," even factually incorrect. They would not accept his *pesak*, because they would not necessarily be persuaded of the legal correctness of the assertions on which it is based. But then, he is not addressing himself to Reform Jews. They are not part of the community he creates in these responsa, and they are not his ideal readers.

The import of community and audience is manifest when we compare Feinstein's ruling with a decision of the Supreme Rabbinic Court of Eretz Yisrael in 1946.[69] Feinstein invalidates the wedding in the Reform temple by invalidating the testimony of the witnesses: individuals who transgress the ritual commandments of the Torah (he mentions Shabbat and the dietary laws explicitly) are by that reason ineligible to serve as witnesses. This is certainly a plausible interpretation of Jewish law: the Torah disqualifies the "evil" *(rasha)* as a witness, and those who habitually violate the Torah's commandments are defined as "wicked."[70] The Jerusalem court, by contrast, suggests that the testimony of such individuals may be accepted. The court holds that the *rasha* is ineligible to be a witness, not merely because he is sinful but because he is untrustworthy. His nonobservance, in and of itself, is not the issue; rather, the fact that he violates any of God's laws leads us to presume that, as he is lawless and immoral, he would not hesitate to violate the rest of them. Thus, one who eats nonkosher food is just as likely to transgress the prohibition against bearing false witness. Today, says the court, against the backdrop of widespread nonobservance, we can no longer make this presumption. The judges write that in a secular age, "when ritual transgressions *(aveirot shebein adam lamakom)*" have become a rampant phenomenon among the Jewish people, "such transgressions do not imply that the witnesses are dishonest." If most Jews in our time are nonobservant, this fact is to be attributed to

178

"general, world-wide forces" beyond their control. In a secular age, when "God's face is hidden" from so many, those who violate the ritual commandments do not do so intentionally, are not necessarily "wicked," and are quite possibly honest and reliable individuals. A court should therefore consider each case on its own merits, and if it should find that an individual is unlikely to deliver false testimony, he should be accepted as a witness even though he is ritually non-observant. This alternative theory of the law of testimony is, to be sure, controversial; the Israeli court concedes as much, writing that "this question demands much clarification." Yet whether or not one accepts it, it does exist, and we might say that Feinstein's failure to mention[71] and to argue against it weakens his claim that, as a matter of halakhic doctrine, those in attendance at Reform weddings are invalid witnesses.

Again, however, the literary method would advise us that the real difference between the two positions is not one of legal doctrine or method but rather of audience. The Israeli rabbinic court issues its ruling in the context of the nascent Jewish state, a community in which, although the institutions of marriage and divorce for Jews are governed by *Halakhah*, the preponderant majority of its citizens are nonobservant of Jewish ritual law.[72] By referring to this majority as "unintentional transgressors" *(shogegim)*, the Court calls on its audience, made up primarily of rabbis and other knowledgeable students of Jewish law, to include *all* Jewish citizens within the circumference of the halakhic communiity. True, this audience, like the Court's judges, are "Orthodox Jews." But the Court's appeal is persuasive to them to the extent that they accept the definition (in the decision) of the Jewish community, *kelal yisrael*, as the entire Jewish people, observant and not. And they will accept this definition to the extent that they are able to see the entire people as engaged in the

179

fulfillment of a common religious destiny. The members of the Court were rabbis closely associated with the Zionist movement and with the dream that *Halakhah*, the law of the Torah, would become the legal foundation for the new Jewish state. The audience they address, therefore, is an audience of rabbis and Jewish legal scholars who share their basic assumptions about the religious meaning of the Jewish national movement, its messianic implications, and the need to draw all Jewish citizens under the umbrella of participation in the legal framework of the state. The *charedim,* those "ultra-Orthodox" Jews who reject the notion that the new state possesses any Jewish religious value, would probably disagree with this argument to include the secularists and nonobservant within the parameters of the legal community. But then, the Court is not addressing itself to that audience. Instead, it evokes an ideal reader who, although Orthodox and observant, can entertain the notion that some degree of pluralism is a necessary and permissible element in the administration of the Jewish legal system.[73]

Feinstein, meanwhile, addresses himself to a very different audience: that group of North American Orthodox Jews that consciously defines itself, over against the larger liberal Jewish community,[74] as the sole embodiment of authentic Judaism. Such a community does not—indeed, cannot—include nonobservant Jews within its notion of *kelal yisrael,* let alone accept them as valid witnesses under the *Halakhah.* Indeed, such a community must regard nonobservant Jews as "libertines," equally liable to violate the moral commandments of the Torah as they are its ritual laws; for this reason, we will recall, the rule "no man makes his intercourse an act of licentiousness" does not apply to anyone outside the Orthodox world. Not all Orthodox rabbis will agree with this assessment of non-Orthodox Jews,[75] yet Feinstein need not argue with them or prove that his view is more correct than theirs. His very language is the tool by

180

which his community of interpretation constitutes itself: by assuming the "wickedness" of the non-Orthodox, by not even discussing the possibility that nonobservant Jews might be allowed to testify, he invites his audience to share in his conviction that the halakhic community, the Jewish religious community, consists solely and exclusively of Orthodox Jews. He offers no proof for this assertion, because no proof is necessary. The apodictic statement, put forward as self-evident fact, allows a community to define itself, to delineate its own realm of existence by excluding others that do not share its sense of identification. Feinstein's words are not so much "proof" of a position as they are a banner, a linguistic formula that enables this particular audience to coalesce around a shared conception of Jewish authenticity. For this reason, even if different halakhic theories exist and no matter how well or poorly Feinstein "proves" his case according to a set of formalist criteria, he has accomplished his task through language that both persuades and defines his intended audience.

2. Flags in the Synagogue. Our second example is a ruling Feinstein issued in 1957.[76] The leaders of a synagogue have decided to place the national flags of the United States and Israel in the sanctuary. This offends some of the members, who have threatened to leave and form a breakaway congregation. What should be done?

Feinstein begins his responsum by noting that a synagogue is not rendered an unfit place for prayer by sinful acts committed within its walls. He cites an incident in which the *shamash* of a synagogue was discovered *in flagrante delicto* with a woman in the sanctuary; after removing him from the place, the congregants prayed there nevertheless.[77] This proves that "the sanctity of a synagogue does not depart, even if it is treated in an unholy manner or if actual sins and disgraceful acts are performed therein." Thus, "even if we say that the

181

placing of flags violates a ritual prohibition, the synagogue is not profaned thereby. And it is preferable to pray there than to form a *minyan* in a place not devoted to prayer *(makom chol)*."

In addition, Feinstein continues, the *Halakhah* contains no explicit prohibition against the presence of national flags in a synagogue sanctuary. This is not a case of idolatry or an appurtenance of idolatry. The leaders of the synagogue, who put the flags there, do not consider them to be holy, objects of religious devotion; they are merely symbols "that the leaders of the synagogue love this country and the state of Israel and that they wish to display this love in a public place." Even though "those who created the flag of Israel [i.e., the Zionists] were wicked people *[resha'im;* that is, nonobservant]," we need not worry that an act of idolatry is being committed because nobody imagines that they are worshipping the flags. For this reason, although "it is certainly improper" to put the flags in the sanctuary, especially *(kol shekhein)* on a permanent basis and especially *(kol shekhein)* next to the ark, this is nothing more than "a matter of nonsense and foolishness" *(hevel veshetut)* that violates no explicit prohibition. It would, of course, be a good thing to remove the flags, particularly that of Israel, which calls to mind the "deeds of the wicked" *(ma'aseh haresha'im),* but such a move should not be taken if it would lead to communal strife and contention *(machloket)*. Feinstein closes with an admonition to the members of the synagogue who threaten to quit the synagogue over the flags. "They think they are doing a great thing, but they are acting improperly; this is nothing more than politics, instigated by the evil impulse."

What is especially noteworthy about this *teshuvah* is the deftness with which Feinstein changes the subject at issue. The central question in this case, one would think, is the propriety of placing

182

national flags in the synagogue sanctuary: is it right or wrong, proper or improper, to introduce these nonreligious symbols into a place that partakes of sanctity *(kedushah)?* To the extent that he discusses this question, Feinstein makes it clear that he agrees with the disgruntled congregants. It is, he writes, an "improper" thing to put national flags in the sanctuary. It is an act of "foolishness" to introduce secular symbols into sacred space, particularly when the presence of one of those symbols would grant undeserved recognition to the deeds of the "wicked" Zionists. The flags do not belong in the synagogue, and they ought to be removed. Therefore, were the *she'lah* to be framed in this way— "is it permissible to put national flags in the synagogue sanctuary?"—there seems little doubt that its answer would be a resounding no. Feinstein, however, asks the question in a very different way: "Does the presence of national flags, which admittedly do not belong in the synagogue, justify an extreme act of opposition (quitting the synagogue) that threatens the unity and perhaps the survival of the congregation?"

The question, in other words, is no longer "about" flags so much as it is "about" *machloket,* communal strife that threatens to divide and perhaps to destroy a synagogue. This changing of the subject is crucial to the answer that Feinstein ultimately renders. Where the original question, the propriety of the flags, would seem to invite a decision in favor of the demands of the disgruntled congregants, this new question directs our sympathies away from them and their otherwise justified claims.

To construct the question thus is a rhetorical accomplishment of real significance. It accomplishes a major shifting of the burden of proof, the drawing of a distinction between the accepted opinion and the opinion that cannot be adopted without sufficient reason.[78] We would normally expect that those who introduce a change into the existing situation (in this case, the leaders of the synagogue) would bear the responsibility of demonstrating that their innovation, which after all has instigated the problem in the first place, does not transgress the *Halakhah* or Jewish religious norms. Feinstein's *teshuvah* transfers that responsibility onto the other side: it is the disgruntled congregants who must now prove that the action of the leaders of the synagogue is odious enough to warrant a breakup of the congregation.

The setting and the shifting of the legal burden of proof is a powerful rhetorical tool in the hands of the judicial writer, and Feinstein wields it here with consummate skill. The disgruntled congregants, who are, as Feinstein himself admits, *right* about the flags in theory, now find themselves at a tactical disadvantage: it is they, and not the synagogue leaders, who must prove their case. This disadvantage becomes insurmountable, moreover, when Feinstein determines just what it is they have to prove. To "win," the disgruntled congregants must demonstrate not only that the synagogue leaders have violated Jewish religious norms but that the presence of the flags somehow desecrates the synagogue and renders it unfit for prayer.

This is an impossible burden, because, as Feinstein notes, a synagogue never loses its holiness as the result of sins committed within the building. Of course, the disgruntled congregants in all probability never raised this concern: their claim is not that the synagogue has become desecrated but simply that the presence of flags is improper there. Feinstein, as we have seen, agrees with this more modest assertion. But because he perceives the "real" issue here as *machloket*, congregational division and strife, he declares that ritual

184

impropriety is no longer sufficient warrant to decide in favor of the disgruntled congregants. He requires, rather, that they prove the stronger claim of desecration. And this is a standard of proof beyond their reach.

All this points to a simple fact: nothing in this case *requires* Feinstein to address it as he does. He might have centered this question, as other responsa have done,[79] around the propriety of national flags in the synagogue; had he followed this course, his answer would presumably have offered support to the outrage of the dissatisfied synagogue members. Neither his answer nor the structure of his argument can thus be said in any way approaching objectivity to be "correct."

The fact that the responsum exists in the form that we have it, expressing an answer very different from the one we might otherwise expect, is the result of a construct its writer places on the facts before him. A responsum, in other words, is a *literary* construct, a text that invites its readers to share in its author's perception of legal reality. Although the legal author is bound to his "data," the facts at issue, and the legal materials from which he is expected to fashion his answer, he is like all authors to a very real extent the creator of his literary universe. It is the author of a responsum that defines the parameters of the issue he addresses, determining what the question is "about," where the burden of proof shall lie, and of precisely what that burden consists. These activities, a necessary feature of every halakhic decision, are at bottom *literary* activities. No science or calculus dictates them to the *posek*. They are not deductions arrived at by a judicial scientist in search of an objectively verifiable legal answer. They are rather judgments of an author constructing a text whose words define the question at hand, the standards of proof that must be

185

met, and the very legal universe in which the *posek* and his readers function.

Judgments are not syllogisms; they do not arrive at truth by way of logical demonstration. But no judicial writing or reasoning is possible without them. If the *posek* exercises these judgments well—that is, to the extent he succeeds in persuading his intended audience to view the question as he does—he has accomplished his task; he has proved, in the best and only way he can, that his answer is a "correct" one.

3. Artificial Insemination—Donor. The third responsum I shall examine pertains to the field we call "medical ethics." In the case before Feinstein, a woman has had herself inseminated with the sperm of a man other than her husband and without her husband's consent. The husband wishes to know whether, according to *Halakhah,* his wife is permitted to him sexually, that is to say, did she commit adultery by having herself inseminated?[80] He inquires as well as to the status of the child. Feinstein[81] rules in favor of the wife on virtually every relevant issue. The wife is not forbidden to her husband, since "adultery" can be committed only by means of sexual intercourse. The child, should it be the offspring of a Jewish semen donor, is not a *mamzer,* since the status of *mamzerut,* too, is effected only through actual intercourse.[82] Moreover, we can assume that in America, where the majority of males are Gentiles, the child is the offspring of a non-Jewish semen donor; this means that *mamzerut* is not an issue[83] and that we need not worry that the child may grow up and marry a relative of his Jewish father. Feinstein even suggests that although the daughter of a non-Jewish male is prohibited from marrying a *kohen,*[84] the prohibition does not apply when the conception took place through artificial means. Hence, if this child is a female, she is permitted to marry a *kohen*. The woman's husband "wins" only to the extent that he is not obliged to support the child, who was after all conceived despite the husband's wishes.

The most significant feature of this responsum, perhaps, is what Feinstein does *not* say. At no point does he indicate that there is something "wrong" with the wife's action or that she has transgressed against some aspect of Jewish law by becoming pregnant in this manner. His ruling therefore stands in sharp opposition to the overwhelming consensus of Orthodox halakhic opinion, which, though it permits artificial insemination when the semen donor is the woman's husband (AIH),[85] prohibits the procedure known as AID, artificial insemination by means of a "foreign" donor,[86] and this for two principal reasons. First, AIH is justifiable if it is the only way in which the husband can father children and thus fulfill his halakhic requirement "to be fruitful and multiply." AID, by contrast, does not produce a child to the husband. And since women are not obligated under the *mitzvah* of procreation,[87] a wife who is impregnated with the semen of a "foreign" donor fulfills no halakhic requirement that would warrant such a radical departure from the normal, natural means of conception.[88] In this case, since the child would not be the husband's offspring, its birth would not help him fulfill his *mitzvah* to bring children into the world. Second, most *poskim* consider the insertion of "foreign" seed into the womb of a married woman to be a revulsive act. If it is not, strictly speaking, adultery, it is nonetheless a *to'evah* ("abomination") and a *ma'aseh ki'ur* ("an act of ugliness"), a transgression against the most fundamental Jewish standards of sexual propriety.[89]

How does R. Moshe Feinstein counter this weight of precedent? How does he prove unobjectionable a procedure that so many authorities condemn so strongly? Once again, I would suggest that "proof," in the sense we normally use this term, has nothing to do with it. Feinstein instead establishes his point by literary means, by constructing a text in which the concerns that occupy the other *poskim* are conspicuous by their absence.

Let us consider, first of all, the language with which Feinstein introduces this *teshuvah:*

> The matter concerns a woman who has been married for ten years and has not given birth to children. The physicians say that the cause of the childlessness lies with her husband. And for this reason the wife went to the doctor, who injected the semen of another man into her womb. She wishes to bear children as is the desire of all women, as we learn in *BT* Yevamot 65b.... Aside from this halakhic evidence, it is well known that our holy matriarchs desired to bear children, as indeed do all women everywhere.

As indicated above, most halakhic authorities classify the issue of artificial insemination as a subset of the *mitzvah* of procreation. The procedure is permissible to the extent that it allows a Jewish man to fulfill his toraitic obligation. *Poskim,* for example, will discuss at some length the question of whether a child conceived by artificial insemination is, under *Halakhah,* the legal offspring of the semen donor. If the answer is "no," they are much less likely to permit the procedure, which in any case is a signifi-cant departure from natural procreation, since a child thus conceived would not be counted toward the male's requirement for procreation.[90] The entire question is framed, in other words, from the perspective of the husband. That the wife may desire to have children is irrelevant to these discussions, because she fulfills no *mitzvah* thereby. In Feinstein's *teshuvah,* however, the wife replaces the husband as the center of our concern. Her wish to have children is taken seriously, for three reasons: (1) it is the desire of all women; (2) the biblical narratives of the matriarchs show that our tradition treats this desire as one of immense importance; and (3) the *Halakhah* itself, in *BT* Yevamot 65b, regards a husband's sterility as grounds for divorce, not because the wife is *required* to procreate but because her wish to have children is actionable, a sufficient warrant for the court to take legal notice.

In the space of a single paragraph, Feinstein has totally redefined the framework in which halakhists generally discuss the question of artificial insemination. No longer do we apprehend this technology primarily as a means of enabling a husband to fulfill his *mitzvah;* it is now chiefly a means of allowing a wife to fulfill her own hopes and dreams. As such, the case for AID becomes a much stronger one. Feinstein does all of this, I must emphasize, without ever mentioning the opinions of all those authorities that disregard the wife's desire to bear children as irrelevant to the question. Those opinions had created a paradigm, a way of thinking and talking about artificial insemination that, because it proceeded from the husband's *mitzvah* to procreate, virtually demanded a negative halakhic response to AID. The "weight of precedent" would seem to impose upon every *posek,* as a member of the halakhic community, the obligation to consider those other rulings. Either he would have to submit to the judgment of all these worthy scholars, or he would have to refute them or at least show why his own decision does not run counter to established rabbinic legal thought. Feinstein does none of this; he simply ignores the other opinions. His introduction, which speaks to the wife's wishes and needs, totally reframes the question. It replaces the established paradigm with a new discourse on the subject, one that leads us inexorably to accept a *pesak* that diverges sharply from the existing halakhic consensus. For when we examine this issue from the standpoint of the wife, listening to her voice, placing her desires rather

189

than her husband's ritual obligations at the foundation of our reasoning, we are much less likely to find a halakhic impediment against AID. In one fell swoop, therefore, Feinstein has turned the halakhic world upside down. What is now "irrelevant" is the fact that the husband will not fulfill a *mitzvah* if his wife is impregnated by another man's semen; what is "relevant" is that the woman will realize a goal that is most proper and natural for her. In the textual universe Feinstein has created, the husband's *mitzvah* is never considered and plays no role in determining the law. The dominant consideration, instead, is our own *mitzvah* to alleviate the suffering of the childless Jewish woman.

How does Feinstein deal with the second objection to AID, that it is a *to'evah* or an "ugly" thing? Here, too, he "refutes" a troublesome legal argument by ignoring it. Feinstein treats the insertion of "foreign" semen as a normal medical procedure, discussing it in language that is entirely free of pejorative terminology and moral judgment. This is true even when the semen donor is a Gentile. Not only does Feinstein analyze this possibility in a dispassionate tone; but he also points out that the use of a Gentile's semen would solve some difficult halakhic problems that would arise were the donor a Jew.[91] Once again he diverges from the position of other halakhists, for they tend to regard the use of Gentile semen as a particularly disgusting thing.[92] And once again, he "proves" his point by ignoring theirs. The moral concerns over Gentile semen do not exist because his text simply does not mention them. Were we to read his responsum in isolation from the others, we would have no idea that AID presents any special moral or even aesthetic problem.[93]

How is it possible that the author of a halakhic responsum can smash the paradigms and ignore the conclusions of his peers? The answer, as was the case with our two previous examples, is the literary nature of halakhic decision. Here, too, we see the *posek* at work as author, the creator of a text. Like an author, it is the *posek* who defines the parameters of his subject matter. It is he who establishes the perspective of the responsum, the vantage point from which he invites his readers to consider the question as a whole. It is he who determines the issues that must be discussed, the points that must be proved, the objections to be ignored or taken seriously. None of these decisions is artificial, a trick, a distortion of formal legal process. Each one of them is a step that must be taken, necessary to the construction of the responsum, the analysis of the halakhic issues involved, and the justification of its ruling. Each one of them is an indispensable element in the creation of a language, a way of speaking and thinking about an issue that the author proposes to his audience. Each one is in other words a quintessentially *literary*, as opposed to a strictly *legal*, activity. The halakhic decisor presents his *pesak* as part of a text that creates a community with its intended readers, that invites them to view halakhic reality in the way that its creator views it, and that suggests to them ways of thinking and speaking about the values that are constitutive of Jewish religious life. In this sense we can say that R. Moshe Feinstein is successful as a *posek* to the extent that he succeeds as an author.

SOME CONCLUDING OBSERVATIONS

We return to our original question: is there such a thing as *"Halakhah"*? Does there exist a distinct process of Jewish legal reasoning, an activity possessing its own intellectual integrity and that cannot without loss be translated or assimilated into any other mode of thinking and speaking? The examples I have cited here suggest both that *Halakhah,* like law, claims an autonomous existence and that this

191

autonomy ought to be acknowledged as real. *Halakhah* is not the same thing as ethics or theology or economics or any other discipline. It expresses its conception of reality, frames its arguments, and derives its conclusions in a language all its own, a discourse that operates according to its own understood procedures and that therefore cannot be reduced to any other form of discourse. It is in this sense that we can describe *Halakhah*, with accuracy, as an "objective" reality: the answers it reaches are not simply the personal proclivities of the rabbis but the product of a process that justifies those answers according to accepted standards of legal validity.

On the other hand, an examination of these *teshuvot* indicates that such "standards of legal validity" are a literary invention. It is the *posek,* the author of this literary text, who determines just what those standards shall be. It is the *posek* who combines the materials at his disposal to persuade his intended audience, his "ideal" readers, that they should view halakhic reality in a specific way as opposed to other plausible ways. The creation of a responsum is therefore an act of language. It is the translation of texts, the substance of Jewish legal tradition, into new patterns of meaning. It is an act of conversation that helps constitute a community through a shared language of values, assumptions, and aspirations that link author to audience in a common culture of argument.

For this reason, although it is possible to speak of law as a distinct discipline, it is much more difficult to speak of legal correctness as the objective outcome of the operation of formal logic or method. Indeed, the word "method," understood as a set of neutral principles by which the answers to all legal questions are tested and evaluated, is inappropriate in the extreme. It would be better, our findings suggest, to measure the correctness of an act of halakhic reasoning in terms of its literary and rhetorical excellence, its success in winning the adherence of a community of readers and in shaping the course of halakhic discourse, the way in which subsequent communities of readers perceive and frame the issues. To put it differently, the question to ask of a rabbinic responsum is not whether it is "right" but whether it meets the standards of excellence we would expect of a well-written work of literature.

Although wide-ranging and general scholarly conclusions concerning rabbinic responsa cannot confidently be based on a reading of but three *teshuvot,* what these examples suggest to us is that the next stage in the study of the responsa literature ought to be their study *as* literature. This is not to say that they should be read and analyzed precisely as we seek to comprehend a poem, a novel, or a play. To impose such standards on responsa would be as out of place as subjecting them to the criteria of formal logic and scientific reasoning. It is to suggest, though, that, as written texts, responsa have much in common with other literary creations and that it is this very literary nature that determines how the responsum functions as an act of rabbinic instruction addressed to and carried on within a community of observant Jews.

And this conclusion is a significant one for our self-understanding as liberal halakhists, as non-Orthodox Jews who seek to construct a language of religious meaning out of the sources of the Jewish legal tradition. It is significant because we carry out our work under the disapproving stares of critics to both our right and our left. The former, representing a formalist stance much like that expressed by J. David Bleich, argue that our activity and conclusions are simply wrong, that they transgress the set, logically determined standards of halakhic validity that exist independently of the individual rabbinic decision and that measure the correctness of every Jewish legal utterance. The latter, who draw to their logical extreme the observations of Louis Jacobs, assert that there *is* no standard of halakhic correctness, that every legal decision is nothing more than the translation of the rabbi's religious or ideological predilections into a neutral-sounding legal vernacular. We err, they say, in thinking that there is a thing called *Halakhah* that is anything other than these predilections, and we waste our time attempting to enlist halakhic language in expressing our notions of Jewish religious truth when the "real" meaning conveyed by Jewish legal teaching is to be found in other forms of discourse.

A literary conception of the activity of *Halakhah,* a conception that accounts for much of what the *posek* actually does, responds to both these criticisms. There *is* such a thing as *Halakhah,* we would assert, but it is properly understood as a culture of argument, a way of thinking and speaking, rather than a collection of discrete conclusions and a "scientific" method for arriving at them. Our *Halakhah* is as "legitimate" as any other version of it, to the extent that our halakhic writings participate in this culture. Our audience differs substantially in fact from the audience of most Orthodox responsa, but all halakhic writing and argument is addressed to *some* Jewish audience that takes halakhic writing and argument seriously and considers it prayerfully. And, in principle, we present our arguments and conclusions to all Jews, for though we know that many will reject what we say, we believe that they could be persuaded by our words, were they to open themselves to persuasion. For these reasons we need not regard our work as halakhically suspect, let alone inauthentic. For these reasons, we can proclaim the importance and the necessity of our work, take pride in what we have accomplished, and turn our energies to the completion of the halakhic tasks that yet lie before us.

Notes

1.   Throughout this paper, I use masculine pronouns to refer to antecedents of indeterminate gender. Although I generally try to write in a more gender-inclusive style, it is a fact that most "rabbis" and "halakhic scholars," historically speaking, have been men, and those *poskim* who function in the world of R. Moshe Feinstein are to this day exclusively male. Today, of course, the halakhic process in the liberal Jewish world is open to the active participation of female as well as male scholars, a subject about which I will have some things to say below.

2.   J. David Bleich, *Contemporary Halakhic Problems* (New York: Ktav/Yeshiva, 1977), xiii–xviii.

3.   Bleich cites in this context the *agadah* of R. Eliezer and his dispute with his colleagues over the "oven of Akhnai" (*B. Bava Metzi'a* 59b), a passage which famously stresses that halakhic decision cannot be fixed according to miracles or even according to an act of divine revelation. Once God gives His Torah at Sinai, it no longer belongs to Him and He no longer declares its meaning; the legal interpretation of the Torah is set by the majority opinion among the sages (cf. Exod. 23:2).

4.   Louis Jacobs, *A Tree of Life: Diversity, Flexibility, and Creativity in Jewish Law* (Oxford: Oxford U. Press, 1984), 11–12.

5.   The chief example is that of the *mamzer,* the offspring of an incestuous or adulterous union, who is forbidden to marry most other Jews; see Jacobs, pp. 236 and 257–75.

6.   Ronald Dworkin, *Freedom's Law: The Moral Reading of the American Constitution* (Cambridge: Harvard, 1996), 36.

7.   The list of authors is huge, even if we restrict it to scholars of the post-talmudic *Halakhah,* that is, of Jewish law *after* its most "classical" and creative period. A few of the leading works, however, can be mentioned, beginning with those of our colleagues Moshe Zemer (*Halakhah shefuyah* [Tel Aviv: Dvir, 1993]) and David Ellenson (*Tradition in Transition: Orthodoxy, Halakhah, and the Boundaries of Modern Jewish Identity* [Lanham, MD: University Press of America, 1989]). Among other scholars, Jacob Katz surely leads the field; see his collected studies in *Halakhah vekabalah* (Jerusalem: Magnes, 1984), as well as his monographs *Masoret umashber* (Jerusalem: Bialik, 1958); *Exclusiveness and Tolerance* (Oxford: Oxford U. Press, 1961); and *Hahalakhah bameitzar* (Jerusalem: Magnes, 1992). Yisrael Ta-Shema and Haym Soloveitchik have also devoted much of their research to the influence of social and intellectual history upon the *Halakhah.* For an appreciation of the writings of these and other scholars in the field, see Mark Washofsky, "Medieval Halakhic Literature and the Reform Rabbi: A Neglected Relationship," *CCAR Journal,* Fall (1993), 61–74.

RESPONSA AND THE ART OF WRITING

8.   Solomon B. Freehof, *Modern Reform Responsa* (Cincinnati: Hebrew Union College Press, 1971), Introduction, 1–13. This is actually a theme propounded by Freehof in the introductions to his various responsa volumes.

9.   Menachem Elon, *Jewish Law* (Philadelphia: Jewish Publication Society of America, 1994), 1576–84. Freehof (note 8, above) makes a similar point.

10.   Jacob Katz, *Le'umiut yehudit: masot umechkarim* (Jerusalem: World Zionist Organization, 1983), 188–190, and *Goy shel shabbat* (Jerusalem: Merkaz Zalman Shazar, 1984), 180ff.

11.   An interesting, if tentative essay in this regard is Chaim I. Waxman, "Toward a Sociology of *Pesak*," in Moshe Z. Sokol, ed., *Rabbinic Authority and Personal Autonomy* (Northvale, NJ: Jason Aronson, 1992), 217–37. (The volume is a publication of the Orthodox Forum, a project of the Rabbi Isaac Elchanan Theological Seminary of Yeshivah University.) Waxman notes that the social conditions that dominate *yeshivah* communities and distinguish them from those of the "modern" Orthodox encourage a preference toward stringency in all matters of religious observance.

12.   On the rise of the *gedoley hador* and the decline of the community rabbinate, see Lawrence Kaplan, "Daas Torah: A Modern Conception of Rabbinic Authority," in Moshe Sokol, ed., *Rabbinic Authority and Personal Autonomy* (Northvale, NJ: Jason Aronson, 1992), pp. 1–60; Haym Soloveitchik, "Rupture and Reconstruction: The Transformation of Contemporary Orthodoxy," *Tradition* 28:4 (1994), 64–130; R. Immanuel Jakobovits, "Rabbanim verashey yeshivah," in Y. Izner, ed., *Ish 'al Ha'eidah* (Jerusalem: Ministry of Education and Culture, 1973), 373–82; Waxman, 233–34.

13.   Emanuel Feldman, in Reuven P. Bulka, ed., *Dimensions of Orthodox Judaism* (New York: Ktav, 1983), 334–35.

14.   Bernard Weinberger in *Jewish Observer* 1:2 (October 1963), 11.

15.   Some trace it to the growing influence of the chasidic ideology upon the mitnagdic world. The chasidic style of rabbinic leadership champions the belief in the centrality of the *tzadik* as the unquestioned religious authority in all walks of life; today, the role and spiritual authority of the "Lithuanian-style" *rosh yeshivah*, who has largely replaced the community rabbi as the religious leader of the non-chasidic Orthodox world, have come to resemble those of the chasidic *rebbe*. See Kaplan, 48–49, and Soloveitchik, 94ff. Gershon C. Bacon ("Da'at torah vechavaley mashiach," *Tarbitz* 52 [1983] 497–508) links the phenomenon more directly to the emergence of the Agudat Yisrael as a political party, an institutional advocate for a rejectionist Orthodoxy. In this view, the concept of *da'at torah*, based upon the unerring judgment of the *gedoley hador*, enabled the Agudah to fulfill its ideological commitment to, in the words of R. Chaim Ozer Grodzinsky, "solve all the problems of the day in the spirit of Torah and tradition."

16.   See Jakobovits, pp. 374–75: although the community rabbi issues halakhic rulings on the basis of an intimate knowledge of the community and its problems, the *yeshivah* head by his nature is relatively isolated from the day-to-day world of the average observant Jew. The latter's legal

decisions, accordingly, reflect a theoretical approach to Jewish law rather than a respect for established *minhag* (legal custom), the traditions by which the community lives.

17.   See R. Simchah Eilberg's laudatory description of an approach to observance that he terms "Beney Berakism," in *Hapardes* 38:3 (Kislev, 5724): a *yeshivah* student educated in the spirit of the Chazon Ish quite properly searches out the more or most stringent options to observance, so that *chumra* (stringency) quickly becomes the norm rather than an "option" per se. Feldman (at p. 335) denies the charge (raised by Oscar Z. Fasman in an article in Bulka, 317–30) that the *gedoley hador* are out of touch with community concerns or "subjective" in their decision making. On the contrary, men blessed with the charismatic (Platonic?) ability to perceive truth as it is, rather than its pale reflection, *by definition* cannot suffer from these faults.

18.   As Nachmanides wrote some seven hundred years ago, absolute certainty is the property of mathematics and *not* of "talmudic science." See his introduction to *Sefer Milchamot Hashem,* printed immediately before the Alfasi in the Romm/Vilna editions of tractate *Berakhot.*

19.   Stanley Fish, "The Law Wishes to Have a Formal Existence," in Austin Sarat and Thomas R. Kearns, *The Fate of Law* (Ann Arbor: University of Michigan Press, 1994), 159ff. Although Fish is most definitely *not* a legal formalist, this is the best brief and least polemical description of legal formalism I have seen.

20.   Hans Kelsen, *The Pure Theory of Law,* tr. Max Knight (Berkeley: University of California Press, 1967), 192.

21.   Ernest J. Weinrib, "The Jurisprudence of Legal Formalism," *Harvard Journal of Law and Public Policy* 16 (1993), 592. See also his "Legal Formalism: On the Immanent Rationality of Law," *Yale Law Journal* 97 (1988), 949ff.

22.   Ernest J. Weinrib, "Jurisprudence," 594.

23.   Owen Fiss, "Objectivity and Interpretation," *Stanford Law Review* 34 (1982), 739ff.

24.   See H.L.A. Hart, *The Concept of Law* (Oxford: Clarendon Press, 1961), p. 136: without definable rules, law possesses no authority; in the absence of rules, there is nothing to distinguish the decision of a private person from that of a court.

25.   Upon this notion, Herbert Wechsler based his critique of "unprincipled" if popular judicial decisions; see "Toward Neutral Principles of Constitutional Law," *Harvard Law Review* 73 (1959), 1ff.

26.   Oliver Wendell Holmes, Jr., *The Common Law* (Boston: Little, Brown, 1881), 5.

27.   Lochner v. New York, 198 U.S. at 76 (Holmes, J., dissenting).

28.   "The Path of the Law," in Oliver Wendell Holmes, Jr., *Collected Legal Papers* (New York: Pantheon Books, 1982), 200.

29.   Holmes, *The Common Law*, 1.

30.   It is generally recognized that Holmes's views were shaped by the reigning pragmatist philosophy of his time; see Thomas C. Grey, "Holmes and Legal Pragmatism," *Stanford Law Review* 41 (1989), 787ff.

31.   On the history of the movement, see Gary Aichele, *Legal Realism and Twentieth-Century American Jurisprudence* (New York: Garland, 1990). That Holmes was a "forerunner" of the realist movement is a judgment made by realists and others who note the skeptical and pragmatic tendencies in some of his writings. This in not to say, however, that Holmes *was* a "realist" or that his complex approach to law is composed solely of "realist" elements. See Neil Duxbury, "The Birth of Legal Realism and the Myth of Justice Holmes," *Anglo-American Law Review* 20 (1981), 81ff.

32.   For the strongest presentations of this point of view from a "legal realist" see Jerome Frank, *Law and the Modern Mind* (New York; Doubleday, 1930), and Felix Cohen, "Transcendental Nonsense and the Functional Approach," *Columbia Law Review* 35 (1935), 809ff.

33.   For introductions to this movement, see Mark Kelman, *A Guide to Critical Legal Studies* (Cambridge: Harvard University Press, 1987); David Kairys, ed., *The Politics of Law: A Progressive Critique* (New York, Pantheon, 1982); and Gary Minda, *Postmodern Legal Movements: Law and Jurisprudence at Century's End* (New York: New York University Press, 1995), Chap. 6.

34.   See Richard Posner, "The Decline of Law as an Autonomous Discipline," *Harvard Law Review* 100 (1987), 761ff.

35.   Duncan Kennedy, "Legal Education as Training for Hierarchy," in Kairys, *The Politics of Law,* 47.

36.   "One of my few expectations regarding judicial opinions...is that they will almost always be written in a tone of impersonality suggesting that the legal materials themselves, rather than the personal desires of the judge, required the result in question"; Sanford Levinson, "The Rhetoric of the Judicial Opinion," in Peter Brooks and Paul Gewirtz, *Law's Stories: Narrative and Rhetoric in Law* (New Haven: Yale University Press, 1996), 188.

37.   Joseph Singer, "The Player and the Cards: Nihilism and Legal Theory," *Yale Law Journal* 94 (1984), 5. This description is more obviously suited to Critical Legal Studies than to Law and Economics, a movement much more favorably disposed to free-market capitalism and that aspires to the scientific rationality of economic thought. Richard Posner, however, one of the leading Law and Economics scholars, has lately become a legal pragmatist and has accordingly written some words whose skepticism rivals that of the "crits." See his "The Jurisprudence of Skepticism," *Michigan Law Review* 86 (1988), 827–91, and *Problems of Jurisprudence* (Cambridge: Harvard

MARK WASHOFSKY

University Press, 1990), 454–69.

38.   Costas Douzinas, *Postmodern Jurisprudence: The Law of Texts in the Texts of Law* (New York: Routledge, 1991), 1ff.: postmodernists doubt that "there is a 'real' world or legal system 'out there,' perfected, formed, complete and coherent, waiting to be discovered by theory."

39.   See Richard Rorty, *Philosophy and the Mirror of Nature* (Princeton: Princeton University Press, 1979), 3: "the notion of knowledge as accurate representation...needs to be abandoned." And p. 11: the traditional program of epistemology, which held that "rationality" and "objectivity" could offer accurate representations of reality, is now seen to be "a self-deceptive effort to eternalize the normal discourse of the day."

40.   See Paul Carrington's condemnation of Critical Legal Studies in "Of Law and the River," *Journal of Legal Education* 34 (1984), 222ff.

41.   See Owen Fiss, "The Death of the Law?" *Cornell Law Review* 72 (1986), 1ff.

42.   The best-known exposition of legal positivism is Hart, *The Concept of Law.* See at p. 136: "In every legal system a large and important field is left open for the exercise of discretion by courts and other officials in rendering initially vague standards determinate.... Nonetheless these activities...must not disguise the fact that both the framework within which they take place and their chief end-product is one of general rules." On the "moderate" and nonthreatening nature of legal indeterminacy see Frederik Schauer, "Easy Cases," *Southern California Law Review* 58 (1985), 399ff., and Ken Kress, "Legal Indeterminacy," *California Law Review* 77 (1989), 283ff.

43.   See Ronald Dworkin, *Law's Empire* (Cambridge: Harvard University Press, 1986); *A Matter of Principle* (Cambridge: Harvard University Press, 1985); and *Taking Rights Seriously* (Cambridge: Harvard University Press, 1977).

44.   H.G. Gadamer, *Truth and Method,* tr. J. Weinsheimer and D.G. Marshall (New York: Crossroad, 1989).

45.   Thomas Kuhn, *The Structure of Scientific Revolutions,* 2nd ed. (Chicago: University of Chicago Press, 1970).

46.   See the Introduction by James F. Bohman, David R. Hiley, and Richard Shusterman, the editors of *The Interpretive Turn: Philosophy, Science, Culture* (Ithaca: Cornell University Press, 1991), 1–14.

47.   Thomas C. Grey, "The Constitution as Scripture," *Stanford Law Review* 37 (1984), 1ff; Sanford Levinson, *Constitutional Faith* (Princeton: Princeton University Press, 1988).

48.   Shall the meaning of a text, for example, be identified with the intention of its author, or does that meaning lie inherent in the text apart from what its author might think? Does the reader entirely construct a meaning of a text, either in accordance with a set of objective standards of literary excellence or as the result of a conversation within an identified "community of interpretation"? Is "truth in interpretation" in fact discoverable at all, or does any standard of "truth" imply an artificial construct that represses other competing standards?

49.   Sanford Levinson and Steven Mailloux, *Interpreting Law and Literature: A Hermeneutic Reader:* (Evanston: Northwestern University Press, 1988), x.

50.   This expansive view of the domain of "rhetoric" is commonly associated with Chaim Perelman; see his *The Realm of Rhetoric* (South Bend, Ind.: Notre Dame University Press, 1982) for a summary of his theories. Perelman draws upon the Aristotelian tradition, in which "rhetoric" includes the forms of evidence used in disciplines such as ethics and politics where argumentation, rather than the formal syllogism, is the way in which conclusions are ultimately drawn. Rhetoric therefore *is* a form of reasoning, rather than simply a collection of speakers' tricks, but it differs from formal logical reasoning in that it admits such standards as shared values, common sense, and other criteria accepted as persuasive within a particular culture.

51.   James Boyd White, *Heracles' Bow: Essays on the Rhetoric and Poetics of the Law* (Madison: University of Wisconsin Press, 1985), 78, 98.

52.   Richard Weisberg, *Poethics, and Other Strategies of Law and Literature* (New York: Columbia University Press, 1992), 16–17.

53.   Weisberg, *Poethics,* 7–8: "No opinion with a misguided outcome has ever in fact been 'well-crafted.'" Richard Posner responds that it is entirely possible for a judge to present a horrendous ruling in a felicitous style; see "Judges Writing Styles (And Do They Matter?)" *University of Chicago Law Review* 62 (1995), 1421ff. See also John Fischer, "Reading Literature/Reading Law: Is There Really a Literary Jurisprudence?" *Texas Law Review* 72 (1993), 135ff.

54.   Despite his acknowledgment of the significance of "metanarratives" for the understanding of law and legal institutions (see *"Nomos* and Narrative," *Harvard Law Review* 97 [1984] 4ff). Robert Cover also noted that law, at bottom, is an exercise in authority and the controlled imposition of violence on the members of a community; "Violence and the Word," *Yale Law Journal* 95 (1986), 1601–29. See also Robin West, "Adjudication Is Not Interpretation: Some Reservations about the Law and Literature Movement," *Tennessee Law Review* 54 (1987), 203–78, and Sanford Levinson, "The Rhetoric of the Judicial Opinion."

55.   See Thomas Morawetz, "Understanding Disagreement, The Root Issue of Jurisprudence: Applying Wittgenstein to Positivism, Critical Theory, and Judging," *University of Pennsylvania Law Review* 141 (1992), 371–456.

56. Peter J. Haas, *Responsa: Literary History of a Rabbinic Genre* (Atlanta: Scholars Press, 1996); Solomon B. Freehof, *The Responsa Literature* (Philadelphia: Jewish Publication Society of America, 1955); Mark Washofsky, "Responsa and Rhetoric: On Law, Literature, and the Rabbinic Decision," in John C. Reeves and John Kampen, eds., *Pursuing the Text: Studies in Honor of Ben Zion Wacholder on the Occasion of his Seventieth Birthday* (Sheffield: Sheffield Academic Press, 1994), 360–409.

57. *Resp. Igerot Moshe,* EHE 1:76–77.

58. Feinstein spells this word phonetically in Hebrew letters, rather than using the customary Hebrew word *rav,* to emphasize the foreign nature of Reform Judaism: their clergy are not real rabbis, but merely transliterated ones!

59. In 1:77, Feinstein spells this word out in Hebrew letters, obviously to distinguish the Reform house of worship from a true *bet knesset* (synagogue).

60. *Resp. Chatam Sofer,* EHE 100.

61. The technical term for this presumptive evidence is *anan sahadey,* "we are the witnesses," i.e., it is common knowledge that such and such occurred, even if no valid eyewitness testimony exists to that event.

62. *BT* Gitin 81b.

63. On this method of betrothal, *kiddushey bi'ah,* see *M.* Kiddushin 1:1; *B.* Kiddushin 9b; *Yad,* Ishut 3:5. This method of effecting betrothal, although halakhically valid, has been in disfavor since the days of the third-century amora Rav; see *B.* Yevamot 52a and Kiddushin 12b.

64. Indeed, R. Yosef Eliyahu Henkin asks, in his critique of Feinstein, "who knows what Reform Judaism is or that for a certainty no 'kosher' witnesses are present at those weddings?" (*Resp. Teshuvot Ibra,* no. 76).

65. Joel Roth, *The Halakhic Process: A Systemic Analysis* (New York: Jewish Theological Seminary, 1986), 71–74. The decision in question is *Resp. Igerot Moshe,* YD 1:139.

66. Roth's conceptual approach to law, as he notes on p. 5, footnote 1, relies heavily on the works of John Salmond (P. J. Fitzgerald, ed., *Salmond on Jurisprudence,* 12th ed. [London: Sweet and Maxwell, 1966]) and Menachem Elon, *Mishpat ivri* (Jerusalem: Magnes, 1977). These works speak at length about the discrete "sources" of the law, a central aspect of positivistic legal thought.

67. See, for example, *M.* Sanhedrin 11:1.

68.   Roth, 73. And see n. 50: Feinstein declares the Conservatives to be "heretics" presumably because of their supposed widespread denial of the Mosaic authorship of the Torah and their apparent lack of commitment to *Halakhah*. "What he ignores, however, is the possibility that there may be legitimate *machloket* between him and the Conservative movement about the nature of the halakhic process, such that neither he nor they are heretics."

69.   Chief Rabbinate of Israel, *Osef Piskey Din* (1950), 337–38. The court (chief rabbis Yitzchak Halevy Herzog and Benzion Meir Hai Ouziel, along with R. Meshulam Ratta) refused to annul a marriage on the grounds that the wedding was not conducted according to proper halakhic form.

70.   Exod. 23:1; *BT* Sanhedrin 27a; *Yad*, Edut 9:1ff.

71.   It is, of course, quite likely that Feinstein was unaware of the ruling, which is published in an obscure pamphlet of the Jewish Law Institute of Israel's Ministry of Justice.

72.   For an analysis of this ruling see Menachem Elon, *Miba'ayot hahalakhah vehamishpat bemedinat yisrael* (Jerusalem: Hebrew University, Institute for Contemporary Judaism, 1973), 22ff.

73.   See Mark Washofsky, "Halakhah and Political Theory: A Study in Jewish Legal Response to Modernity," *Modern Judaism* 9 (1989), 289–310. That the "Zionist rabbis" were aware that they were speaking to a particular, identified audience that did not include the anti-Zionist *charedim* is made clear by R. Shaul Yisraeli, the editor of the Zionist-halakhic journal *Hatorah vehamedinah,* 1 (1949), 11, and by Shelomo Zalman Shragai, the noted theorist of Hapo'el Hamizrachi, in *Sha'ah venetzach* (Jerusalem: Mosad Harav Kook, 1960), 326–36. That such an inclusive *"kelal yisrael"* approach to the *Halakhah* is no longer taken by Israeli rabbinic courts is stressed by Elon, *Miba'ayot.* This change, too, can be attributed to the notion of audience, to the particular public to which contemporary rabbinic authorities believe they are addressing themselves.

74.   These responsa were written during the decade of the 1950s, at a time when American Orthodoxy was just beginning to emerge into an era of self-confidence.

75.   Compare Feinstein's approach to that of his American contemporary R. Yosef Eliyahu Henkin, *Resp. Teshuvot Ibra,* no. 76. Henkin criticizes Feinstein on this very point. Even the secular and nonobservant Jew wishes that his marital relations be "legitimate"; therefore, by his act of intercourse he does intend to constitute a valid Jewish marriage, regardless of the ritual circumstances of the wedding. The marriage is valid and requires a *get* to dissolve it. Henkin also does not attempt to "prove" this assertion; rather, like the rabbinic court of Eretz Yisrael, he states it as a fact, assuming that his intended audience will find it persuasive as a basis for deriving conclusions of law.

76.   *Resp. Igerot Moshe,* OC 1:46.

77.   Feinstein cites this incident simply in the name of the *Magen Avraham,* providing no additional information. I have not succeeded in locating the reference.

78. On the role of burden of proof—and its shifting—in legal argument, see R.H. Gaskins, *Burdens of Proof in Modern Discourse* (New Haven: Yale University Press, 1992). See also Chaim Perelman and M. Olbrechts-Tyteca, *The New Rhetoric* (South Bend, Ind: Notre Dame University Press, 1969), 106: the very existence of a burden of proof, which denotes that there *are* presumptions and norms that we accept as valid without the need to demonstrate their validity, makes argument possible in the first place.

79. Reform responsa have addressed the issue in this way. See *American Reform Responsa,* nos. 21 and 22, and *Teshuvot for the Nineties,* no. 5753.8.

80. *M.* Sotah 5:1; *SA* EHE 11:1.

81. *Resp. Igerot Moshe,* EHE 1:10.

82. See *Turey Zahav,* YD 195, no. 7.

83. *BT* Yevamot 45b; *Yad,* Isurey Bi'ah 15:3; *SA* EHE 4:5.

84. *BT* Yevamot 45a; *SA* EHE 4:5. The matter, however, is controversial; see *Beit Shmuel* and *Chelkat Mechokek* to *SA* ad loc.

85. R. Sholom M. Schwadron, *Resp. Maharsham* 3:268; R. Zvi Pesach Frank, cited in *Otzar Haposkim* 23:1, no. 1; R. Yechiel Ya'akov Weinberg, *Resp. Seridey Esh* 3:5; R. S.Z. Auerbach in *No'am* 1 (1958), 157.

86. R. Eliezer Yehudah Waldenberg, *Resp. Tzitz Eliezer* 9:51, end; R. S.Z. Auerbach, in *No'am* 1 (1958), 165; R. Ovadyah Yosef, *Resp. Yabi'a Omer* 2, EHE 1, end ("Heaven forbid that we should permit such a thing"); R. Yechiel Ya'akov Weinberg, *Resp. Seridey Esh* 3:5 ("this is an ugly act, one which resembles the abominations of Egypt"); R. Ya'akov Breisch, *Resp. Chelkat Ya'akov* 3:45ff.

87. Gen. 1:28; *BT* Yevamot 65b; *Yad,* Ishut 15:2; *SA* EHE 1:1.

88. On Judaism's preferences in this regard see Daniel Schiff, "Developing Halakhic Attitudes to Sex Preselection," in Walter Jacob and Moshe Zemer, eds., *The Fetus and Fertility in Jewish Law* (Pittsburgh and Tel Aviv: Freehof Institute of Progressive Halakhah, 1995), 91–117.

89. For a summary of the opinions see A.S. Avraham, *Nishmat Avraham,* EHE 1, 5–13.

90. Thus, R. Benzion Ouziel prohibits AIH on the grounds that, as the child is not legally that of the husband, there is no warrant for the procedure that would supersede the prohibition against the improper emission of seed *(hotza'at zera levatalah); Resp. Mishpetey Ouziel* 2:19. The authorities cited in note 85, by contrast, do regard the child as the semen donor's legal offspring.

91.   See as well *Resp. Igerot Moshe,* EHE 1:71.

92.   See, for example, R. S.Z. Auerbach in *No'am* 1 (1958), 159–66. Although he recognizes the seriousness of a woman's desire for children, and although he admits that "it is possible that this is not prohibited" (165–66), he is quite clear that a child born of a Gentile's sperm is "dirty" *(mezuham;*164) and that it is an act of unquestioned ugliness *(ke'ur)* to bring Gentile seed into the community of Israel.

93.   It is true that Feinstein subsequently withdrew from the more radical implications of his decision, writing that his words should not be taken as a blanket permit of AID; see his letter reprinted in *Resp. Chelkat Ya'akov* 3:47. Yet this does not affect our analysis of the approach he takes in his original ruling.

RESPONSE TO DR. MARK WASHOFSKY
Responsa and the Art of Writing

Richard S. Rheins*

How appropriate it is for Rodef Shalom to honor Dr.Walter Jacob by hosting an academic symposium. By virtue of his distinguished career, Walter has established, what for me, is the ideal rabbinate. He has combined an extraordinary talent for serving a large and most demanding congregation with making academic contributions of the highest order of scholarship. Service and study, these are the attributes of a well-rounded rabbi, and Walter is the role model *par excellence*. But these accomplishments alone hardly define how special he is. For those of us who have studied with and worked alongside him, what is most impressive is that Walter's heart is as great as his intellect. I shall be forever grateful to Dr. Mark Staitman for giving me the opportunity to pay tribute to my teacher and colleague, Dr. Walter Jacob.

My task this morning is made even more daunting by the fact that I have been asked to comment about the work in progress by my teacher (indeed, he is my *Rav Muvhak)* and my friend, Dr. Mark Washofsky. It is Mark who instilled in me a love of halakhic literature and, to date, my greatest honor as a rabbi has been that Mark and Walter thought I was sufficiently competent to serve on the Responsa Committee of the Central Conference of American Rabbis (CCAR). As my term of five or six years on the committee is coming to a close, this is a most fitting moment for me to publicly express my profound appreciation, respect, and gratitude to my teachers, Walter Jacob and Mark Washofsky.

Now, let me try and justify the time you have given me. Mark outlines two different models that attempt to define the ha-

---

*In tribute to my rabbi, Dr. Walter Jacob.

lakhic process. One is halakhic formalism, as championed by J. David Bleich. Formalism, as Mark describes it, means that "the halakhic process is one of thoroughgoing rationality, a mental operation in which intellectual detachment and impartial analysis overpower whatever desire the *posek* may have to place his own subjective and individual stamp upon the *Halakhah.*" The methodology of *Halakhah* is not a matter of arbitrary choice, and the law must be, in Bleich's own words, "determined on its own merits and let the chips fall where they may."[1]

The other halakhic model is conveyed by scholars like Louis Jacobs, who can be described, perhaps, as "rule skeptics," scholars who emphasize the subjectiveness of the halakhic process. For Jacobs, the *posek* manipulates the sources and the methodology to reach a particular conclusion. Though Mark notes that Bleich and Jacobs should not be so sharply contrasted, in point of fact, neither scholar demonstrates in his work a complete agreement with either model. Although J. David Bleich may tend toward halakhic formalism, he admits in several of his halakhic articles that the process is secondary to the conclusion either because the decision is a foregone conclusion or because the authorities of this age simply do not feel empowered to confirm such a decision.

In his discussion of the issue of intermarriage, for example, Bleich says simply, *"Men tor nisht!* It is not permitted." Declaring that there is very little more to say about intermarriage, he wrote: *"Hamefursamot einan zrikhot ra'ayah.* Matters which are well known do not require substantiation."[2] Of course, he then goes on for several pages with a detailed analysis of some of the crucial halakhic issues. Nevertheless, the conclusion is never in doubt. The analysis was given to clarify and justify the longstanding rabbinic opposition to intermarriage.

In addition, Bleich admits, contrary to the theory of formalism, that even if the halakhic process could reach a radical decision, the authorities of this age do not feel empowered to confirm such a decision. A good example of this is Bleich's review of the theoretical possibility of a kosher pig.[3] The Babirussa is a species of swine that appeared to both chew its cud and, like all swine, have split hooves. Theoretically, if such an animal existed, it would qualify under the Torah's definition of permitted animals to be included among those that may provide kosher meat. And yet, Bleich ultimately concluded: "It is forbidden to eat meat of any hitherto unknown species even if it possesses the characteristics of a kosher animal."[4] Quoting *Chockmat Adam* 36.1, Bleich makes the further point that observant Jews are permitted to eat only those animals that our ancestors determined were kosher. Far from employing an objective methodology to decide the fitness of an animal and letting "the chips fall where they may," Bleich demonstrates that in some cases the answer is known and fixed, regardless of the theoretical halakhic flexibility.

Louis Jacobs maintains that halakhic reasoning is often subjective; a *posek* musters citations to justify preconceived positions because, as Jacobs writes, "his general approach to Judaism compels him to come up with a conclusion that must not be at variance with Jewish ideas and ideals as he and his contemporaries or his 'school' sees them."[5] But, as surely Jacobs would acknowledge, the *posek* and his contemporaries are limited to what *chidushim* they can make not only by the perspective of their particular school of thought, but also by the overwhelming momentum from the weight of tradition.

Menachem Elon identified six different legal sources of Jewish law: Tradition *(kabbalah)*, Interpretation *(midrash)*, Legislation *(takkanah* and *gezerah)*, Custom *(minhag)*, Case *(ma'aseh)*, and Legal reasoning *(severah)*.[6] But of those laws derived from tradition he wrote: "This legal source is fundamentally different from the other legal sources of Jewish law in that it is inherently not amenable to development; it does not change but remains fixed—a static source of Jewish law."[7] Indeed, when one speaks about *Halakhah* and the halakhic process, one must differentiate between the rulings of *poskim* that deal with laws and practices that are firmly rooted in tradition and the attempts by *poskim* to create laws to fill a void unaddressed by tradition or in reaction to some pressing contemporary issue.

Contrary to Jacobs's claim of halakhic subjectiveness, the halakhic process cannot be arbitrarily used to overturn tradition or to establish a *chidush*. This point is illustrated in a passage from the *Yerushalmi, Pesachim* 6.1. R. Jose bar Rab Bun taught in the name of Rabbi Abba bar Memel:

> If a man creates a *gezerah shavah* of his own, he can make a crawling thing transmit ritual impurity in a tent [even though this is not the law]....

> A person may create a *gezerah shavah* to uphold what he has learned [by tradition] but not to negate what he has learned.

True, halakhic authorities could make rulings that overturned Toraitic law when the times demanded it.[8] *Et la'asot* (Psalm 119:126), which the Rabbis understood to say: "When a time comes to do something for the sake of God's name, it is permitted to violate the Torah." "There are times when setting aside the Torah is the only way to preserve it" (TB *Mehachot* 99a/b). "It is better that one letter of the Torah should be uprooted than that God's name should be openly

208

profaned" (TB *Yebamot* 79a). And yet this legislative power was used with the utmost care and caution and only with the ultimate goal of strengthening the Torah as a whole and safeguarding the health, security, and religious fidelity of the Jewish people.

Since we can generally assume that *poskim* of all generations strive to make decisions that will have the most positive influence on Jews and Judaism—namely, strengthening our faith and fortifying our Covenant with God, all the while sensitive to our human needs for survival and prosperity—Louis Jacobs's point of subjectivity can be best understood insofar as he establishes that different schools of thought may have different perspectives as to what is best for Jews and Judaism. It is in pursuing these different perspectives that the *poskim* employ different methodologies and/or conflicting sources and precedent. The traditional *posek* serves neither as a mere functionary to the halakhic system nor as a subjective maverick free to rule and create at will. The *posek* is given the tools of flexibility and is called on to use those tools when the need arises.

Jacobs's definition of the halakhic process is best illustrated in Jacob Katz's marvelous history concerning the halakhic development of the *Shabbes Goy*. The phenomenon of halakhic subjectivity is clearly evidenced as we see in the rulings of Rabbi Moses Schick,[9] who relates that, in certain instances, even when he could rule leniently he would not, explaining:

> I stay away from such rulings, especially in this unruly generation when one should be as strict as possible.... Permissive rulings are of no help to the light-headed, for relying on them, they then permit themselves even more, saying: "The pious permit it!"[10]

209

Here Schick recognized that he could have ruled differently, and yet he felt restricted, not by *Halakhah,* but by the need to impose discipline on an unruly generation. In this he was following the principle expressed by many in his generation, that an unruly generation will become more unruly only if the authorities are permissive. It was their opinion that such a generation required higher standards and strict interpretations to safeguard the Jewish people and our Covenant with God.[11] In their eyes, following the overwhelming trend one finds among *poskim* in every generation of our people, the community requires rulings that will preserve the Jewish people and safeguard the unique and sacred practices, principles, and teachings we received from our ancestors. There may be differences of opinion as to which is the best way to preserve us and safeguard our way; there may be differences of opinion as to what is best for Jews and Judaism; but the *poskim* all are guided by the ultimate goal of striving to discover the will of God in keeping with God's Covenant with Israel.[12]

Finally, the question arises: "What significance does this have for those who follow a Progressive halakhic methodology?" I believe that one of the most important lessons we should keep in mind is that the role of tradition is preeminent. Although tradition alone should not veto Reform *chidushim,* nevertheless, knowing the preeminence of tradition should make us much more cautious in our experimentation than we have been wont to be. Even when faced with an issue for which there is no established tradition, we should strive to follow the model established by generations of *poskim* who, regardless of theological differences of opinion, were unified in the sincerity of their approach to decide that issue in a way that would best safeguard both the immediate health and welfare of the Jewish people and the long-term standards of our faith.

Appropriately, the general Progressive halakhic guideline as currently employed by the CCAR Responsa Committee is to look first to the traditional principles and customs and seek to alter those traditions only when they are obviously at variance with preeminent Progressive principles (such as the equal participation of men and women in the performance of mitzvot). When a recent case came up wherein the questioner was seeking to expand the definition of what would be an acceptable Sukkah, the committee, seeing no Progressive principle that required us to alter the traditional definition of a kosher Sukkah, rejected the plea.[13]

Although Orthodox *poskim* have made a conscious decision to be more conservative than they need to be, this is not solely a product of political orientation. Rather, many are strict out of their concern for the "unruliness" of the current generation. When faced with the decision to fall on the side of leniency or stringency, it is most interesting that the traditional response has been to be lenient when there are destructive pressures against Jews from the outside (oppressions, persecutions, etc.) but to be stringent when there is evidence of the abandonment of Jewish law, morality, or fidelity from within the Jewish people. In contrast, our "natural" Reform reaction to evidence of the abandonment of Jewish values and observance is, all too often, to lower our standards and lessen our requirements.

The great and ultimate achievement of Solomon Freehof, Walter Jacob, Gunther Plaut, and Mark Washofsky is that they have established a Reform/Progressive alternative to the chaos that currently plagues so many Reform congregations and our movement as a whole. The vanity some pursue by the name of "autonomy" has led to a de facto polydoxy whereby Reform Jews and far too many of our Reform rabbinic colleagues do only what is fitting in their own eyes without regard to tradition and are seemingly oblivious to the long-term impact of their actions (or lack thereof) on the broader Jewish community. In contrast to the evidence of *hefkerut* among us, our teachers have given us an authentic, modern Jewish model for the establishment of Progressive Judaism that remains loyal to the heritage of our ancestors while, at the same time, responding to the modern world. For their great efforts, the future generations will sing their praises.

Notes

1. J. David Bleich, *Contemporary Halakhic Problems,* Vol. 1, p. xv.

2. Ibid., Vol. 2, pp. 268ff.

3. Ibid., Vol. 3, pp. 66ff.

4. Ibid., Vol. 3, p. 74.

5. As quoted in Mark Washofsky's paper.

6. Menachem Elon, *Jewish Law,* Vol. 1, pp. 238–39.

7. Ibid., p. 239. Compare also pp. 283 and following, where Elon reviews the scholarly debate between J.N. Epstein and Hanokh Albeck that has interesting parallels to the debate Mark reviews between Bleich and Jacobs. Epstein takes the position that halakhic midrash merely attributes an existing law to a source biblical verse, whereas Albeck maintains that midrash not only supports the existing law but is also a source for deducing new rules of law.

8. Ibid., Vol. 2, pp. 503ff.

9. Jacob Katz, *The "Shabbes Goy,"* pp. 202–203.

10. Ibid., pp. 196ff.

11. Ibid., pp. 196ff.

12. Since God promised our ancestors an eternal *brit* and God's revelation is "not in heaven," but can be determined by means of our sacred text and God-given ability to reason, Israel's preservation and safety is God's will, even when Israel's preservation seems to contradict a law stated in the Torah. Thus, *Vachai bahem* (Lev. 18:5), One shall live by them and not die because of them (TB *Sanhedrin* 74a); "One should violate one Shabbat in order that he may live to observe many Sabbaths" (TB *Yoma* 85b).

13. For an excellent review of Progressive halakhic principles, see *Dynamic Jewish Law* (Pittsburgh: Freehof Institute of Progressive Judaism, 1991).

THE LESSER EVIL
A MAIMONIDEAN HERMENEUTIC FOR LENIENCY*

Moshe Zemer

PRECEDENTS OF THE RESPONSUM

The elders of a twelfth-century Egyptian Jewish community asked Maimonides what action they should take regarding a young Jewish man of their community who was living with his female slave *(shifhah)*. May he keep his Gentile maidservant or must the elders compel him to send her away?[1]

The Rambam's reply should have been obvious, since he had already codified this issue in his *Mishneh Torah:*

> If a man was suspected of having intercourse with a slave girl who was later emancipated, or with a Gentile woman who afterward became a proselyte, he may not marry her; but if he has already taken her in marriage, they need not be parted.[2]

Instead of applying his own halakhic ruling, Maimonides surprisingly responds:

> After this evil tale [you have related], a *beit din* should force him either to send her away or to emancipate and marry her, even though [this latter action involves] something of a sin *[aveirah]*, because a man suspected of intercourse with a slave girl who was later emancipated, may not marry her *ab initio (lekhat'hilah);* in accordance with my ruling in a number of similar cases, he should manumit her and marry her. We have done this [relying on the sages' pronouncements]:

---
* I am grateful to the Memorial Foundation for Jewish Culture for the award of a research grant to prepare this paper. It is based in part on my book *Halakhah Shefuyah* (Tel Aviv: Dvir Press, 1993), 23–29, and on an unpublished paper presented to the Eighth Jewish Law Association Conference in Jerusalem.

(a) *Takanat Hashavim* (the decree of the repentant)[3]
(b) We have proclaimed: 'It is better for him to eat the
gravy and not the fat itself.'[4]
(c) We rely on the edict of the rabbis: *Eit la'asot ladonai*—
"It is time to act for the Lord, they have voided
your Torah."[5]

Maimonides not only contradicted his own ruling in the
Mishneh Torah, but admitted to his questioners that he had helped, on
more than one occasion, in the commission of this *aveirah.* Then he
mentions, *en passant,* with no explanation, three talmudic *takanot* (or
regulations). He seemed to have found justification for his
contradictory action in these rabbinic edicts. This paper will attempt
to understand the Rambam's use of the following three *takanot:*

1. Takanat hashavim. A talmudic *beraita* recounts a
controversy between Beit Shammai and Beit Hillel about a man who
stole the main beam of a building and built it into his own mansion
(bira). Beit Shammai says he should demolish the entire structure and
return the beam to its rightful owner. Beit Hillel says that he need only
pay its monetary value to the owner, because of *takanat
hashavim*—the decree of the penitent.[6] Beit Shammai literally
interpreted the biblical injunction "He shall return the stolen object,
which he took by robbery,"[7] to mean that the thief must restore the
original object to its owner. This would be the case even if it meant
that he must lay waste his own home to return the original pillar.

Beit Hillel, on the other hand, understood that if a penitent
thief is faced with the choice of either destroying his dwelling or
taking the path of inaction, he may never make restitution. Therefore
the House of Hillel allowed him to return in repentance—*lahzor
be'teshuva*—and right the wrong without undue damage to himself.

216

Rashi explains Beit Hillel's reasoning—*mipnei takanat hashavim:* "For if you force him to destroy his dwelling and return the beam to its owner, he will avoid the act of repentance."[8] Beit Shammai ruled according to the literal meaning of biblical law, but Beit Hillel chose the lesser evil. Maimonides found a close parallel between Beit Hillel's decree and his own case. Beit Hillel allowed the thief to retain the stolen beam and his house yet make restitution and become a *ba'al teshuvah.* The Rambam allowed the young man to retain his *shifah,* but only after she had gone through a change of status.

The emancipation of a slave is the equivalent of conversion. Every Gentile slave was actually a kind of preconverted individual that was circumcised (if male) and immersed, and accepted the yoke of the commandments *leshem avdut.*[9] As soon as the master freed the slave, he or she attained the status of a proselyte Jew, with all rights and prohibitions thereunto pertaining.[10]

The slave girl in our case, therefore, does indeed become eligible for marriage to a Jew after she is manumitted. That is, she could marry any Jew except her master, who as we have seen, was suspected of living with her while she was a slave. On the other hand, according to Maimonides' ruling, if the young Jew and the *shifhah* are married in spite of the prohibition, *post factum,* the marriage is valid and they need not be separated.

Maimonides understood that if the young Egyptian Jew had not been allowed to manumit his beloved *shifhah,* he would undoubtedly have continued living with her in her slave status, which is a serious violation (as we shall see), and would never have been able to repent. The Rambam considered this situation, which prevented one

217

from doing *teshuvah,* to be much more serious than the rabbinic violation of marrying her. The young man was no less in need of becoming a *ba'al teshuvah* than the thief who stole the beam.

The great teacher considered that any obstacle to repentance must be removed. This is consistent with the Rambam's view of *teshuvah,* to which he attributes the highest religious value:

> How great is repentance that it draws one close to the Divine Presence...yesterday this person was hated before God, defamed, cast away and abominable—and today he is beloved, charming favorite and friend![11]

If the violation of the marriage prohibition was wrong, without doubt, obstructing repentance was a greater wrong. Maimonides, like Beit Hillel before him, chose the lesser evil.

2. "It is better for him to eat the gravy and not the fat itself." Maimonides uses the aphorism "It is better for him to eat the gravy and not the fat itself" as another justification of his verdict. This enigmatic adage is an invention of the decisor based on two talmudic sources:[12]

(a) "If a pregnant woman smelled the [forbidden] flesh of a sacrifice, or of pork (for which she has a morbid craving), we put a reed into the gravy and place it in her mouth. If she then feels that her craving has been satisfied, it is well; if not, she is fed the fat meat itself."[13] The gravy, of course, is forbidden, but not to the same degree as the fat flesh.

The woman is fed this forbidden meat because she, her fetus, or both might be in danger. This is a matter of *pikuah nefesh,* saving human life, which overrides almost all other *mitzvot*. The pork gravy, of course, is prohibited, but licking less than an olive's bulk is but a minor infraction, not at all as severe as eating the fat flesh.

(b) The second talmudic *takanah* supplies the rest of the wording of Maimonides' aphorism: "It is better for Israel to eat flesh of animals about to die, yet ritually slaughtered, than the flesh of animals that have perished." Slaughtering a dying animal, of course, is repulsive, but if we don't allow its hungry owner to have the creature ritually slaughtered, he is liable to eat the carcass after its natural death, which is an immeasurably more serious violation of the Scriptural commandment concerning *neveilah* (carrion).[14] In both these cases, the Talmud recognizes human frailty and chooses the lesser of the evils.

So it is with the young man and the slave girl. On the one hand is a rabbinic prohibition forbidding him to give her manumission and then to marry her. On the other is a greater evil, a more stringent prohibition forbidding one to cohabit with a slave, as Maimonides ruled: "Therefore a female slave is forbidden to a free man, whether she belongs to him or to someone else" and further warned us, "Do not think that this is a minor sin because the Torah did not prescribe flogging for one who violates the prohibition, for this connection also causes the son to turn away from the Lord,[15] since a son born to a maidservant is a slave and not from Israel. The result is that holy seed is profaned by becoming slaves."[16]

Maimonides considered the young man's action in continuing to live with his enslaved *shifhah* to be a grave sin.

More than three centuries later, Joseph Caro codified the punishment for this offense in much harsher tones:

> If one is caught with his female slave, they take her away from him, sell her and distribute the sale price among the poor of Israel. The man is beaten, his head is shaved and he is placed under the ban for thirty days.[17]

As we have seen, Maimonides testified that he had given a lenient decision in a number of cases where a man freed his slave and then married her. According to this testimony, such relationships between female slaves and their owners were not uncommon.[18] Many documents dealing with *sh'fahot* were found in the Cairo *Geniza.* M. A. Friedman published twelve of them that bear witness to the prevalence of this phenomenon.

The most significant for this present study is the case of the daughter of the Nubian *shifhah,* whom Eli ben Yefet had purchased in Ashkelon.[19] He was ordered to appear before the *beit din* of the *Rosh Golah,* Nassi David ben Daniel, in Fustat, Egypt, to clarify the status of his daughter, Malah ("the beauty of beauties"), who had just come of age. It was explained that Eli had manumitted his Nubian slave and then married her. Their daughter, Malah, was born only after her mother had become Jewish. The document, states: "Her birth was in holiness, she is permitted to marry in the Congregation of the Lord." We can thus see that freeing his beloved, transforming her into "a nice Jewish girl," and then marrying her is by far the lesser evil.

3. "It is time to act for the Lord, your Torah has been violated." The third justification for the Rambam's decision is this oft-quoted talmudic precept based on Psalm 119:126. Rashi interpreted this verse to mean that there are times when Torah commandments may be violated to do the Lord's work. "When there comes a time to do a deed for God it is permissible to violate therewith His Torah."[20]

Here we can note the application of this *takanah* by Rabbi Yohanan and Rabbi Shimon be Lakish, third-century C.E. scholars of the Palestinian Talmud. They were studying a book of *aggadah* on the Sabbath, in spite of the prohibition against committing the Oral Law to writing. The two sages justified their action, stating: "It is time to act for the Lord, for your Torah has been broken— It is preferable that [a specific law of] the Torah be uprooted, so that the entire Torah not be forgotten by Israel."[21] This action was justified, because by the time of R. Yohanan and Resh Lakish, it had become almost impossible to commit the entire body of the oral Torah to memory and thus to preserve it.[22]

Which is more serious, neglecting one single law or forgetting the entire Torah? Our decisor's third talmudic justification is also based on choosing the lesser evil.

YEFAT TOAR—THE BEAUTIFUL CAPTIVE

The responsum contains an additional justification, although it is somewhat elusive. The lack of clarity is due to the befuddled nature of the question and the manner in which Maimonides chose to reply.

The questioners describe the situation of a young man *(bahur)*, who purchased a *shifhah, yefat toar.*[23] He lives in a courtyard with his father's wife and her small daughters. They continue with a stream of information or, more likely, misinformation: the young man's brother informed on him to a judge with the accusation that he had bought a

Christian slave and converted her to Judaism.[24] The judge returned the woman to the *bahur,* who took her to his home; all the community was gossiping about this.

The *shoelim* apparently tried to ask a scholarly question, *healat hakham,* hinting at rabbinic solutions to his queries. The questioners debate whether there was a violation of *yihud* (forbidden privacy or the couple in a closed room). They conclude that there is no prohibition of *yihud* with a Gentile woman. They wonder if she must be sent away and why. Finally, they speculate whether the woman has the status of a *yefat toar,* beautiful woman taken as a prisoner of war.[25]

How does Maimonides deal with each of these questions and the offer of scholarly help for their solution? He virtually ignores almost all the questions. There is no discussion of brother informing on brother to a Gentile judge; he does not even mention the matter of conversion to Judaism in his responsum. The Rambam chooses only two issues to discuss: (a) What is the standing of the couple that, according to rumor, is living together? (b) Does the woman have the status of *yefat toar?*

We have explored in detail his ruling of a man living with a female slave *(nitan al hashifhah),* which is the heart of his answer. The case of the beautiful prisoner of war is another issue. Maimonides begins the responsum by stating that this matter of the female slave is not the same as the case of the *yefat toar* before him. The Torah made a special ruling at that time; that is, in a time of conquest, that the warrior may take the woman while she is still a Gentile. This would ordinarily be forbidden, but the Torah permitted it, making allowance for human passions. This is the same situation as in the heat of battle, when the sages permitted soldiers to eat forbidden foods, as it is written: "[The Lord will give you] houses full of good things, which you did not fill."[26] The sages interpreted this to include sides of pork.[27]

Why does the Rambam include this enlightening elucidation of the *halakhot* of wine, women, and war in this responsum? Do these issues have any relevance to the young man living with his slave girl? There is no prima facie connection. The author opens his *teshuvah* with the demurrer that the subject of the responsum is not the captive woman. He then concludes this section of the responsum about the *yefat toar* with the following guideline to his readers: "Do not make an inference by comparison with this case."[28]

The Rambam continues to protest that there is no relation between the war ruling and that of the *shifhah*. We may ask further, if there is no relation between these *sugyot,* why does the respondent, who is such a stickler on brevity in responsa, devote one-third of the responsa to this subject?[29] Why does he begin the *teshuvah* with a denial of any connection with the *yefat toar* and then proceed to discuss its regulations?

The question of the captive woman proves to be the key to the entire responsum. The Talmud provides us with the *ta'am hamitzvah,* which the Rambam quotes: "The Torah provides for human passions."[30] The Talmud recognizes the weakness of human beings in resisting temptation to their bodily appetites. Maimonides adopts this talmudic explanation for leniency in cases where one has no control over lust and craving: "The Torah takes into consideration a person's *yetzer."[31]* We have already seen the continuation of this tannaitic statement: "It is better for Israel to eat flesh of animals about to die, yet ritually slaughtered, than the flesh of animals that have perished."[32]

Both situations deal with the weakness of those who are enslaved by their appetites.

The case of the captive woman is employed as an indirect, but logical, justification of the marriage of the slave woman. It appears, prima facie, to be entirely different from the three rabbinic *takanot*, which are all variations of choosing the lesser evil. The case of the captive woman is plainly a biblically lenient commandment taking into consideration the behavior of men in wartime.

On the contrary, we shall see that the *mitzvah* of the beautiful captive, as codified by the Rambam and others,[33] is also an issue of selecting the lesser evil. In his *Moreh Nevukhim*, the Maimoni suggested that by allowing the captive Gentile woman to the warrior, the Oral Law places him in a framework of restraint. We realize that the soldier may be unable to suppress his lust for her, but the *Halakhah* requires him to "bring her inside his home."[34] He is not allowed to take her forcibly in the army camp. He is forbidden to take more than one woman. He may not have sexual relations with her a second time until she has finished the process of mourning. He may not hinder her grieving and crying for her parents or prevent her from looking repulsive for the thirty days of her mourning period. She may not be sold or treated like a slave.[35]

Once this biblical law is placed in a framework of *halakhot*, limitations are placed on his lust. One may wonder whether all these restrictions on this permissive law were the reason the law of the captive woman fell into disuse.

If the Torah and the rabbis had not legislated this matter, the warrior who lusted for a woman would have taken her without any

224

restraints. He might have forced her at any time, in any way, with any frequency and with as many other foreign women as he wished. By permitting the soldier to take the captive woman as his wife under strict limitations, the Torah and the rabbis chose the lesser evil.

P'SAK HALAKHAH—THE VERDICT

Why did the author select these four talmudic precedents, all of which are based on choosing between two problematic alternatives? What is the significance of the resolution of the conflict by choosing the less severe option? It does not appear to be mere chance that he quotes these halakhic models.

The Rambam used these precedents to buttress his own decision. Allowing the young man to marry the slave girl after her manumission is "a sort of sin *(k'ein aveirah)*."[36] The great *posek* does not admit that this action actually constitutes a sin. It is only "a kind of sin." Do not ask what is the source of Maimonides' category of *k'ein aveirah*, because it appears nowhere else in halakhic literature.[37] Even if it is only "a sort of sin" and not a full-fledged *aveirah,* this action is against the *Halakhah.* Self-evidently, the Rambam took the halakhic process seriously.[38] He had codified this law, which he now took into his own hands. On the other hand, he had been an accessory to this "sort of sin" several times in the past.

Here he was confronted by a conflict between two *halakhot* codified in his *Mishneh Torah.* According to the first, the young man was said to have had intercourse with the slave girl, who was thereby forbidden to him after her emancipation. Yet, once freed, she became a full-fledged Jew. Their marriage, although forbidden, would be valid, and they need not be divorced.

225

The talmudic *ta'am hamitzvah* was that allowing this marriage might confirm the rumor that he, indeed, did have sexual intercourse with her while she was still a slave. This rabbinic ruling is particularly concerned with the public creditability of the original rumor.[39]

This ruling, which gives *post-factum* recognition to the forbidden marriage and is founded on the believability of gossip, obviously cannot be considered a stringent *Halakhah*. If it were transgressed, this would be only a "sort of sin."

In the second ruling a man is forbidden to have his slave serve as his mistress.[40] The great decisor strictly warned his reader not to consider this iniquity *(avon)*[41] to be a light matter, because the perpetrator would be flogged in accordance with rabbinic ordinance *(makot mardut)*. Living with his *shifhah* is a grave offense, for which severe punishment is prescribed.

The original form of the last *takanah* that Maimonides presents, "It is time to act for the Lord," is the *hora'at sha'ah,* "an emergency situation." Maimonides undoubtedly saw the widespread practice of Jewish men having intimate relations with their slave girls as constituting an emergency situation. This justified an emergency decision and the Rambam's deviation from his own halakhic norm.

When the Rambam compared this grave iniquity and its resultant corporal punishment with the alternative of a valid and lasting marriage with the freed slave, he could only term the latter "a sort of sin." Only in comparison with the severe "iniquity" and the perspective of the situation, does this forbidden marriage appear to be a slight matter and therefore permissible. There was no doubt in his mind which was the lesser evil, for he had so decided in a number of cases.

Now all he had to do was to hint at the precedents for his decision, and, on the rare chance that a scholar was among the questioners, this hint would be sufficient.[42] Neither the author nor his many commentators explained the full meaning of the four *nimmukim*.

Now the Rambam instructs the local *beit din* of the young man's community to present to him the alternatives. The time for his decision has arrived and cannot be postponed. The choice is presented to the young man, who is compelled to decide: choose now: manumit and marry her or send her away. The slave and her owner have been cohabiting long enough. No further time for reflection is needed. The procrastination must come to an end. 34-Maimonides is permissive, but firm. He has set his verdict: the *beit din* will set a date for him to marry her or send her away.[43]

Maimonides responded to the ethical imperative of the couple's plight by ruling against his own Code. Here is an instance of case law (responsa) overcoming code law. Yet the Rambam was ruling not for just the one couple, but for a whole class of people, for whom he had previously adjudged.

The respondent realizes that his resolution of the issue does not constitute a perfect solution. Only God will repair our moral damage, as was promised in the words of the prophet: "I shall remove all your dross" (Isaiah 1:25).

Moses ben Maimon was not content with just presenting to the couple his radically lenient responsum, which allowed them to be joined together. He related to the pair with tenderness. He exhibited a warm, humane understanding of their predicament and wounded feelings. This is illustrated by his *obiter dicta* concluding the responsum: "Gently and with tenderness we help him to marry her."

"THE LESSER EVIL" AS A HERMENEUTIC PRINCIPLE

Choosing the lesser evil is an ancient rule of interpretation that can be found in the Bible but, of course, not by this term. Let us look at the following three examples:

In the Book of Genesis, we find Joseph, the unrecognized Egyptian ruler, telling his brothers that Benjamin must remain with him as a slave. Judah pleads that he himself will remain as a slave to the unknown Egyptian instead of Benjamin "and let the lad go back with his brothers. For how can I go back to my father if the lad is not with me? I fear to see the evil that would come upon my father" (Genesis 44:33–34).

It would be terrible to be a slave in Egypt, but not as bad as being the cause of the disaster that might befall his aged father. This is, indeed, a case of choosing the lesser evil.

The prophet Gad came to King David to tell him that it had been decreed that pestilence or famine or exile would be inflicted on him and his people. David replied: "I am in great distress; let us fall into the hand of the Lord, for his mercy is great; but let me not fall into the hand of man." This is clearly a case of David's choice of the lesser evil from the hands of God.[44]

Another instance is found in the book of Esther. At Mordecai's urging, Esther goes to King Ahasuerus, although it is forbidden
by law and she might be executed. When she weighs this danger to
herself against the decree calling for the destruction of all the Jews of
Persia, Esther chooses the lesser evil (Esther 4:8–16).

We cannot find the expression "choosing the lesser evil" in the
responsum about the *shifha*. This is not surprising, because it does not
appear anywhere else in Maimonides' writing. Furthermore, the
phrase is not to be found in biblical or rabbinic literature,[45] although,
as we have seen, the principle of *hara b'miuto* is most definitely
present. It is not mentioned among the seven *middot* attributed to
Hillel the Elder,[46] the thirteen *middot* of R. Ishmael, or the 32 *middot*
ascribed to Eliezer ben Jose HaGelili.[47]

What then, is the source of "the lesser evil" if it is not found
in any of these lists? It would appear to be a variation of *kal vahomer*,
an inference from the light or less important to the heavy or more
important, and vice versa.

Unlike the usual inference known in the western world as *a
minori ad maius* (from the minor to the major) or *a fortiori*, each of
which deals with matters of greater or lesser importance or stringency,
hara b'miuto compares and evaluates two phenomena that are both
evil. A decision is made by clarifying which is the worse and which is
the lesser evil.

Justice Haim Cohn claims that the source of this hermeneutic
is ancient Greece and Rome.[48] Socrates (fifth century B.C.E.) was
quoted as saying: "One who must choose between two evils should
not choose the greater evil if one is able to choose the lesser."[49]

229

Aristotle (384–322 B.C.E.) developed this idea: "A small evil appears good in comparison with a larger evil, for people prefer a smaller evil to a greater evil."[50] Cicero (106–43 B.C.E.) used the expression *"minima ex malis,"* which is indeed *hara b'miuto.*[51]

If the Greeks and Romans knew this principle, called it by name, and put it into writing, why did it not appear in rabbinic literature? We have seen that the rule was put into practice, but for some reason it did not acquire a name in ancient times, in the periods of the Mishnah and Talmud, nor even in the early responsa literature. There was no *middah* in Maimonides' time known by any particular nomenclature.

It was about 200 years after Maimonides' responsum that we find the first mention of this rule in rabbinic literature. Rabbi Isaac ben Sheshet Perfet (1326–1408), known as Ribash, was the chief rabbi of Algiers and head of its rabbinic court. Hundreds of the decisions in his responsa were included in the *Shulhan Arukh.* In one of his *teshuvot,* we find for the first time an explicit reference to the hermeneutic rule, in a somewhat different style: "I chose the least part of the evil."[52] The phrase does not appear again for a number of generations until R. David ibn Zimra (1479–1573) responded to a question about a conflict among members of a community. He advises them that it would be preferable if they could pray together in harmony. If they quarrel most of the time, however, it would be better to worship separately as the lesser evil.[53] From the fifteenth or sixteenth centuries until this century, the rule is in use and is called by its name.[54]

In a penetrating analysis of this responsum, Mark Washofsky partially adopts the concept of choosing the lesser evil. He notes that "by waiving the 'lesser' rabbinic decree against conversion and

230

marriage of this woman (= gravy), Rambam saves the man from violating the 'weightier' toraitic prohibition against cohabitation with Gentiles (= forbidden fat)." The tannaitic *takanat hashavim* is a means of pursuing "this 'lesser of two evils' line." He sees this *takanah* as an implied *kal vahomer:* if the law of the Torah that requires the return of the stolen object can be set aside, this must be the case with the rabbinic interdiction of the marriage.[55]

Prof. Washofsky cites this responsum to illustrate rabbinic discretion in conversion: "[The Rambam] allows a conversion which is clearly not undertaken *leshem shamayim.* "[56] Similarly, Daniel Sinclair states that this case submitted to Maimonides concerned the marriage—following conversion—of a female slave to her Jewish master.[57] He, too, refers to the above-noted choice between the grave sin of living with the slave girl and the lighter sin of marrying her after conversion. These scholars do note, directly or obliquely, the issue of choosing the lesser evil.

Once again we must emphasize that the subject of our *teshuvah* is not conversion, but manumission. Conversion required circumcision (for males), immersion, and accepting the yoke of the commandments in the presence of a *beit din* of three worthy judges. Manumission required only that the slave's owner free her. Conversion might take some time; the *beit din* might or might not be helpful; and manumission was instantaneous. Furthermore, as we have seen, Rambam completely ignored the question about conversion and made no mention of *giyur* or any of its components in his responsum. The *coup de grâce* to the interpretation of this responsum as conversion can be found in Maimonides' instructions to the *beit din* in the young man's community to compel him to free his slave. He says absolutely nothing about her being converted by this *beit din,* which would have been expected, if this were indeed the respondent's understanding of his responsum.

A number of other scholars interpret this *teshuvah* as establishing a halakhic stance on *giyur*.[58] In the next section we shall try to understand the reasons for this interpretation.

RESURRECTION AND TRANSFORMATION: THE CASE OF THE MISSING RESPONSUM

The Rambam wrote the responsum between his immigration to Egypt from the Land of Israel in 1165 and his death in 1204. As far as we can determine, Maimonides' responsum was never cited by his contemporaries or by any *rishonim* or *aharonim*. No medieval or premodern scholar ever mentioned this ruling. It appears that the manuscript of the *teshuvah* was stored away and did not see the light of day for four centuries.

The first written evidence of the destiny of this responsum is found in *Melekhet Shlomo,* the *Mishnah* commentary of R. Shlomo Adani (born in Yemen, 1567; died in Safed, 1625). His work is considered one of the foremost exegeses of the *Mishnah,* bringing together innumerable talmudic commentaries and halakhic decisions. The final edition of his work was written from 1621 to 1624. Adani, in his commentary to the *Mishnah* quotes the source that serves as the basis of Maimonides' *pesikah* in his *Laws of Divorce* forbidding a female slave to be married to her suspected lover.[59]

For the first time since it was written, Adani quotes this Maimonidean responsum: "I found a hand-written manuscript composed by our Rabbi, the author, of blessed memory. He wrote this as a responsum to a question, which was copied from the Arabic." He then goes on to quote the Rambam's *teshuvah,* which is almost identical to the modern Hebrew translation. Most likely, he recognized the importance of his find, but he added nothing other than to literally quote part of the answer. The responsum was not published and disappeared again for more than a century.

In 1765, about six hundred years after its composition, Rabbi Yitzhak ben Mordecai Tamah of Amsterdam translated and published this responsum in the collection of Maimonides' responsa. He called this collection *Pe'er HaDor* (The Glory of the Generation)—one of the honorific titles his questioners gave to Moses ben Maimon.[60] Yitzhak Tamah, using an ancient manuscript, translated it from Arabic to Hebrew.

Finally, these long-lost *teshuvot* had become accessible to rabbis and scholars, yet, the rediscovered *teshuvah* about the *shifhah* is not quoted again for a century. Then began a series of citations in the responsa literature. As far as I could determine, the first respondent to quote it as a precedent was R. Abraham b. Hayyim Palache (1809–1899), the Chief Rabbi of Ismir. He replied to a question about a Gentile woman who had lived with a Jew and then became a convert. Could the couple now get married? R. Palache, after extensive *shakla v'tarya,* permits the marriage. He triumphantly quotes the Rambam's responsum from the *Pe'er HaDor,* not only because it supports his answer to the questioner, but because it affirms his position in a polemical debate with a rabbinical colleague: "This responsum was not discovered by the Rabbi, author of *Hina v'Hisda,* who struggled to understand the Rambam's position which is clearly revealed in the *teshuvah.* "[61]

Palache's responsum was followed by a steady stream of responsa written by Sephardic and Ashkenazic rabbis who quoted the responsum about the slave girl as a precedent. What engendered the renaissance of this halakhic ruling that was over six hundred years old? How do we explain the resurrection of a responsum that had never been part of the process of discussion in later responsa?

First, we would have to uncover the reason for the silence of the rabbinic world during the century since its publication in 1765. This may be accounted for by the fact that slavery among Jews was not prevalent at this time, and a question about a young master purchasing a female slave was rare. Since there were few, if any, questions on this subject, no responsa were written on the issue, and the Rambam's precedent was not needed.

The Jewish community was faced with another conundrum, however: intermarriage and conversion to Judaism. With the Enlightenment and the Emancipation as well as legislation, official intermarriage was sanctioned by European governments. This raised the problem of allowing conversion for the sake of marriage. Although, as we have seen, the Rambam does not deal with *giyur* in his responsum,[62] in the *Mishneh Torah* he showed the close parallel between a *shifhah* that was freed and a Gentile woman that was converted.[63] It would therefore be most reasonable for these learned decisors to transform Maimonides' six-century-old decision and apply it to their current halakhic needs.[64]

An analysis of this responsa revolution is beyond the scope of this paper, but a brief quote from the responsum of Chief Rabbi Ben Zion Uziel (1890–1953) may give us an idea of this transformation. R. Uziel was asked whether it was permissible to convert a Gentile woman who had married a Jew in a civil ceremony. There are many halakhic difficulties, but R. Uziel relies on the Rambam's *pesikah* to overcome all obstacles:

> Our generation is experiencing a disaster with mixed marriages performed under civil auspices, so we must in many instances convert the man or the woman in order to save the Jewish woman or man from the sin of living with a Gentile. We act thus also to save their children, who otherwise would be lost for Israel. We rely on the responsum of our Rabbi and Light, the Rambam, of blessed memory.[65]

Notes

1. Maimonides, *Responsa,* Jehoshua Blau Edition, Vol. 2, Responsum 211 (Jerusalem: R. Mass, 1986), 373–75.

2. Maimonides, *Hilkhot Gerushim* 10:14, based on *m. Yevamot* 2:8; *b. Yevamot* 24b. This marriage might confirm the rumor that he had had sexual intercourse with her while she was forbidden to him in her Gentile status. This rabbinic ruling is only a *siyag,* concerned with what people might think and say. See Rashi *s.v. hanitan.*

3. *b. Gittin* 55a.

4. As we shall see, this is a composite statement comprising certain Talmudic rulings.

5. *b. Berakhot* 54a.

6. Above, n. 3.

7. Leviticus 5:23.

8. Rashi to b. *Gittin* 55a *s.v. mipnei takanat hashavin.*

9. Maimonides, *Hilkhot Shabbat* 20:13; *Hilkhot Issurei Biah* 12.11.

10. Maimonides, *Hilkhot Issurei Biah* 14:19.

11. Maimonides, *Hilkhot Teshuvah* 7:6.

12.　　A check of the sources indicates that this phrase was not used before the Rambam. See Haim Yehoshua Kasoveski, *Concordance to the Talmud* (Jerusalem, 1971) and *Concordance to Tannaitic Literature* (New York, 1968) and Bar Ilan University Responsa Project, 4th version, 1994.

13.　　*m. Yoma* 8:1; *Yoma* 82a.

14.　　*b. Kiddushin* 21b–22a; Leviticus 22:8.

15.　　Deuteronomy 7:3–4 relates the biblical prohibition against making marriages with the seven Canaanite nations.

16.　　Maimonides, *Hilkhot Issurei Biah* 12:11, 13.

17.　　*Shulhan Arukh,* Even HaEzer 16:14.

18.　　Cf. Blau, *Responsa Rambam*, 353 and 372.

19.　　*Jewish Polygamy in the Middle Ages* (Jerusalem: Bialik Institute, 1986), 31–19.

20.　　*b. Yoma* 69a, *s.v. eit la'asot ladonai.*

21.　　*b. Temurah* 14b.

22.　　Eliezer Berkovits, *Not in Heaven: The Nature and Function of Halakhah* (New York: Ktav, 1983), 67.

23.　　See below, n. 31.

24.　　In Egypt it was a crime to convert a slave to Christianity or Judaism. See Blau, n. 1 above, p. 373.

25.　　Deuteronomy 21:11–14.

26.　　Deuteronomy 6:10.

27.　　*b. Hullin* 17a. "During the seven years of Conquest [of the Land] they were permitted to eat unclean things, for it is written 'and houses full of good things' (ibid.), and Rav Jeremiah b. Abba stated in the name of Rav that even sides of bacon were permitted!" Maimonides codified this in *Hilkhot Melakhim* 8:1:

> When the vanguard of the army conquered a foreign land and settled in it, it was permitted for them to eat unkosher meat *[neveilot u'treifot],* pork and similar foods,

if they were hungry and could find only these forbidden foods. The same applied to drinking wine used for idolatrous libation *[yein nesekh]*. We have learned from oral tradition that the biblical phrase "housed full of good things" includes sides of bacon and similar food.

28.   His expression *v'ein l'vhakish al zeh* is based on a modified form of the *hekesh,* which is one of the *middot* or hermeneutical rules ascribed to Hillel the Elder. See *Tosefta Pesachin* 4:1. See Hermann L. Strack, *Introduction to the Talmud and Midrash* (Philadelphia: Jewish Publication Society, 1932), 93ff.

29.   See Mark Washofsky, "Halakhah and Ulterior Motives: Rabbinic Discretion and the Law of Conversion," in Walter Jacob and Moshe Zemer, eds., *Conversion to Judaism in Jewish Law,* (Pittsburgh and Tel Aviv, 1974), p. 7, on the brevity of Maimonides' responsa. He refers the reader on this subject to Menahem Eilon, *HaMishpat Halvri,* 2, p. 1233 and n. 78.

30.   *b. Kiddushin* 21b.

31.   Maimonides, *Hilkhot Melakhim* 8:4.

32.   Above, n. 14.

33.   Maimonides, *Sefer Hamitzvot,* ed. Heller (Jerusalem, 1980), positive commandment 221; negative commandments 263 and 264; and *Hilkhot Melakhim,* above, n. 31.

34.   Deuteronomy 21:12.

35.   *Moreh Nevukhim,* ed. Yosef Kapah (Jerusalem, 1977), 3:41, 372.

36.   The Hebrew term, *k'ein aveirah,* was translated by Prof. Jehoshua Blau from the original Judeo-Arabic *n'hu ta'di.* I am grateful to Professor Blau for explaining this and other aspects of the responsum. See above, n. 1.

37.   The term appears again only in the eighteenth century in the work of R. Ezekiel Landau, *Noda BiYehudah, Even HaEzer,* No. 75.

38.   In his introduction to the *Mishneh Torah s v. ud'varim halalu,* Maimonides states that he has included all Talmudic statements (and especially those of the *Bavli),* which are "mandatory for all Israel." See Jacob Levinger, *Maimonides' Techniques of Codification* (Hebrew) (Jerusalem: Magnes Press, 1965), 88–89.

39.   See above, n. 2.

40.   See above, n. 18.

41.   Maimonides does not always distinguish between *aveirah* and *avon*. The latter, however, is usually used as a severer category of wrongdoing. He uses the term *avon,* for example, for shaming a person in public (*Hilkhot Deot* 6:8), for tale-bearing (which is termed *avon gadol*—ibid., 7:1), for slander (ibid., 7:2), etc.

42.   Cf. *Midrash Proverbs* (Buber), 22:15: "A hint is sufficient for the wise, but only a fist for the foolish."

43.   The author compares this act with that of Ezra the Scribe, in Ezra 10:10–44. Unlike Ezra, who ordered that foreign women be driven away without any option, Maimonides gave a choice.

44.   Samuel 24:14. I am grateful to Justice Haim Cohn for the suggestion of this verse. See below, n. 46.

45.   Above, n. 12.

46.   *Avot d'Rabbi Natan* 16:10.

47.   Strack, above, n. 28, pp. 93–98; Yosef Schechter, *Otzar HaTalmud* (Tel Aviv: D'vir, 1962), p. 224, *s.v. middot.*

48.   Letter to the author, dated 18 May 1994.

49.   Plato, *Dialogue with Protagoras,* p. 358D.

50.   Aristotle, *Nicomachean Ethics,* V 3:20–23.

51.   Marcus Tullius (106–43 B.C.E.), *De officiis,* III, 3.

52.   *Responsa HaRibash* (New York, 1954; photocopy Vilna, 1879), 171, *Et la'asot l'Adonai, hefeiru Toratekcha, uvaharta min hara miuto.*

53.   *Responsa Radbaz* (Jerusalem, 1972; photocopy, Vilna, 1882), 472.

54.   The most recent work to use this term is Ovadia Yosef's *Responsa Yabia Omer* (Jerusalem, 1956–1993) 5:49.

55.   Mark Washofsky, "Halakhah and Ulterior Motives, n. 28, pp. 7–8.

56.   Ibid., p. 7.

238

57.   Daniel Sinclair, "Trends in Rabbinic Policy in Relation to Insincere Conversions in Post Emancipation Responsa," *Dine Israel,* A. Kirschenbaum, ed., 16 (1991-1992), 49-50. Although the author speaks about conversion of slave girls throughout, he exhibits some irresolution on the matter: "It is not quite clear whether or not the slave-girl needed to be converted or merely manumitted.... Many authorities, however, assume that the conversion issue is also at stake in this responsum" (p. 49, n. 15). He refers the reader to a number of Sephardic sages who had a *tendenz* to read their contemporary problems of proselytism into the responsum. Rabbi Dr. Sinclair is the principal of Jews College in London.

58.   See Avi Sagi and Zvi Zohar, *Conversion to Judaism and the Meaning of Jewish Identity* (Jerusalem: Bialik Institute, 1994), pp. 34-35 and 59-60, in their otherwise excellent book make this claim.

59.   Shlomo Adani, *Melekhet Shlomo, The Mishnah* (Vilna, 1905), *m. Yevamot* 2:8, *s.v. hanitan al hashifhah.* See above, n. 2.

60.   Among the many superlative designations are found "The Strong Hammer, The Light of the West, The Flag of the Rabbis, The Sign and Wonder of the World" (Blau, *Resp. Rambam,* 112); "The Light of the World and Its Marvel from the Rising of the Sun until Sunset, The Only One of the Generation" (ibid., 277). There are many more such appellations. Maimonides usually dictated his answer to a scribe, who wrote on the same sheet as the question. After his responsum, which follows, the praise poured out to him in the question above, the Rambam adds: "Signed, Moshe."

61.   This responsum is found in his father's book *Hayyim ve'Shalom, Even Haezer,* Ismir, 1862-1879, v. 2, p. 108. R. Hayyim Palache (1788-1869), his father and predecessor as Chief Rabbi added a short imprimatur praising the *teshuvah.*

62.   See p. 236 of this text.

63.   Above, n. 2.

64.   Among those who quoted the Rambam's decision in their responsa on intermarriage and conversion are Eliyahu Hazan, *Ta'alumot Lev* 28; Meir Simhah HaCohen, *Or Sameah* 32; Hayyim Fischel Epstein, *Teshuvah Shleimah,* E.H. 10; Shalom Mordecai Shwadron, *Maharsham,* Vol. 6, p. 109; Hayyim Ozer Grodzinsky, *Ahiezer* 26; Ben Zion Uziel, *Piskei Uziel,* 59, 60, 63; and Ya'akov Yehiel Weinberg, *Seridei Esh* 3:3; Moshe HaCohen, *Ve'heishiv Moshe* 51.

65.   Ben Zion Uziel, *Piskei Uziel,* 63.

RESPONSE TO RABBI ZEMER

Daniel Schiff

I am deeply gratified to have been asked to participate in this symposium in honor of Rabbi Walter Jacob and Irene. I first met Rabbi Jacob in the offices of the World Union for Progressive Judaism when he was the President of the Central Conference of American Rabbis.

At the time, I had been ordained for maybe two or three years. I vividly remember the conversation. Rabbi Jacob's first question to me that day was, "What is your field of interest?" Now the colleagues in the room will know that the first question asked by most rabbis is usually something like, "How big is your congregation?" or, "How many worshippers are in your synagogue on Shabbat morning?" But Rabbi Jacob's first question—which was so typical of him—was, what is your field of interest? At the time, I was already intrigued by the responsa literature and was a close friend of the man to whom I am responding this afternoon, Moshe Zemer. So, I immediately replied, "Being a good friend of Moshe Zemer, it is natural that my field of interest is the responsa literature!" Rabbi Jacob responded, "Really? Well, in that case, I have a number of volumes in my library that are duplicates, and if you would like them I would be happy to send them to you." I, of course, thinking that this was classic American politeness said, "How wonderful, Dr. Jacob, that would be very nice of you," and the conversation concluded. Soon after my arrival back in Australia, I was absolutely shocked—although those who have known Rabbi Jacob for much longer than I would not have been—when a package arrived from Rodef Shalom with Rabbi Jacob's promised books. They are an important part of my library to this day. I continue to marvel at the fact that they came from a rabbi whom I had met only once.

I relate this story because I think it is so very characteristic of the person we honor at this hour. It is surely clear to us all that Rabbi Jacob will be one of the very few Reform rabbis that history will remember from the twentieth century—because of his prodigious contributions to scholarship, but also because Rabbi Jacob is a mensch in every way. He is a person I am very proud to call a friend. It would indeed have been a great surprise to me on that first day we met to have thought that I would one day end up in Pittsburgh and would know Rabbi Jacob and be a part of his community. How greatly I have been blessed!

I want, very briefly, to make some points about the fine paper Rabbi Zemer presented. Rabbi Zemer has elucidated for us a complex responsum of the Rambam concerning the "lesser evil." When you have the opportunity to read the full paper you will see that Dr. Zemer makes the claim that this concept of the "lesser evil" is a significant hermeneutic principle. In fact, Dr. Zemer holds that one can use the "lesser evil" as a tool for trying to evaluate instances beyond the one Maimonides introduced. Indeed, Dr. Zemer informs us that, through the course of history, the principle of the "lesser evil" has come to be used much more than it had ever been before Maimonides gave it the shape he did in the course of this responsum. Dr. Zemer's implication is that the "lesser evil" may be readily applied to evaluate the correct, or the most appropriate, halakhic path to choose in a given set of circumstances.

It seems to me, however, that this assertion is problematic. I will illustrate the primary difficulty inherent in Rabbi Zemer's position by bringing two halakhic examples and by asking whether the "lesser evil" principle can really be logically and appropriately applied and whether the principle can actually be made to "work" dispassionately every time. For, in contradistinction to Rabbi Zemer's position, I claim that the "lesser evil" is a principle that, at the least, has great flexibility in its application, if not a large measure of subjectivity as well. I am not claiming that this should be either surprising or disturbing to us—merely that we should not be under any illusions that this is a tool that can be wielded regularly with detached objectivity.

The first halakhic illustration arises from an event that occurred during World War I, at the time that Germany invaded Poland and Lithuania. The late Ashkenazi Chief Rabbi of the State of Israel, Rabbi Isser Yehuda Unterman, describes the situation in these terms:

> It happened that in the ranks of the German soldiers and officers stationed in Jewish towns, one of the officers had intimate relations with a Jewish girl. When she revealed to him that she was pregnant and asked that he take responsibility for the results of his actions, he requested that she go to a doctor for an abortion in order to get out of this situation. They turned to a Jewish doctor in the town in order to carry out the abortion, and even though the girl did not desire it [the abortion], [the officer] pressed her to agree. However, the doctor refused [to carry out the abortion] because it was forbidden according to the law of the Torah (and also, according to the law of the state, such an act was regarded as a criminal transgression). Thereupon the officer threatened [the doctor's life] with a drawn revolver (for they [the Germans] regarded themselves as having absolute dominance over the lives of the inhabitants). The doctor requested the postponement of his decision [as to whether he would choose to perform the abortion or be killed] in the matter for one day, and, in the meantime, he brought the question to a rabbi. The rabbi gave serious contemplation to this problem of the "appurtenance of spilling blood," and could not come to a decision.

Now it is plain that the rabbi who was consulted in this case had a great deal of trouble trying to work out what the correct solution to the problem should be. Ought the doctor say, "Shoot me, for it would be better that I should give up my life rather than that I should be compelled to take the life of the fetus?" After all, abortion might be warranted in some cases, but here the mother does not want an abortion, there is no obvious indication for an abortion, and the doctor's actions could be construed as an appurtenance of murder if he performs the procedure. Or ought we contend that the doctor should destroy the fetus against the wishes of the woman and terminate the life that would otherwise come to be? Rabbi Unterman regards this as a particularly difficult question and finds compelling things to say on both sides of the issue before he ultimately comes up with his solution. By no means, then, is his solution arrived at simply or without struggle.

Rabbi Unterman's conclusion, parenthetically, is that the doctor ought to perform the abortion. But the conclusion is far less significant for our purposes than is the point that Rabbi Unterman finds this to be such a difficult question. After all, in the middle of the nineteenth century, Rabbi Joseph Babad, the author of the *Minchat Chinnukh,* when faced with a similar sort of issue, wrote that it was an inescapable conclusion that when confronted with a choice between taking the life of a full human being—not the mother—or killing the unborn child, killing the unborn child was the lesser of two evils. Now if, therefore, we are to assume that the "lesser evil" is a hermeneutic principle that can be applied reliably and then remains an effective compass for locating the "correct path," why was Unterman in such doubt? Why does Unterman need to follow such a tortuous process of consideration to arrive at a conclusion? And why does he never quote Babad? Why does he not allude to the fact that others have said

244

that killing the fetus is the "lesser evil," and, therefore, this must be the answer? My view is that the most cogent response to these inquiries is that the "lesser evil" is regularly to be found "in the eye of the beholder." Unterman, therefore, was not prepared to use the "lesser evil" as the basis on which he would construct his answer to the problem before him. Although the "lesser evil" might, then, be given as a reason for taking a particular stance, its status as a solid hermeneutic principle should be seen as being at least somewhat pliable.

The second halakhic illustration comes not from a *teshuvah* within the Orthodox context, but, rather, from the Reform milieu. This *teshuvah*, number 192 in Contemporary American Reform Responsa and written by Rabbi Jacob, deals with the complex issue of adultery. Interestingly, it does, in fact, bear similarities to Rabbi Zemer's *teshuvah* of Maimonides. The question brought to Rabbi Jacob, however, deals not with a *shifhah*, a slave girl, but rather with a couple, in which one party has committed adultery. A divorce occurs, and now the person who has committed adultery would like to be married to the individual with whom the adultery was committed. So the question is: ought the rabbi officiate at the wedding of the person who has committed adultery together with the paramour?

Now, before I give you Rabbi Jacob's answer, it is important to demonstrate just how this connects to the idea of the "lesser evil." In the course of considering one's response, one might say, as the Rambam said in his *teshuvah,* that it would be unseemly, unsightly, and an insult to the institution of marriage if such a couple were to go on living together, and, therefore, it would be preferable for them to be married. Or, conversely, one might say that it would be a gross insult to the former spouse and to the former marriage, and, in some

245

ways, would bless the adultery that has occurred if the rabbi were to officiate at the marriage of an acknowledged adulterer. Both alternatives clearly contain evils, and the essential question that needs to be decided is, "Which is the lesser evil?"

Now, Rabbi Jacob's answer will not surprise you because Rabbi Jacob is by nature like Maimonides, very compassionate and understanding, particularly when it comes to human foibles. Hence, Rabbi Jacob is of the view that the couple ought to be married because it would be worse for them to be living together and bring the institution of marriage into disrepute. Consequently, writes Rabbi Jacob, the rabbi should officiate at some type of private, low-key ceremony and should speak to the couple about the seriousness of marital commitments.

Now I, who cannot claim for myself quite the highly developed sense of compassion for which Rabbi Jacob is known, am of the opposite point of view. I contend that to officiate at the marriage of such a couple is actually to reward adultery and that if people become aware that officiation is encouraged, a significant statement disapproving of adultery is removed from our communal life. So now we must ask the question—how do we evaluate which is really the lesser of two evils? I would submit that it all depends on what you think is truly evil. I happen to think that a profound societal evil is involved in rewarding adultery. Rabbi Jacob has great compassion for the people involved here and effectively says that one ought to understand that, although they have certainly done bad things, they are now repentant, so we ought to normalize their status; it would be worse to require them to live together. Which is the lesser evil? It depends on what particular spectacles you use to view the question.

246

Before, then, we get overly impressed with the notion that Maimonides has struck a blow for leniency through his use of the "lesser evil" idea, perhaps we ought to pause to ask ourselves, is leniency always what we seek? For, in actuality, there may well be more than a few instances in which Reform Jews might want to articulate rigorous standards as being critical norms for a society in which we can function appropriately with each other. If we do not establish such standards, the leniency we might set in place could actually lead to an ever-diminishing observance of traditions that we regard as critical for the sanctity and the effectiveness of the Jewish people. The idea of the "lesser evil," then, represents an important and logical justification for choosing a particular road to take. But we should be under no illusions: the particular road taken is very much a choice structured around the priorities of those making the determination. The "lesser evil" is by no means a "preset" principle that can automatically guide us to a determined destination.

Rabbi Zemer has presented to us a paper that he titled "The Lesser Evil." As I read it and heard his presentation, though, I found that, in fact, his paper—my minor quibbles notwithstanding —depicts "the greater virtue" of his own scholarship. To have been able to be the last speaker honoring Rabbi Jacob this afternoon, and to have been given the opportunity to respond to my good friend and the cofounder of the Freehof Institute for Progressive Judaism, Rabbi Zemer, has been a great pleasure, indeed. We have all been enriched to have been in the presence of such great scholars and teachers.

Annette and Ernest Jacob

Irene Jacob

Irene and Walter Jacob

Lynn and Herbert Jacob

Claire and Irene

Kenneth, Walter, and Daniel

Bari, Eslyn, and Daniel

Zachary and Madeliene Jacob

BIBLIOGRAPHY OF WALTER JACOB:
BOOKS, ESSAYS, AND ARTICLES

This bibliography contains books, essays, articles, and sermons published in the general or Jewish press.[*]

Books:

1. *Paths of Faithfulness, A Collection of Sermons,* by Ernest I. Jacob. Ed. with Herbert Jacob, Pittsburgh, 1964, 212 pp.
2. *Essays in Honor of Solomon B. Freehof.* Ed. and au. with Frederick C. Schwartz and Vigdor Kavaler, Pittsburgh, 1964, 333 pp.
3. *Our Biblical Heritage,* New York, 1965, 101 pp.
4. *Christianity through Jewish Eyes,* New York, 1982, 1974, 287 pp.
5. *Genesis, Interpreted by Benno Jacob.* Ed. and trans. with Ernest I. Jacob, New York, 1974, 358 pp.
6. *American Reform Responsa.* Ed. and au., New York, 1983, 563 pp.
7. *Books of Fifty Years.* Ed. and au., Pittsburgh, 1984, 197 pp.
8. *The Pittsburgh Platform in Retrospect: The Changing World of Reform Judaism.* Ed. And au., Pittsburgh, 1985, 123 pp.
9. *Gardens of North America and Hawaii, A Traveler's Guide.* With Irene Jacob, Portland, 1985, 368 pp.
10. *Essays in Jewish Theology of Samuel Cohon.* Ed. with S. Dreyfus and S. Brooks, New York, 1987, 366 pp.
11. *Contemporary American Reform Responsa,* New York, 1987, 322 pp.

---

[*]Abbreviations: SP—Sabbath Pulpit, a regular column in *Rodef Shalom Temple Bulletin,* containing summaries of Saturday morning sermons.
RSTB—Rodef Shalom Temple Bulletin, Pittsburgh, Pa.
CCAR—Central Conference of American Rabbis.

12. *Liberal Judaism and Halakhah.* Ed. and au., Pittsburgh, 1988, 155 pp.
13. *Dynamic Jewish Law—Progressive Halakhah, Essence and Application.* Ed. and au. with Moshe Zemer, Tel Aviv and Pittsburgh, 1991, 148 pp.
14. *Exodus, A Commentary by Benno Jacob.* Ed. and trans., Hoboken, N.J., 1992, 1099 pp.
15. *The Healing Past—Pharmaceuticals in the Biblical and Rabbinic World.* Ed. and au. with Irene Jacob, Leiden, 1993, 127 pp.
16. *Questions and Reform Jewish Answers—New American Reform Responsa,* New York, 1992, 443 pp.
17. *Rabbinic—Lay Relations in Jewish Law.* Ed. and au. with Moshe Zemer, Pittsburgh and Tel Aviv, 1993, 128 pp.
18. *Conversion to Judaism in Jewish Law—Essays and Responsa.* Ed. and au. with Moshe Zemer, Pittsburgh and Tel Aviv, 1994, 216 pp.
19. *Death and Euthanasia in Jewish Law—Essays and Responsa.* Ed. and au. with Moshe Zemer, Pittsburgh and Tel Aviv, 1995, 204 pp.
20. *The Fetus and Fertility in Jewish Law—Essays and Responsa.* Ed. and au. with Moshe Zemer, Pittsburgh and Tel Aviv, 1995, 224 pp.
21. *Israel and the Diaspora in Jewish Law—Essays and Responsa.* Ed. and au. with Moshe Zemer, Pittsburgh and Tel Aviv, 1997, 198 pp.
22. *Not by Birth Alone.* Ed. and au. with Walter Homolka and Esther Seidel, London and New York, 1997, 209 pp.
23. *Aging and the Aged in Jewish Law—Essays and Responsa.* Ed. and au. with Moshe Zemer, Pittsburgh, 1998, 176 pp.

24. *Crime and Punishment in Jewish Law—Essays and Responsa.* Ed. and au. with Moshe Zemer, New York and London, 1999, 201 pp.
25. *Marriage and Its Obstacles in Jewish Law—Essays and Responsa,* Ed. and au. with Moshe Zemer, Pittsburgh, and Tel Aviv, 1999, xii, 248 pp.
26. *Gender Issues in Jewish Law - Essays and Responsa,* Ed. and au. with Moshe Zemer, New York and London, 2001.

1955

1. "Modern Education and Modern Religion," (SP) *RSTB,* April 20: 3–4.
2. "An Enduring Classic," (SP) *RSTB,* May 7: 3–4.
3. "Heroism," (SP) *RSTB,* May 21: 3–4.
4. "A Picture of Judaism," *The Sabbath Pulpit, Chapel Bulletin,* Clark Air Base, Subic Bay, Sangley Point, November 25, No. 1: 2, 3.
5. "Militant Loyalty," *The Sabbath Pulpit,* Clark Air Base, December 16, No. 5: 2, 3.

1956

6. "The Symbols of Judaism," *Chapel Bulletin,* Clark Air Base, January 6, No. 11: 2, 3.
7. "Escape from Freedom," *The Sabbath Pulpit,* Clark Air Base, January 20, No. 10: 2, 3.
8. "Progress and Despair," *The Sabbath Pulpit,* Clark Air Base, January 27, No. 11: 2, 3.
9. "Jews in the Far East," *Chapel Bulletin,* Clark Air Base, February 17, No. 14: 2, 3.

10. "Victory or Defeat," *Chapel Bulletin,* Clark Air Base, Manila Air Station, Subic Bay, Cubi Point, Sangley Point, Linkou Air Base, Taipei, Taiwan, March 20, No. 20: 2, 3.
11. "Revolution and Reflection," a Passover sermon broadcast on "The Message of Israel," March 25, 1956 (with an Introduction by Nelson Glueck), Union of American Hebrew Congregations, New York, 3 pp.
12. "Israel I," *Chapel Bulletin,* Clark Air Base, April 13, No. 22: 2, 3.
13. "Israel II," *Chapel Bulletin,* Clark Air Base, April 20, No. 23: 2, 3.
14. "Israel III," *Chapel Bulletin,* Clark Air Base, April 27, No. 24: 2, 3.
15. "Report to the Congregation," *Chapel Bulletin,* Clark Air Base, June 8, No. 30: 2.
16. "Jews in the Far East—Tokyo," *Chapel Bulletin,* Clark Air Base, June 15, No. 31: 2, 3.
17. "Reform Judaism," *Chapel Bulletin,* Clark Air Base, October 19, No. 47: 2, 3.
18. "Orthodox Judaism," *Chapel Bulletin,* Clark Air Base, October 26, No. 48: 2, 3.
19. "In Memoriam for the Ninth of November," *Chapel Bulletin,* Clark Air Base, November 9, No. 50: 2.
20. "Hannukah," *Chapel Bulletin,* Clark Air Base, December 7, No. 54: 2
21. "Prayer," *Chapel Bulletin,* Clark Air Base, December 14, No. 55: 2

1957

22. "Jewish Music—Its History," *Chapel Bulletin,* Clark Air Base, January 4, No. 58: 2, 3.

23. "Jews in the Philippines," *Congress Weekly,* January 7, No. 1: 10, 11.
24. "Even in Manila," *World Jewish Affairs,* News and Feature Service, London, 21 January: 1, 2.
25. "Even in Manila," *Sidney Jewish News,* February 8.
26. "Jewish Music—The Sabbath," *Chapel Bulletin,* Clark Air Base, January 11, No. 59: 2.
27. "Jewish Music—The Folk Song," *Chapel Bulletin,* Clark Air Base, January 18, No. 60: 2.
28. "Jews in the Far East—Bangkok," *Chapel Bulletin,* Clark Air Base, February 1, No. 62: 2, 3.
29. "Modern Jewish Thinkers—Theodore Herzl," *Chapel Bulletin,* Clark Air Base, February 15, No. 64: 2, 3.
30. "Modern Jewish Thinkers—Martin Buber," *Chapel Bulletin,* Clark Air Base, February 22, No. 65: 2, 3.
31. "Modern Jewish Thinkers—Ahad Ha-Am," *Chapel Bulletin,* Clark Air Base, March 8, No. 67: 2, 3.
32. "Esther," *Chapel Bulletin,* Clark Air Base, March 15, No. 68: 2.
33. "Modern Jewish Thinkers—Franz Rosenzweig," *Chapel Bulletin,* Clark Air Base, March 29, No. 70: 2, 3.
34. "Modern Jewish Thinkers—Abraham J. Heschel," *Chapel Bulletin,* Clark Air Base, April 5, No. 71: 3.
35. "Eighteen Months—A Review," *Chapel Bulletin,* Clark Air Base, April 12, No. 72: 2, 3.
36. "A Farewell Letter," *Chapel Bulletin,* Clark Air Base, April 19, No. 73: 2, 3.
37. "A Visit to the Orient," *The Reconstructionist,* June 14, 9: 23–25.
38. "The Struggle for Life," (SP) *RSTB,* November 1: 3–5.
39. "The Spirit of Learning," (SP) *RSTB,* November 20: 3.

40. "From Generation to Generation," (SP) *RSTB*, December 18: 3.
41. "The Quiet Life," (SP) *RSTB*, December 25: 3.

1958

42. "Escape," (SP) *RSTB*, February 19: 4–6.
43. "Misplaced Moods," *RSTB*, March 5: 3.
44. "Be Precise," (SP) *RSTB*, May 2: 3.
45. "Who is Wise?" (SP) *RSTB*, May 21: 3.
46. "Judge Carefully," (SP) *RSTB*, May 28: 3.
47. "Rosh Hashono, The Days of Our Youth," (SP) *RSTB*, October 15: 3–4.
48. "Yom Kippur, Out of the Past," (SP) *RSTB*, October 22: 3–6.
49. "Foundations for Life," (SP) *RSTB*, October 29: 3–6.
50. "Holy or Profane, Last Day of Succos," (SP) *RSTB*, November 19: 3–4.
51. "A World of Hope," (SP) *RSTB*, November 26: 3.
52. "Follies—Old and New," (SP) *RSTB*, December 24: 3–4.

1959

53. "Growing Up," (SP) *RSTB*, January 7: 3.
54. "Three Paths to Freedom," (SP) *RSTB*, January 21: 3.
55. "Our Home," (SP) *RSTB*, January 28: 3–4.
56. "Ideas into Action, (SP) *RSTB*, February 4: 3.
57. "Our Foes," (SP) *RSTB*, February 11: 3
58. "Survival," (SP) *RSTB*, February 18: 3.
59. "Views of the Past," (SP) *RSTB*, February 25: 3.
60. "Outside Influence," (SP) *RSTB*, March 4: 3–5.

61. "Principles Are Not Enough," (SP) *RSTB*, March 11: 3.
62. "Old Words with New Meanings," (SP) *RSTB*, March 18: 3.
63. "To Observe the Sabbath," (SP) *RSTB*, April 1: 3.
64. "Permanent Ideas, (SP) *RSTB*, April 15: 3.
65. "Evil into Good, Book of Esther," (SP) *RSTB*, April 22: 3.
66. "Sickness and Health," (SP) *RSTB*, May 15: 2–4.
67. "Learning," (SP) *RSTB*, October 7: 3–6.
68. "Personal Religion," (SP) *RSTB*, October 28: 3–4.
69. "Two Paths," (SP) *RSTB*, November 25: 2–3.
70. "The Struggle for Justice," (SP) *RSTB*, December 16: 3–4.
71. "To Our Critics," (SP) *RSTB*, December 23: 2–3.

1960

72. "Paths to Success," (SP) *RSTB*, January 6: 3–4.
73. "From Day to Day," (SP) *RSTB*, January 20: 3–4.
74. "The Road to Victory," (SP) *RSTB*, February 3: 3–4.
75. "Dreams and Reality," (SP) *RSTB*, February 17: 3.
76. "Stumbling Blocks into Stepping Stones," (SP) *RSTB*, March 2: 3–7.
77. "Remember This Day," (SP) *RSTB*, March 9: 3.
78. "A Lost Mood," (SP) *RSTB*, March 30: 3.
79. "Purim and Personality," (SP) *RSTB*, April 13: 3.
80. "Our Spiritual Vocation," (SP) *RSTB*, April 27: 3–6.
81. "Bitter-Sweet Freedom," (SP) *RSTB*, May 25: 3–4.
82. "Sabbath Pulpit," (SP) *RSTB*, September 28: 3–4.
83. "Holidays," (SP) *RSTB*, October 26: 3.
84. "The Space Age," (SP) *RSTB*, November 12: 3.
85. "Youth Service, (SP) *RSTB*, December 7: 3.

1961

86. "Delayed Action," (SP) *RSTB*, February 8: 3–8.
87. "The Songs of Our Life," (SP) *RSTB*, February 22: 3.
88. "Freedom for Us and Our Neighbors," (SP) *RSTB*, March 22: 3.
89. "The Contributions of the Weak," (SP) *RSTB*, April 5: 3–4.
90. "Weak Links," (SP) *RSTB*, April 19: 3.
91. "The New Synagogue: Success or Failure," *Jewish Spectator* (April): 26.
92. "From Generation to Generation," (SP) *RSTB*, May 3: 3–6.
93. "Israel and Her Critics," (SP) *RSTB*, May 17: 3–4.
94. "Oh, Jerusalem," (SP) *RSTB*, October 4: 3–4.
95. "Hear, O Israel, High Holydays," (SP) *RSTB*, November 8: 3–6.
96. "A True Classic," (SP) *RSTB*, November 22: 3–4.
97. "The Tin Menorah: A Symbol of Neglect," *Congress Bi-Weekly* 28: 17, November 27.
98. "Back to Paradise," (SP) *RSTB*, November 29: 3.

1962

99. "Social Justice and the Synagogue," (SP) *RSTB*, January 3: 3–5.
100. "Family Problems," (SP) *RSTB*, January 17: pp. 3-5.
101. "The Twice Forgotten Man," (SP) *RSTB*, January 24: 3–4.
102. "Pattern for a People," (SP) *RSTB*, February 14: 3–4.

103. "Rebuilding the *Bible*," (SP) *RSTB*, March 21: 3–4.

104. "A Nightmare into a Dream," (SP) *RSTB*, April 4: 3–6.

105. "When Religion Fails Us," (SP) *RSTB*, April 11: 3.

106. "Time Value," (SP) *RSTB*, March 2: 3–4.

107. "The Lighter Side," (SP) *RSTB*, May 16: 3.

108. "The New Teen-Ager," (SP) *RSTB*, October 10: 3–6.

109. "Failure or Success," (SP) *RSTB*, October 24: 3–4.

110. "Free Will," (SP) *RSTB*, October 31: 3.

111. "High Holydays, 1962," (SP) *RSTB*, November 14: 3–4.

112. "Grant Us Peace," (SP) *RSTB*, December 5: 3–4.

113. Review: "Objective Study of Holy Scripture, *The Birth of the Torah*, by Edward Zerin," *Pittsburgh Press*, December 9.

114. "Let's Get Rid of the Tin Menorah: A Symbol of Neglect," *The Jewish Digest*, December: 21–23.

1963

115. "The Tower of Babel, A Fable for Adults," Sabbath Sermon, Rodef Shalom Congregation, booklet, 5 pp.

116. "In Memoriam," Memorial Sermonette Given at Vesper Services, November 22, President John F. Kennedy, Rodef Shalom Congregation, Pittsburgh, Pa., pp. 10–11.

117. "The Bible and the City," (SP) *RSTB*, January 2: 3–4.

118. "How Bad Is Our Family Life?," (SP) *RSTB*, January 16: 3–4.

119. "Review: Translation of 'Torah' Follows New Paths," *The Pittsburgh Press*, January 26, Section 2: 9.

120. "Military Might to Religious Achievements," (SP) *RSTB*, February 6: 3–5.

121. "The Dark Past," (SP) *RSTB*, February 27: 3–6.

122. "Friends and Foes," (SP) *RSTB*, March 13: 3–6.

123. "Our Share in Survival," (SP) *RSTB,* April 10: 3–6.
124. "Why Indifference?" (SP) *RSTB,* May 1: 5–6.
125. "Birmingham: Our Conflict and Theirs," Sabbath Sermon, Rodef Shalom Congregation, Pittsburgh, Pa., May 18, booklet, 6 pp.
126. "The New Jewish Bible Translation—Success or Failure," Sermon, Rodef Shalom Congregation, Pittsburgh, Pa., Sunday, March 13, booklet, 15 pp.
127. "Education and the Jew: A German View," *Religious Edu cation,* May–June, pp. 269–75.
128. "The Jewish Retreat," *Jewish Spectator* (June), pp. 25–26.
129. "Shaping the New World," (SP) *RSTB,* June 6: pp. 3–4.
130. "Frustrations into Blessing," Rosh Hashannah Sermon, Rodef Shalom Congregation, Pittsburgh, Pa., September 18, booklet, 10 pp.
131. "The Inter-Religious Dialogue," *Jewish Heritage* (Fall), pp. 31–35.
132. "The March on Washington," (SP) *RSTB,* October 2, pp. 3–5.
133. "Toward the New Year," (SP) *RSTB,* October 30, p. 3.
134. *Anti-Semitism in the Soviet Union—Myth or Reality?,* Sermon, Rodef Shalom Congregation, Pittsburgh, Pa., November 17, booklet, 12 pp.
135. "A Fable for Adults," (SP) *RSTB,* November 20: pp. 3–5.
136. "The Book of Promise," (SP) *RSTB,* December 18: pp. 3–4.
137. "A Bibliography of Novels & Short Stories by German Jewish Authors 1800–1914, *Studies in Bibliography & Booklore* 6: 2 (Winter), pp. 75–92.

1964

138. "Our Chanuka—Victory or Defeat?" (SP) *RSTB*, January 8, pp. 3–4.

139. "Archaeology and Scripture," (SP) *RSTB*, January 22, pp. 3–6.

140. "The Decline of the Sermon," *CCAR Journal* (January), pp. 48–50.

141. "The Decalogue—A Modest Beginning," (SP) *RSTB*, March 4: pp. 3–6.

142. "Brotherhood versus the Ideal," (SP) *RSTB*, March 11: pp. 3–6.

143. "Negro Anti-Semitism," (SP) *RSTB*, April 22: pp. 3–5.

144. "Wisdom for Life," (SP) *RSTB*, May 13: p. 3.

145. "Has the Jewish Retreat Failed," *The Jewish Digest* (May), pp. 58–60.

146. "A Mirror of Our Life, The Book of Ruth," (SP) *RSTB*, June 3: pp. 3–5.

147. *The Enemies within Us*, High Holiday Sermon, Rodef Shalom Congregation, Pittsburgh, Pa., September, booklet, 12 pp.

148. "Review: The Teaching of Contempt, *Christian Roots of Anti-Semitism*, by Jules Isaac," *The Jewish Teacher* 33: 1 (October), p. 31.

149. Benno Jacob, "The First and Second Commandments," An Excerpt from the *Commentary on Exodus*, Translator, *Judaism* 13: 1 (Winter), pp. 318.

150. Review of T. H. Tetens, *The New Germany and The Old Nazis* (New York: Random House, 1961), *Jewish Social Studies, A Quarterly Journal Devoted to Contemporary and Historical Aspects of Jewish Life* 24: 4 (October), pp. 255–56.

151. "Hitler and Christianity," *Jewish Spectator* 29 (October). 152. "Bored? Lonely?" Family Worship Service, November 7, Rodef Shalom Congregation, Pittsburgh, Pa., 4 pp, booklet.

153. "The American Jewish Novel— A Mirror of Our Intellectuals," (SP) *RSTB*, November 18: p. 3.

154. "A Style of Life," (SP) *RSTB,* December 9: p. 3.

155. "The Winter of Our Lives," a Sabbath Sermon, December 19, Rodef Shalom Congregation, Pittsburgh, Pa., booklet, 4 pp.

156. "Science Challenges Religion—A Jewish Response," Sunday Sermon, December 13, Rodef Shalom Congregation, Pittsburgh, Pa., booklet, 9 pp.

157. "Bored? Lonely?" (SP) *RSTB,* December 16: pp. 3–6.

1965

158. "Gloomy Days," (SP) *RSTB,* January 27: pp. 3–4.

159. "Success—Sweet or Sour," A Sabbath Sermon, February 6, Rodef Shalom Congregation, Pittsburgh, Pa., booklet, 5 pp.

160. "Techniques Which Fail Us," (SP) *RSTB,* February 24: pp. 3–4.

161. "The United Jewish Federation: An Appraisal and a Critique," Sermon preached at Rodef Shalom Congregation, Pittsburgh, Pa., Sunday, February 28, booklet, 14 pp.

162. "The Little Genius," (SP) *RSTB,* March 17: pp. 3–4.

163. "We Are Not Religious," (SP) *RSTB,* March 31: p. 3.

164. "Too Sweet, Too Kind," (SP) *RSTB,* April 21: pp. 3–6.

165. "From the Mouth of Babes," (SP) *RSTB,* May 19: p. 3.

166. "World Union Leaders: Solomon B. Freehof," *Reform Review, Monthly Journal of Modern Judaism, South Africa* 1: 3 (May), pp. 8–9.

167. "Thank You, Thank You Very Much," (SP) *RSTB*, June 2: pp. 3–6.

168. "In a Divided Secular Age," (SP) *RSTB*, October 13: pp. 3–7.

169. "Leo Baeck on Christianity," *The Jewish Quarterly Review* 56: 2 (October), pp. 158—72; 195–211.

170. "Sorrow in a Time of Joy," Succot Sermon, Rodef Shalom Congregation, Pittsburgh, Pa., October 16, booklet, 5 pp.

171. "An Appraisal of the U.J.F.," Excerpts from a Sermon, Rodef Shalom Congregation," *The Jewish Leader*, Pittsburgh, Pa., 75: 16 (October); also reference, p. 1.

172. "Moses Mendelssohn and the Jewish-Christian Dialogue," *CCAR Journal* 13: 3 (October), pp. 45–51.

173. "Judaism and the New Catholicism—The Price of New Found Love," Sunday Sermon, Rodef Shalom Congregation, Pittsburgh, Pa., November 14, booklet, 11 pp.

174. "Sorrow in a Time of Joy," (SP) *RSTB*, November 17: pp. 3–7.

175. "Soviet Jews—Progress of Despair?" (SP) *RSTB*, November 24: pp. 3–4.

176. "'God Is Dead'—Really?" (SP) *RSTB*, December 8: pp. 3–4.

177. "Viet Nam—Our Forgotten Dead," (SP) *RSTB*, December 2: p. 3.

1966

178. "The Tower of Babel, A Fable for Adults," *Best Jewish Sermons of 5725–5726*, edited by Saul I. Teplitz, New York, pp. 128–34.

179. "High Hopes—Little Luck," (SP) *RSTB*, January 12: pp. 3–4.

180. "Is Judaism Too Staid?" (SP) *RSTB*, January 19: p. 3.
181. "The Pangs of Pacifism," Sermon, Rodef Shalom Congregation, Pittsburgh, Pa., February 6, booklet, 12 pp.
182. "Fuzzy Vision," (SP) *RSTB*, February 23: p. 3.
183. "It Could Have Been Worse," (SP) *RSTB*, March 9: p. 3.
184. "For Those Who Think Young," (SP) *RSTB*, April 6: pp. 3–4.
185. "Eternal Springtime," (SP) *RSTB*, April 13: p. 3.
186. "Quaint Old Ways," (SP) *RSTB*, May 4: p. 5.
187. "Our Hymns—Our Psalms," (SP) *RSTB*, September 14: p. 3.
188. "Who Envies the Farmer?" (SP) *RSTB*, September 29: p. 3.
189. "Isaac Mayer Wise's Views on Christianity," *Judaism* 15: 4 (Fall), pp. 437–49.
190. "Who Wants Paradise?" (SP) *RSTB*, November 2: p. 3.
191. "Will We Disappear?" (SP) *RSTB*, November 16: p. 3.
192. "The Pace of Our Life," (SP) *RSTB*, November 30: p. 3.
193. "Service of Installation of Dr. Walter Jacob as Rabbi," Rodef Shalom Congregation, Pittsburgh, Pa., November 6, booklet, pp. 17–20.
194. "In the Shadows," (SP) *RSTB*, December 7: p. 3.
195. "The Delusions of History," (SP) *RSTB*, December 21: p. 3.

1967

196. "Bored? Lonely?" *Sermonic Talks on Jewish Ideas and Ideals, for Lay Leaders in the Armed Forces of the United States*, National Jewish Welfare Board, pp. 35–36.

197. "Sorrow in Time of Joy, A Succot Sermon," *Sermonic Talks on the Jewish Holidays and Festivals,* National Jewish Welfare Board, pp. 15–16.

198. "The Interreligious Dialogue: Three Jewish Pioneers," *Face to Face,* Washington, D.C., pp. 13–18.

199. "Success: Sweet or Sour," *The American Rabbi* 2:5 (January), pp. 30–33.

200. "The Permanent Revolution," (SP) *RSTB,* January 4: p. 3.

201. "Sick or Just Nervous," (SP) *RSTB,* January 11: p. 3.

202. "What Is Wrong with Israel?" (SP) *RSTB,* January 18: p. 8.

203. "View from the Bottom," (SP) *RSTB,* February 1: p. 3.

204. "Believe It or Not," (SP) *RSTB,* March 1: p. 3.

205. "It's the Law," (SP) *RSTB,* March 8: p. 3.

206. "I Wish I Had," (SP) *RSTB,* March 22: p. 3.

207. "One, Two, Three," (SP) *RSTB,* April 5: pp. 3–4.

208. "A Sense of Adventure," (SP) *RSTB,* April 19: p. 3.

209. "J. Leonard Levy—A Man of Action," Sunday Sermon, Rodef Shalom Congregation, Pittsburgh, Pa., April 23, *J.Leonard Levy Fiftieth Anniversary Memorial Service,* booklet, pp. 11–14.

210. "Enthusiasm or Bureaucracy," (SP) *RSTB,* April 26: p. 3.

211. "Judaism as Eternal Springtime," (SP) *RSTB,* May 3: p. 3.

212. "Little Nations," (SP) *RSTB,* May 10: p. 3.

213. "Excuse Us, Please!, Rest," (SP) *RSTB,* September 6: pp. 3–4.

214. "Pilgrims Lost," (SP) *RSTB,* September 15: p. 3.

215. "Wall of Sorrow—Wall of Joy," (SP) *RSTB,* September 27: p. 3.

216. *High Holiday Sermons, 1967–5728* 2: 1–3, 26 pp; "Down to Earth"; "Revolution Now"; "In the Family Circle."

217. *A Selection of Sermons, 1966–1967, 5726–5727,* Rodef Shalom Pulpit—Second Series, 1: 1–6, 52 pp;

"What Do We Want?"; "New Ghetto Walls"; "What Can We Believe?"; "View from the Bottom"; "Believe It or Not"; "Extremism in Judaism."

218. "What Remained Unsaid," (SP) *RSTB*, October 11: p. 3.
219. "They Suffer Still," (SP) *RSTB*, October 18: p. 3.
220. "When You Have Arrived," (SP) *RSTB*, November 1: p. 3.
221. "Addresses in Honor of the Seventy-Fifth Birthday of Solomon B. Freehof," Rodef Shalom Congregation, Pittsburgh, Pa., Sunday, November 5, booklet, 19 pp.
222. "Who Is a Cynic?," (SP) *RSTB*, November 22: pp. 2–6.
223. "Mission Impossible," (SP) *RSTB*, December 6: p. 3.
224. "Beyond the Spoken Word, Three Thousand Delegates," (SP) *RSTB*, December 20: p. 3.

1968

225. "Bridge the Gap," (SP) *RSTB*, January 3: p. 3.
226. "What of Our Names?," (SP) *RSTB*, January 17: p. 3.
227. "The Other Side," (SP) *RSTB*, January 24: p. 8.
228. "Don't Get Lost," (SP) *RSTB*, February 7, p. 3.
229. "Sisterhood Sabbath," (SP) *RSTB*, February 21: p. 3.
230. "Poetry in an Age of Prose," (SP) *RSTB*, March 6: p. 3.
231. "Everybody Loves a Winner," (SP) *RSTB*, March 20: pp. 3–6.
232. "Desert Days," (SP) *RSTB*, March 27: p. 3.
233. "The Old Reliance," (SP) *RSTB*, April 10: pp. 3–5.
234. "Sources of Hatred," (SP) *RSTB*, April 17: p. 3.
235. "Our Story—Their Story," (SP) *RSTB*, May 1: pp. 3–4.
236. "The Forgotten World of Jewish Art," (SP) *RSTB*, May 15: p. 3.
237. "What about Us?," (SP) *RSTB*, May 22: p. 3.
238. "Troubled Springtime," (SP) *RSTB*, May 29: pp. 3–4.

239. "A Deeper Appraisal," (SP) *RSTB*, September 4: p. 7.

240. *A Selection of Sermons, 1967–1968, 5727–5728*, Rodef Shalom Pulpit—Second Series 2: 4–10; 48 pp; "Religious Freedom in Israel, 168 B.C.E.–1968 C.E."; "Where Are We Going?"; "As American Jews"; "Midsummer Night's Dream or Nightmare?"; "Pilgrim's Progress: A Succos Sermon"; "Who Won–Who Lost? A Hannukah Sermon"; "Promised Land—Promised People"; "Desert Days."

241. "Into the Future," (SP) *RSTB*, October 9: p. 3.

242. "We Object," (SP) *RSTB*, October 23: p. 5.

243. "What Is Left," (SP) *RSTB*, October 30: p. 3.

244. "The Natural World," (SP) *RSTB*, November 13: p. 3.

245. "When We Are Tired," (SP) *RSTB*, November 20: p. 3.

246. "How Did It Begin?" (SP) *RSTB*, December 11: p. 3.

247. "Who Is Listening?" (SP) *RSTB*, December 18: p. 3.

248. "Tribute to Our Parents," (SP) *RSTB*, December 25: p. 3.

249. *Our Bible for Adults* 3: 1–3, 1968–5729, Rodef Shalom Pulpit: "Noah & His Ark, Joseph and His Dreams, Moses & His Plagues, 19 pp.

1969

250. "What Is Learning?, (SP) *RSTB*, January 8: p. 3.

251. "Our Warrior Holiday," (SP) *RSTB*, January 29: p. 3.

252. "Our Seminaries and Their Critics," (SP) *RSTB*, February 12: p. 3.

253. "Israeli Best Sellers," (SP) *RSTB*, February 26: p. 3.

254. "Our Desert—Their Desert," (SP) *RSTB*, March 19: p. 3.

255. "Israel—Past and Future," (SP) *RSTB*, March 26: p. 3.

256. "Barren Pittsburgh," (SP) *RSTB*, April 16: p. 3.

257. "The Commandment Is a Light," (SP) *RSTB*, April 23: p. 3.

258. "Shraga Weil, Israeli Artist," (SP) *RSTB*, April 30: p. 3.
259. "Happy to Be Alive," (SP) *RSTB*, May 14: p. 3.
260. "Short and Sweet,"(SP) *RSTB*, May 28: p. 5.
261. "Current Reform Responsa," (SP) *RSTB*, June 4: p. 3.
262. *Goodbye Columbus*, (SP) *RSTB*, September 10: p. 6.
263. "Israel and Our Fading Joy," (SP) *RSTB*, September 24: p. 7.
264. "Not to Condemn," (SP) *RSTB*, October 8: pp. 3–7.
265. "Renewal," (SP) *RSTB*, October 15: p. 3.
266. "Our War—Our Weakness," (SP) *RSTB*, October 29: p. 3.
267. "Lost Hope," (SP) *RSTB*, November 5: p. 3.
268. "Our National Congregational Meeting," (SP) *RSTB*, November 26: p. 3.
269. *"The Estate*—A Review," (SP) *RSTB*, December 3: p. 3.
270. "The Struggle within a Generation," (SP) *RSTB*, December 10: p. 3.
271. "Minsk to Miami," (SP) *RSTB*, December 17: p. 3.
272. "Ethics of the Pilgrims," (SP) *RSTB*, December 31: p. 3.
273. *A Selection of Sermons, 1968–1969, 5728–5729,* Rodef Shalom Pulpit—Second Series 3: 4–8, 23 pp; "Embarrassed Generation"; "The Natural World"; "Tribute to Our Parents"; "Legends of Our Time"; "The Light Is Sweet."

1970

274. "Where Are We Going As American Jews?, *Best Jewish Sermons 5729–5730*, Ed. by Saul I. Teplitz, New York, 1970, pp. 62–71.
275. "Herman Cohen on Christianity," *CCAR Journal* 17: 1 (January), pp. 61–69.
276. "Victory for What?," (SP) *RSTB*, January 7: p. 3.

277. "Good History," (SP) *RSTB*, January 20: pp. 3–5.

278. "Snow," (SP) *RSTB*, January 28: p. 3.

279. "The Meditations of Our Hearts," (SP) *RSTB*, February 4: p. 3.

280. "Bible and Prayer Book," (SP) *RSTB*, February 18: pp. 3–5.

281. "The Art and the Hebrew Book," (SP) *RSTB*, March 4: p. 3.

282. "The Twentieth Century Synagogue," (SP) *RSTB*, March 18: p. 3.

283. "The History of Indifference," (SP) *RSTB*, March 25: p. 3.

284. "How Do We Serve?" (SP) *RSTB*, April 29: p. 3.

285. Review: "Man, Emotion, Eternal Thought: J. Leonard Levy: *Prophetic Voice*, by Solomon B. Freehof and Vigdor W. Kavaler," *The Jewish Chronicle of Pittsburgh*, 9: 24 (August 6), p. 9.

286. "American Jewish Confusion" (SP) *RSTB*, May 6: pp. 3–7.

287. "The Great Sabbath," (SP) *RSTB*, May 20: p. 3.

288. "What Is Missing?" (SP) *RSTB*, May 27: p. 3.

289. "Russia and the Arabs," (SP) *RSTB*, June 3: p. 3.

290. "Off to College," (SP) *RSTB*, September 30: p. 3.

291. "Hijackers," (SP) *RSTB*, October 14: pp. 3–5.

292. *A Selection of Sermons, 1969–1970, 5729–5730*, Rodef Shalom Pulpit—Second Series 4: 1–7, 51 pp; "To Rome with Cardinal Wright"; "Out of the Depths"; "Our New Beginnings"; "Renewal"; "Gloomy Days"; "Victory—For What"; "Our Bible for Adults—Abraham, Father of Judaism."

293. "One Sin at a Time," (SP) *RSTB*, November 4: pp. 3–6.

294. "The World of Nature," (SP) *RSTB*, November 11: p. 3.

295. "What's Wrong?" (SP) *RSTB*, November 24: p. 3.
296. "No Words—Just Pictures," (SP) *RSTB*, December 16: p. 3.

1971

297. "Thanksgiving Puzzle," (SP) *RSTB*, January 6: p. 3.
298. "The Chanuka Puzzle," (SP) *RSTB*, January 27: p. 3.
299. "Our Jewish Future," (SP) *RSTB*, February 10: p. 3.
300. "What Future?" (SP) *RSTB*, February 17: p. 3.
301. "American Jews," (SP) *RSTB*, March 31: p. 3.
302. "Hear, O Israel," by Benno Jacob (translated by Ernest I. Jacob and Walter Jacob), *Jewish Spectator* (April), pp. 5–7.
303. "Max Brod's Critique of Christianity," *CCAR Journal* 18:2 (April), pp. 19–28.
304. "Dissatisfied Generation," (SP) *RSTB*, April 28: p. 3.
305. "Sorrow, But No Regrets," (SP) *RSTB*, May 19: p. 3.
306. "Lieutenant Calley," (SP) *RSTB*, June 2: p. 3.
307. *A Selection of Sermons, 1970–1971, 5730–5731,* Rodef Shalom Pulpit—Second Series 5: 1–8, 57 pp; When Nothing Goes Right"; "The World of Nature"; "Our Times—Our Problems, Judaism on Abortion"; "Turning Point—70 C.E.–1970 C.E., Judaism and Christianity"; Turning Point—70 C.E.–1970 C.E., Victory out of Defeat"; "Sorrow, But No Regrets"; "Israel Now"; "Project Equality."
308. "The Leader and the People," (SP) *RSTB*, September 15: p. 3.
309. "The Star of Redemption," (SP) *RSTB*, September 29: p. 3.
310. "Damn or Praise?" (SP) *RSTB*, October 6: p. 3.
311. "For Those Who Fail," (SP) *RSTB*, October 13: p. 3.
312. "The New Charity," (SP) *RSTB*, November 10: p. 3.

313. "Failure and Laughter," (SP) *RSTB*, December 15: p. 3.

1972

314. "The World of Nature," *Best Jewish Sermons of 5731–5732*, edited by Saul I. Teplitz, New York, pp. 72–79.
315. "Introduction," *Spoken and Heard*, by Solomon B. Freehof, Pittsburgh, Pa., pp. vii–viii.
316. *"Encyclopedia Judaica,"* (SP) *RSTB*, January 19: p. 3.
317. "Time," (SP) *RSTB*, January 26: p. 3.
318. "What of Our Sorrows?" (SP) *RSTB*, February 2: p. 3.
319. "Do We Understand the Ten Commandments?" (SP) *RSTB*, March 8: p. 3.
320. "J. Leonard Levy—Prophetic Voice," (SP) *RSTB*, March 22: p. 3.
321. *"Encyclopedia Talmudic,"* (SP) *RSTB*, April 5: p. 3.
322. "Counting the Days," (SP) *RSTB*, May 3: p. 3.
323. "Honor the Past," (SP) *RSTB*, May 17: p. 3.
324. "Relax, Relax," (SP) *RSTB*, May 31: p. 3.
325. "A New Beginning," (SP) *RSTB*, September 20: p. 3.
326. *A Selection of Sermons, 1971–1972, 5731–5732*, Rodef Shalom Pulpit—Second Series 6: 1–5, 24 pp;" Without Past or Future"; "Find Yourself"; "The Ordinary Hero"; "Time and the Timeless"; "Relax and Dream."
327. "Expect Little," (SP) *RSTB*, October 4: p. 3.
328. "Television and Books," (SP) *RSTB*, October 18: p. 3.
329. "What about Poetry?" (SP) *RSTB*, October 25: p. 3.
330. "What Will Help?" (SP) *RSTB*, November 1: p. 3.
331. "Think Big or Small," (SP) *RSTB*, November 15: p. 3.
332. "Pilgrims," (SP) *RSTB*, December 13: pp. 3–4.
333. "Turning Point," (SP) *RSTB*, December 27: p. 6.

1973

334. "Harry S. Truman: In Memoriam," (SP) *RSTB*, January 17: p. 3.
335. "Quietness & Confidence," (SP) *RSTB*, January 24: p. 3.
336. "War & Peace," (SP) *RSTB*, February 7: pp. 3–4.
337. "Change," (SP) *RSTB*, February 21: p. 3.
338. "The Right Question," (SP) *RSTB*, March 9: p. 6.
339. "From Generation to Generation," (SP) *RSTB*, March 21: p. 3.
340. "Voyage of Discovery," (SP) *RSTB*, April 11: p. 3.
341. "Reform Rabbis as Mystics," (SP) *RSTB*, April 18: pp. 3–5.
342. "The Buber Correspondence—The Early Years," (SP) *RSTB*, April 25: p. 6.
343. "Beyond Despair," (SP) *RSTB*, September 5: pp. 3–6.
344. *A Selection of Sermons, 1972–1973, 5732–5733,* Rodef Shalom Pulpit—Second Series 7: 1–10, 46 pp: "After Munich";" I'm Not Religious"; "What about Poetry?"; "New Religious Experiences II—Meditation Groups"; "Quietness and Confidence"; "Israel at Twenty-Five—Toward a New Zionist Ideology"; "The Right Question"; "Beyond Despair"; "Harry Truman—In Memoriam"; "A Tribute to Dr. Herman Hailperin—A Funeral Address."
345. "Life-Styles," (SP) *RSTB*, September 26: p. 3.
346. "Moses—The Growth of a Legend," (SP) *RSTB*, October 3: p. 3.
347. "He Who Is Wise," (SP) *RSTB*, October 31: pp. 3–6.
348. "Israel at War," (SP) *RSTB*, November 7: p. 3.
349. "Succot in Time of War," (SP) *RSTB*, November 14: p. 3.
350. "It Was Good," (SP) *RSTB*, December 5: p. 3.

1974

351. "An Assessment of Christianity, The Historical Setting," *CCAR Journal* 21:5 (Winter), pp. 47–54.

352. "The Right Question," *Best Sermons of 5732–5733*, edited by Saul I. Teplitz, New York, pp. 51–57.

353. "Union of American Hebrew Congregations Celebration & Critique," (SP) *RSTB*, January 2: p. 3.

354. "Religion in a Secular World," (SP) *RSTB*, January 30: p. 3.

355. "Influence," (SP) *RSTB*, February 6: p. 3.

356. "These Are the Names," (SP) *RSTB*, February 20: p. 3.

357. "The Dead Sea Scrolls, Twenty-Five Years Later," (SP) *RSTB*, March 6: p. 3.

358. "Egypt and the Desert," (SP) *RSTB*, March 27: p. 3.

359. "Purim," (SP) *RSTB*, April 17: p. 3.

360. "Once to Sinai," (SP) *RSTB*, May 29: p. 3.

361. "National-Personal Disaster," (SP) *RSTB*, June 5: p. 3.

362. "For Skeptics," (SP) *RSTB*, September 4: p. 3.

363. "Isaiah," (SP) *RSTB*, September 25: p. 3.

364. *A Selection of Sermons, 1973–1974, 5733–5744*, Rodef Shalom Pulpit—Second Series 8: 1–7, 34 pp:"A Tribute to My Parents"; "Yom Kippur and Hannukah—A High Holiday Sermon"; "Pardon Me"; "It Was Good"; "David Ben Gurion—A Memorial Tribute"; "Happy or Sad—A Purim Sermon"; "Passover in Israel."

365. "Blessings & Curses," (SP) *RSTB*, October 9: p. 3.

366. "A Soft Answer," (SP) *RSTB*, October 23: p. 3.

367. "Desert Days," (SP) *RSTB*, November 6: p. 3.

368. "Is It Jewish?" (SP) *RSTB*, November 13, p. 3.

369. "Names We Use & Avoid," (SP) *RSTB*, December 14: p. 3.

370. "The Close Family, (SP) *RSTB*, December 25: p. 3.

1975

371. "Teaching History," (SP) *RSTB*, January 8: p. 3.
372. "Family Problems, (SP) *RSTB*, January 15: p. 3.
373. "Why Fight?" (SP) *RSTB*, January 22: p. 3.
374. "The Spirit of Jewish Law," (SP) *RSTB*, February 1: p. 3.
375. "We Remember—They Forget," (SP) *RSTB*, February 12: p. 3.
376. "The Birth of a Nation," (SP) *RSTB*, February 26: p. 3.
377. "Tents & Temple," (SP) *RSTB*, March 26: p. 3.
378. "Review: *Genesis, A Modern Commentary*, by Gunther Plaut," *The Jewish Chronicle of Pittsburgh*, April 3, p. 23.
379. "With Malice toward None," (SP) *RSTB*, April 2: p. 3.
380. "Kenney Jacob's Bar Mitzvah," (SP) *RSTB*, April 9: p. 3.
381. "Farm Workers," (SP) *RSTB*, May 7: pp. 3–4.
382. "Young & Old," (SP) *RSTB*, May 14: p. 3.
383. "Contemporary Reform Responsa," (SP) *RSTB*, May 21: p. 3.
384. "Unfashionable Thoughts," (SP) *RSTB*, May 28: p. 3.
385. "In Restless Springtime," (SP) *RSTB*, June 4: p. 3.
386. "Leadership," (SP) *RSTB*, September 3: pp. 3–5.
387. "*Mein Kampf*—Fifty Years Later," (SP) *RSTB*, September 24: p. 3.
388. *A Selection of Sermons, 1974–1975, 5734–5735*, Rodef Shalom Pulpit—Second Series 9: 1–8, 38 pp; "America and Israel"; "Hear, O Israel"; "Isaiah, Our Favorite Prophet"; "Is It Jewish?"; "Our Bible for Adults II—The Tower of Babel"; "Kenney Jacob's Bar Mitzvah"; "Generation Gap"; "Learning from Each Other—Consecration Service."
389. "Collective Guilt," (SP) *RSTB*, October 28.

390. "Cantillation of the Torah, Responsum," *CCAR Journal* (Fall), pp. 77–80.
391. "A Harvest of Leadership," (SP) *RSTB*, October 22: p. 3.
392. "When We Are Gloomy," (SP) *RSTB*, December 31: p. 3.

1976

393. "Theology versus Drama," (SP) *RSTB*, February 4: p. 3.
394. "Outside Advice," (SP) *RSTB*, February 18: p. 3.
395. "Mood or Mondale," (SP) *RSTB*, February 25: p. 3.
396. "Beauty of Holiness," (SP) *RSTB*, March 10: p. 3.
397. "Theology and the Sabbath," (SP) *RSTB*, March 24: p. 3.
398. "Purim Puzzles," (SP) *RSTB*, April 7: p. 3.
399. "'Hester Street'—A Review," (SP) *RSTB*, April 28: p. 3.
400. "Review: *Jesus the Jew, A Historian's Reading of the Gospels*, by Geza Vermes," *CCAR Journal* (Spring), pp. 84–87.
401. "A Better Perspective," (SP) *RSTB*, May 2: p. 3.
402. "The Hebrew Union College at One Hundred Years," (SP) *RSTB*, June 2: p. 3.
403. Review: "Hebrew Union College at One Hundred Years," *The Jewish Chronicle of Pittsburgh*, July 1.
404. "For the Defeated," (SP) *RSTB*, September 8: p. 3.
405. "Review: Marvin Fox, *Modern Jewish Ethics: Theory and Practice*," *Religious Education*, September.
406. *A Selection of Sermons, 1975–1976, 5735–5736*, Rodef Shalom Pulpit—Second Series 10: 1–6, 30 pp; "A High Holiday Sermon"; "Zionism and Racism"; "Theology ver sus Drama"; "The Sabbath"; "For the Defeated."
407. "Looking Forward with America," Sermon given on November21, at Shadyside Presbyterian Church, Pittsburgh, Pa., booklet, 12 pp.

408. "The Tower of Babel," in *Pastoral Services,* Ed. by Harry Essrig and Jonathan David Press, Los Angeles (September), pp. 25–29.
409. "Our Doubts," (SP) *RSTB,* October 13: p. 3.
410. "Return to What?" (SP) *RSTB,* October 27: p. 3.
411. "The Joy of Learning," (SP) *RSTB,* November 10: p. 3.
412. "Good Old Days," (SP) *RSTB,* November 24: p. 3.
413. "Synagogue Models," (SP) *RSTB,* December 15, p. 3.
414. "To Christians: A Jewish Agenda," *The Pittsburgh Jewish Chronicle,* December 23: p. 13.
415. "A Young Man's Road to Religion," (SP) *RSTB,* December 29: p. 3.
416. "Success Sweet or Sour," *Speak to the Children of Israel,* Ed. by M. Appelbaum and Samuel M. Silver, New York, pp. 64–69.
417. "Bored? Lonely?," *Speak to the Children of Israel,* Ed. by M. Appelbaum and Samuel M. Silver, New York, pp. 70–73.

1977

418. "Advice to the Old," (SP) *RSTB,* February 2: p. 3.
419. "Mutual Worries," (SP) *RSTB,* February 9: p. 3.
420. "For Sophisticates," (SP) *RSTB,* March 2: p. 3.
421. "Failure at Sinai," (SP) *RSTB,* March 9: p. 3.
422. "The Purim Spirit," (SP) *RSTB,* March 23: p. 3.
423. "Prose or Poetry," (SP) *RSTB,* April 20: p. 3.
424. "Four Questions We Did Not Ask," (SP) *RSTB,* May 4: p. 3.
425. "Contradictions," (SP) *RSTB,* May 11: p. 3.
426. "The Menora Symbol of Judaism," (SP) *RSTB,* September 9: p. 3.

427. "Introduction on the Occasion of Dr. Freehof's Bar Mitzvah Ceremony," (SP) *RSTB*, September 16: p. 3.

428. "Synagogue Plantings and Christian Legends, Responsum," *CCAR Journal* (Fall), pp. 65–68.

429. "Solomon B. Freehof and Halacha: An Appreciation," *Reform Responsa for Our Time*, New York, pp. 1–27.

430. "Forgotten Words," (SP) *RSTB*, October 7: p. 3.

431. "Not Too Late," (SP) *RSTB*, October 14: p. 3.

432. "The Contemporary Succoh," (SP) *RSTB*, October 21: p. 3.

433. "Theology—No; Stories—Yes," (SP) *RSTB*, November 16: pp. 3–4.

434. "New Wealth—New Possibilities," (SP) *RSTB*, December 7: p. 3.

1978

435. "Liberal Jewish Theology, A Response, Implicit and Explicit Theology," *CCAR Yearbook* 87, pp. 175–78.

436. "May Non-Jewish Clergy Participate in a Jewish Wedding?" *CCAR Yearbook* 87, New York, pp. 100–102.

437. "May a Marriage Be Performed on Shabbat or Yom Tov?" *CCAR Yearbook* 87, New York, pp. 96–99.

438. "Our Cantor—Their Cantor," (SP) *RSTB*, January 11: pp. 3–5.

439. "Martin Buber—After a Century," (SP) *RSTB*, February 12: p. 3.

440. "What Kind of Balance?," (SP) *RSTB*, March 8: p. 3.

441. "What Is a Synagogue?" (SP) *RSTB*, April 12: p. 3.

442. "Our New Officers," (SP) *RSTB*, April 19, pp: 3–4.

443. "Survival & Background," (SP) *RSTB*, April 26: p. 3.

444. "Our Arts Weekend," (SP) *RSTB*, May 3: pp. 3–4.

445. "The Reform Achievement," (SP) *RSTB*, May 10: pp. 3–4.
446. "Review: "150 Years of Reform Responsa, Solomon B. Freehof. *Responsa for Our Times*; Alexander Guttmann, *The Struggle over Reform in Rabbinic Literature*," The Jewish Chronicle of Pittsburgh, May 25, p. 20.
447. "Review: *Jewish Philosophical Polemics against Christianity in the Middle Ages*, by Daniel L. Lasker," *Religious Edu cation* 73: 3 (May/June), p. 371.
448. "Review: David Bleich, *Contemporary Halakhic Problems*, and Emanuel Feldman, *Biblical and Post-Biblical Defilement and Mourning: Law as Theology*," *Journal of Reform Judaism* 25: 3 (Summer), pp. 93–96.
449. "Review: *The Struggle over Reform Judaism*, by Alexander Guttmann, *Journal of Reform Judaism* 7: 1 (September), p. 13.
450. "An Exchange of Correspondence with Lou H. Silberman," *Journal of Reform Judaism* (Fall), pp. 83–84.
451. "Toward the New Year," (SP) *RSTB*, October 25: p. 3.
452. "Return O Israel," (SP) *RSTB*, November 15: p. 3.
453. "Pilgrimage," (SP) *RSTB* November 28: pp. 3–4.
454. Review: "*Anti-Judaism in Christian Theology*, Charlotte Klein," *Religious Education* 58: 6 (November/December) p. 27.
455. "The Natural World," (SP) *RSTB*, December 13: p. 3.

1979

456. "Should the Table of Consanguinity Be Changed?," *CCAR Yearbook* 88, pp. 55–56.
457. "The Marriage of Transsexuals," *CCAR Yearbook* 88, pp. 52–54.

458. "Dialogue in Europe Today," *Sonderheft Zeifschrift für Religions und Geistesgeschichte*, Band 31, Heft 1 (January), pp. 48–61.

459. "Conservative Judaism and Halachah," *Journal of Reform Judaism* 26: 1 (Winter), pp. 17–24.

460. "Partners," (SP) *RSTB*, January 3: p. 3.

461. "The Average Man As Our Hero," (SP) *RSTB*, January 17: p. 3.

462. "Influences on Our Children," (SP) *RSTB*, February 28: p. 3.

463. "The Vision & the Visionary," (SP) *RSTB*, March 14: p. 3.

464. "Theology through Song," (SP) *RSTB*, March 28: p. 3.

465. "Zinberg's *History of Jewish Literature,*" (SP) *RSTB*, April 11: p. 3.

466. "The Playful Element in Judaism" (SP) *RSTB*, April 25: p. 3.

467. "Prophetic Judaism: The History of a Term," *Journal of Reform Judaism* (Spring), pp. 33–45.

468. *A Selection of Sermons, 1977–1979, 5737–5739*, Rodef Shalom Pulpit—Second Series 11: 1–8, 53 pp: "Daniel Benjamin Jacob's Bar Mitzvah"; "When Did We Last Meet?"; "Is There Any Hope?"; "*Kristallnacht*—A Fortieth Anniversary"; "Good Old Days"; "Advice to the Old, 'The Purim Spirit'"; "May God Bless You and Keep You"; "Our Pledge to My Son and Yours."

469. "What Is Holiness?" (SP) *RSTB*, September 5: p. 3.

470. "Tribute to Dr. S. B. Freehof on His Birthday," (SP) *RSTB*, September 12: p. 3.

471. "Tribute to John Cardinal Wright," (SP) *RSTB*, September 18: p. 3.

472. "World War II, Forty Years Later," (SP) *RSTB*, September 26: p. 3.

473. "Approaching the New Year," (SP) *RSTB*, October 10: p. 3.
474. "Convenants & Treaties," (SP) *RSTB*, October 17: p. 3.
475. "The Natural World," (SP) *RSTB*, October 24: p. 3.
476. "We Are Family," (SP) *RSTB*, November 21: p. 3.
477. "Pictures of Our Past," (SP) *RSTB*, November 28, p. 3.
478. "Initiation into Judaism," *Religious Education* 74: 6 (November/December), pp. 597–603.
479. "Extraordinary & Ordinary," (SP) *RSTB*, December 5: p. 3.
480. "Migration As Pilgrimage," (SP) *RSTB*, December 12: p. 3.
481. "Death & Dying," (SP) *RSTB*, December 19: p. 3.
482. "May a Synagogue Use a Lottery for Fund Raising? 'Jewish Questions and Answers,'" *Reform Judaism* 8: 3, Decem ber, p. 9.

1980

483. "May Laymen Perform Marriage Ceremonies?" *CCAR Year book* 89, pp. 110–111.
484. "Adoption and Adopted Children," *CCAR Yearbook* 89, pp. 112–115.
485. "Lottery for Synagogue Fund Raising," *CCAR Yearbook* 89, pp. 115–116.
486. "Report, Responsa Committee," *CCAR Yearbook* 89, pp. 108–110.
487. "Family Problems," (SP) *RSTB*, January 16: p. 3.
488. "The Other Side," (SP) *RSTB*, January 30: p. 3.
489. "Bless These Lads," (SP) *RSTB*, February 6: p. 3.
490. "Sympathy but Not Sorrow," (SP) *RSTB*, March 12: p. 3.
491. "Sinai Desert," (SP) *RSTB*, March 19: pp. 3–5.
492. "Jewish Theology," (SP) *RSTB*, March 26: p. 3.
493. "Humble Forms—Grand Ideas," (SP) *RSTB*, April 9: p. 3.

494. "The Dead Sea Scrolls—A Generation Later," (SP) *RSTB*, April 17: p. 3.

495. "Phillip Sigal's *The Emergency of Contemporary Judaism*," (SP) *RSTB*, April 23: p. 3.

496. "Isaac Mayer Wise—Perfect American," (SP) *RSTB*, April 30: p. 3.

497. "Hand in Hand," (SP) *RSTB*, May 7: p. 3.

498. "Memories Which Count," (SP) *RSTB*, May 14: p. 3.

499. "An Interview with Solomon B. Freehof," *Journal of Reform Judaism* 27: 3 (Summer), pp. 16–21.

500. *A Selection of Sermons, 1979–1980, 5739–5740*, Rodef Shalom Pulpit—Second Series 11: 1–5, 47 pp; "A Special Gift"; "A Tribute to John Cardinal Wright"; Our Pilgrimage"; "The Synagogue in Our Life—A Dedication Sermon"; "The Roots of Reform Halakhah—A Lecture to the New York Association of Reform Rabbis."

501. "Introduction on the Occasion of Dr. Freehof's Bar Mitzvah," (SP) *RSTB*, September 3: p. 3.

502. "Ethics of the Fathers—II," (SP) *RSTB*, September 17: p. 3.

503. "Our Permanent Harvest," (SP) *RSTB*, October 15: p. 3.

504. "What Kind of Paradise?" (SP) *RSTB*, October 22: p. 3.

505. "Our Founding Father," (SP) *RSTB*, November 5: p. 3.

506. "Initiation into Judaism," *Religious Education* 74: 6 (November–December) pp. 597–602.

507. "Our New Russian Settlers," (SP) *RSTB*, December 10: p. 3.

508. "Toward Maturity," (SP) *RSTB*, December 17: p. 3.

509. "The Gifts of the Egyptians: A Critical Commentary by Benno Jacob," (Tr.), *Journal of Reform Judaism* 27: 3, pp. 59–69.

510. "The Roots of Reform Halakhah: A Lecture to the New York Association of Reform Rabbis."

1981

511. "An Unmarried Couple Joining the Synagogue, Responsum," *CCAR Yearbook* 90, pp. 83–84.
512. "Reform Judaism and Mixed Marriage, Responsum," *CCAR Yearbook* 90, pp. 86–102.
513. "Reform Judaism and Divorce, Responsum," *CCAR Year book* 90, pp. 84–86.
514. "Report, Committee on Responsa, A Responsum," *CCAR Yearbook* 90.
515. *A Selection of Sermons, 1980–1981, 5740–5741,* Rodef Shalom Pulpit—Second Series 12: 1–8, 49 pp: "I Am Religious in My Heart"; "Masada, Television, History, and Theology"; "A Tribute to Dr. Iwan J. Gruen"; "Memories Which Count"; "Sympathy but Not Sorrow"; "Theodore Herzl and J. Leonard Levy"; "The Sources of Reform Halakhic Authority."
516. "The Sources of Reform Halakhic Authority," Lecture to the CCAR, 18 pp.
517. "Our Love of History," (SP) *RSTB,* January 7: p. 3.
518. "Family Ties," (SP) *RSTB,* January 14: p. 3.
519. "Better Future," (SP) *RSTB,* February 4: p. 3.
520. "Music in Jewish Life," (SP) *RSTB,* February 11: p. 3.
521. "The Hostages," (SP) *RSTB,* February 18: p. 3.
522. "New Reform Responsa," (SP) *RSTB,* March 25: p. 3.
523. "Our Path," (SP) *RSTB,* April 1: p. 3.
524. "Purim," (SP) *RSTB,* April 15: p. 3.
525. "Prosaic Religion," (SP) *RSTB,* April 22: p. 3.
526. "Violence," (SP) *RSTB,* April 29: p. 3.

527. "Masada in Retrospect," (SP) *RSTB*, May 6: p. 3.
528. "The New Generation," (SP) *RSTB*, May 13: p. 3.
529. "Review: *Responsa Reflects Life*, S. B. Freehof," New Reform Responsa, *The Jewish Chronicle of Pittsburgh*, August 8, p. 15.
530. "Tribute to Dr. Freehof on His 89th Birthday," (SP) *RSTB*, September 2: p. 3.
531. "Our Volunteers," (SP) *RSTB*, September 9: pp. 2–3.
532. "In Despair," (SP) *RSTB*, September 23: p. 3.
533. "I Shall Study, You Shall Study," (SP) *RSTB*, October 7: p. 3.
534. "The Difficult Encounter," (SP) *RSTB*, October 22: p. 3.
535. "On a Full Stomach," (SP) *RSTB*, November 11: p. 3.
536. "It Was Good," (SP) *RSTB*, November 18: p. 3.
537. "Abraham, Our Father," (SP) *RSTB*, December 2: p. 3.
538. "Two Types of Exile," (SP) *RSTB*, December 23: p. 3.
539. *"The Torah:* A New Commentary," (SP) *RSTB*, December 30: p. 3.

1982

540. "War & Peace," (SP) *RSTB*, January 20: p. 3.
541. "The Old & New Diaspora," (SP) *RSTB*, January 27: p. 3.
542. "Review, *The Torah: Modern Commentary*, by W. Gunther Plaut," *The Jewish Chronicle of Pittsburgh*, February 11, p. 27.
543. "Ludwig Wolpert, Eminent Artist," (SP) *RSTB*, March 17: p. 3.
544. "The Law of the Lord Is Perfect?" (SP) *RSTB*, March 31: p. 3.
545. "Waanseeh," (SP) *RSTB*, April 14: p. 3.
546. "Concessions & Ideals," (SP) *RSTB*, April 21: p. 3.

547. "In the Desert," (SP) *RSTB*, May 5: p. 3.
548. "Interview: Solomon B. Freehof: Pioneer—Jewish Educator, *Reach* 12: 2 (Summer), pp. 4ff.
549. *A Selection of Sermons, 1981–1982, 5741–5742*, Rodef Shalom Pulpit—Second Series 14: 1–7, 40 pp; "Your Child's Confirmation and Mine"; "You Have Not Changed a Bit"; "Our Conversation with God"; "War and Peace"; "The Law of the Lord Is Perfect"; "Presidential Address," Religious Education Association.
550. "Installation of Albert I. Raizman, President," (SP) *RSTB*, September 1: pp. 3–4.
551. "Introduction to Dr. Freehof's 90th Birthday," (SP) *RSTB*, September 8: p. 3.
552. "Hebrew for Us," *RSTB*, September 22: p. 3.
553. "View from the Bottom," Presidential Address, *Religious Education* 77: 5 (September–October), pp. 468–71.
554. "Dialogue & Conflict: Jewish Christian Relations Today," *Religious Education* 76: 6 (Fall), pp. 587–93.
555. "Look Ahead," (SP) *RSTB*, October 6: p. 3.
556. "Probe Deeply," (SP) *RSTB*, October 20: pp. 3–4.
557. "Focus Beirut, Three Rabbis View Moral Issues," *The Jewish Chronicle of Pittsburgh*, October 21: p. 28.
558. "Out of the Desert," (SP) *RSTB*, October 27: p. 3.
559. "Review: *The Middle East, Abstract and Index*, by Amy C. Lowenstein," *Journal of Reform Judaism* (Winter), pp. 59–60.
560. "Adolescent Sexuality—Sex Education," *Central Conference of American Rabbis on Sexuality*, November, CCAR, New York, 4 pp.
561. "Building a Caring Community." *Sh'ma*, 13/241 (November 12), pp. 3–4.
562. "The Garden of Eden," (SP) *RSTB*, November 10: p. 3.

286

563. "Israeli Reform Judaism," (SP) *RSTB*, December 1: p. 3.
564. "From Generation to Generation," (SP) *RSTB*, December 15: p. 3.
565. "Human Sexuality in the Jewish Tradition," Lecture, CCAR, New York, 13 pp.
566. "Burial of a Prospective Convert," Responsum, *CCAR Year book* 91, New York, pp. 7ff.
567. "A Statement on Homosexuals in Leadership Positions," Responsum, *CCAR Yearbook* 91, New York, pp. 69–71.
568. "Marriage with a 'Messianic Jew,'" Responsum, *CCAR Yearbook* 91, New York, pp. 67–69.
569. "The Source of Reform Halachic Authority," *Rabbinic Authority*, New York, pp. 31–41.
570. "A Convert with a Christian Family," Responsum, *CCAR Yearbook* 92, pp. 219–20.
571. "Circumcision of Infants," Responsum, *CCAR Yearbook* 92, pp. 218–19.
572. "Havdalah Bar/Bat Mitzvah," Responsum, *CCAR Yearbook* 92, pp. 216-18.
573. "Synagogue Membership of a Mixed Couple," Responsum, *CCAR Yearbook* 92, pp. 215–16.
574. "Rabbi Officiating at a Mixed Marriage," Responsum, *CCAR Yearbook* 92, pp. 213–15.
575. "Conversion without Formal Instruction," Responsum, *CCAR Yearbook* 92, pp. 209–211.
576. "Responsibility of Children to Their Parents," Responsum, *CCAR Yearbook* 92, pp. 207–209.
577. "Surrogate Mother," Responsum, *CCAR Yearbook* 92, pp. 205–207.

1983

578. "Portion of the Week," *The Jewish Chronicle of Pittsburgh,* January 6, p. 4.

579. "Victory & Change," (SP) *RSTB,* January 5: p. 3.

580. "Rabbi Staitman's Wedding," (SP) *RSTB,* January 12: p. 3.

581. "Our First Diaspora," (SP) *RSTB,* January 19: p. 3.

582. "Providing Understanding, A review of Betty Merti's *Understanding the Holocaust,*" *The Jewish Chronicle of Pittsburgh,* February 10, pp. 26.

583. "Computers, (SP) *RSTB,* February 16: p. 3.

584. "Memories of Freedom," (SP) *RSTB,* February 23: p. 3.

585. "Portion of the Week," *The Jewish Chronicle of Pittsburgh,* March 10, p. 3.

586. "Which Is the Right Way?" (SP) *RSTB,* March 16: p. 3.

587. "Our Sanctuaries," (SP) *RSTB,* March 23: p. 3.

588. "Boring or Exciting," (SP) *RSTB,* April 13: p. 3.

589. "Food for Thought," (SP) *RSTB,* April 20: p. 3.

590. "What Will They Say about You?" (SP) *RSTB,* May 11: p. 3.

591. "Pittsburgh & the Synagogue Tradition," *Carnegie Magazine* 56:8 (May/June), pp. 16–18.

592. "Resources for Teaching the Holocaust, A Review Essay," *Religious Education Journal* 78: 3 (Summer), pp. 444–46.

593. *A Selection of Sermons, 1982–1983, 5742–5743,* Rodef Shalom Pulpit—Second Series 15: 1–6, 39 pp; "Ghandi— The Film and Beyond"; "The Haggadah—A Different View"; "Rabbi Staitman's Wedding"; "The Diaspora— Then and Now"; "How Will They Remember You?"; "God Helps Those Who Help Themselves."

594. "God Helps Those Who Help Themselves," (SP) *RSTB,* September 7: p. 3.

595. "Dr. Freehof's 91st Birthday," (SP) *RSTB,* September 14: p. 3.

596. "View of the Jewish Problem Lacks Depth, A Review of Roberta Strauss Feuerlicht's *Fate of the Jews,*" *Pittsburgh Press,* Wednesday, September 21, p. C–16.

597. "In Memoriam: Charles A. Pearson," (SP) *RSTB,* September 21: p. 3.

598. "'History of the Religious Education Association' by Stephen Schmidt," *Religious Education* 78: 4 (Fall), pp. 578–79.

599. "Pursuing Justice and Peace—Why Is It So Difficult?" *Religious Education* 78: 4 (Fall), 487–90.

600. "Changes," (SP) *RSTB,* October 19: p. 3.

601. "The Apple," (SP) *RSTB,* October 26: p. 3.

602. "Write or Read, (SP) *RSTB,* November 2: p. 3.

603. "How Great Are You?" (SP) *RSTB,* November 16: p. 3.

604. "One Hundred & Ten Years of the Union of American Hebrew Congregations, (SP) *RSTB,* December 7: p. 3.

605. "The Next Generation's Road to Religion, (SP) *RSTB,* December 21: p. 3.

606. "The Real Hannukah," (SP) *RSTB,* December 28: p. 3.

607. With Mark Staitman, "Response to Cohon-Sherbok's Law & Freedom in Reform Judaism," *Journal of Reform Judaism* (Winter), pp. 98–104.

1984

608. "The Gates of the Season," (SP) *RSTB,* January 18: p. 3.

609. "The Larger Jewish Family," (SP) *RSTB,* January 25: p. 3.

610. "Portion of the Week," *The Jewish Chronicle of Pittsburgh,* January 26, p. 4.

611. "Happy New Year," (SP) *RSTB,* February 1: p. 3.

612. "What You Don't See," (SP) *RSTB,* February 8: p. 3.

613. "After the Mountain Top," (SP) *RSTB,* March 7: p. 3.

614. "Israel As an Emerging Nation," (SP) *RSTB*, March 14:
p. 3.

615. "Worries," (SP) *RSTB*, April 4: p. 3.

616. "Reform Rabbinate's Passover Statement," *The Jewish Chronicle of Pittsburgh*, April 12, p. 19.

617. "Jewish Learning," (SP) *RSTB*, April 18: p. 3.

618. "Prayer in the Public Schools," (SP) *RSTB*, April 25: p. 3.

619. "Prayer & Sacrifice," (SP) *RSTB*, May 2: p. 3.

620. "Theocracy—Democracy," (SP) *RSTB*, May 9: p. 3.

621. "Introduction to Sermons of Solomon B. Freehof," *S. B. Freehof, The Sermon Continues*, V. Kavaler, ed., Pittsburgh, Pa., Introduction, pp. 23–24; Introduction, pp. 54–55; Tribute, pp. 64–66; Introduction, pp. 70–71; Tribute, pp. 74–76; Tribute, pp. 80–81; Words of Thanks, p. 85.

622. *A Selection of Sermons & Lectures, 1983–1984, 4543–4544*, Rodef Shalom Pulpit—Second Series 16: 1–6, "German Nationalism—Jewish Nationalism"; "Down from the Mountain";"Ancient Israel and the Third World";
"Learning and Jewish Learning"; "Revolution and Tradition"; "Jesse Jackson."

623. "Revolution," (SP) *RSTB*, September 5: p. 3.

624. "Reform Rabbinate's New Year Message," *The Jewish Chronicle of Pittsburgh*, September 20, p. 20.

625. "An Aliya to the Torah and Congregational Dues, A Reform Responsum," *Journal of Reform Judaism* (Fall), pp. 57f.

626. "Feeling More Religious?" (SP) *RSTB*, October 10: p. 3.

627. "The Prophet Who Failed," (SP) *RSTB*, October 24: p. 3.

628. "The Melody & Its Overtones," (SP) *RSTB*, November 4:
p. 3.

629. "The Garden of the Future," (SP) *RSTB*, November 21:
p. 3.

630. "Who Is Important?" (SP) *RSTB*, December 12: p. 3.

631. "Our Beginnings," (SP) *RSTB*, December 19: p. 3.

632. "The Limits of History," (SP) *RSTB*, December 26: p. 3.

633. "On Teaching the Holocaust, A Review Essay," *Journal of Reform Judaism* 31: 1 (Winter), pp. 81–85.

634. "Huntington's Disease & Suicide, A Responsum," *CCAR Yearbook* 93, pp. 198ff.

635. "The Origin of the Mikveh for Conversion, A Responsum," *CCAR Yearbook* 93, pp. 196.

636. "Dual Wedding Ceremonies, A Responsum," *CCAR Yearbook* 93, pp. 194–95.

637. "Christian Music at Jewish Weddings, A Responsum," *CCAR Yearbook* 93, pp. 195ff.

638. "Adopted Children & Their Biological Parents, A Responsum," *CCAR Yearbook* 93, 196ff.

639. "Jewish Wedding in a Non-Jewish Home, A Responsum," *CCAR Yearbook* 93, pp. 199f.

640. "Non-Jew Raising Jewish Children, A Responsum," *CCAR Yearbook* 93, pp. 200f.

641. "Non-Jewish Participation in a Bar/Bat Mitzvah Service, A Responsum," *CCAR Yearbook* 93, p. 201f.

1985

642. "Status of a 'Completed' Jew in the Jewish Community," *Journal of Reform Judaism* 32: 1 (Winter), pp. 88–91.

643. "Crises Overcome," (SP) *RSTB*, January 23: p. 3.

644. "The Slow Road," (SP) *RSTB*, February 6: p. 3.

645. "Optimism," (SP) *RSTB*, February 13: p. 3.

646. "Ethiopian Jews," (SP) *RSTB*, February 20: p. 3.

647. "First Day of Pesah Sermonette," *The Jewish Chronicle of Pittsburgh*, April 4, p. 4.

648. "Preparations," (SP) *RSTB*, April 24: p. 3.

649. *"Had Gadya,"* (SP) *RSTB*, May 8: p. 3.

650. "Non-Lineal Descent," *Judaism* 34: 1, pp. 51–54.

651. "The Right to Create a New Congregation," *Journal of Reform Judaism* 32: 2 (Spring), pp. 59–61.

652. "Leap-Year Yahrzeit Observance," *CCAR Yearbook* 94, pp. 171f.

653. "Two Soviet Jews of Doubtful Descent," *CCAR Yearbook* 94, p. 171.

654. "Problems in a Family Tree," *CCAR Yearbook* 94, pp. 171f.

655. "A Child Raised in Two Religious Traditions," *CCAR Year book* 94, pp. 172f.

656. "Three Generations of Mixed Marriage," *CCAR Yearbook* 94, pp. 173f.

657. "Patrilineal and Matrilineal Descent," *CCAR Yearbook* 94, pp. 174–79.

658. "The Fortune Teller," *CCAR Yearbook* 94, pp. 169f.

659. "Extending the Privilege of Burial from the Synagogue," *CCAR Yearbook* 94, pp. 166ff.

660. "Congregational Membership for a Non-Jewish Partner," *CCAR Yearbook* 94, pp. 167–69.

661. "Virginity and the Ketuba," *CCAR Yearbook* 94, pp. 164–66.

662. *A Selection of Sermons, 1984–1985, 5744–5745,* Rodef Shalom Pulpit—Second Series 17: 1–4, 32 pp;
"The Pittsburgh Platform A Century Later"; "Playing with Numbers"; "The Permanent Garden"; "Religion and Politics—Toward a New Basis."

663. "Memories," (SP) *RSTB*, 4 September 11: p. 3.

664. "In Memoriam for Rabbi Phillip Sigal," (SP) *RSTB*, Septem ber 18: p. 3.

665. "Introduction to S.B. Freehof," (SP) *RSTB*, October 2:

p. 3.

666. "From Generation to Generation," (SP) *RSTB*, October 9: p. 3.

667. "Worte des Rabbiners," *Festzeitung der Israelitischen Kultusgemeinde Schwaben-Augsburg zur Wiedereinweihung der Synagogue,* Augsburg, 1 September, pp. 8f.

668. "Another Road to *Rosh Hashannah,*" (SP) *RSTB*, October 16: p. 3.

669. "Another Road to *Yom Kippur,*" (SP) *RSTB*, October 30: p. 3.

670. "Hebrew Name for a Child with One Jewish Parent, A Reform Responsum," *Journal of Reform Judaism* 32: 4 (Fall), pp. 95f.

671. "Sukkot in America," (SP) *RSTB*, November 6: p. 3.

672. "Hope & Despair," (SP) *RSTB*, November 13: p. 3.

673. "Paradise or Not," (SP) *RSTB*, November 20: p. 3.

674. "Life & Theology," (SP) *RSTB*, November 27: p. 3.

675. "Vatican II and Farrakhan," (SP) *RSTB*, December 4: p. 3.

676. "Our Beloved Dead," (SP) *RSTB*, December 11: p. 3.

677. "A Pittsburgh Centennial," (SP) *RSTB*, December 18: p. 3. 678. "Hannukah Sedra, Portion of the Week," *The Jewish Chronicle of Pittsburgh,* December 5, p. 37.

679. *The Pittsburgh Platform in Retrospect: The Changing World of Reform Judaism,* Rodef Shalom Congregation Press, Pittsburgh, Pa., 123 pp.

1986

680. "'Mitnagdim vs. Hassidim,' *Halakhic Man,* by Joseph B. Soloveitchik, A Review," *The Jewish Chronicle of Pittsburgh,* January 9, p. 23.

681. "Dedication of Spear Windows," (SP) *RSTB*, January 15: p. 3.

682. "Idealism and Reality," (SP) *RSTB*, January 29: p. 3.

683. "'Introducing the Festivals,' *Shaarei Mo-ed, Gates of the Season*, edited by Peter S. Knobel, A Review," *The Jewish Chronicle of Pittsburgh*, February 6, p. 8.

684. "Who Is a Jew?" (SP) *RSTB*, February 12: p. 3.

685. "Before and After Persecution," (SP) *RSTB*, February 19: p. 3.

686. "Words and Melodies," (SP) *RSTB*, February 26: p. 3.

687. "Organization," (SP) *RSTB*, March 12: p. 3.

688. "American and the Old Country," (SP) *RSTB*, April 23: p. 3.

689. "Lost Visions," (SP) *RSTB*, April 30: p. 3.

690. "Guide or Command," (SP) *RSTB*, May 14: p. 3.

691. "Report of the Committee on Responsa," *CCAR Yearbook* 95, p. 248.

692. "Mind Altering Drugs for Pleasure, A Responsum," *CCAR Yearbook* 95, pp. 256ff.

693. "Drugs and Mystical Experiences, A Responsum," *CCAR Yearbook* 95, p. 256.

694. "Medical Use of Psychedelic Drugs, A Responsum," *CCAR Yearbook* 95, pp. 255ff.

695. "When Is Abortion Permitted?, A Responsum," *CCAR Yearbook* 95, pp. 252ff.

696. "Non-Jewish Voices in Congregational Choir, A Responsum," *CCAR Yearbook* 95, pp. 251ff.

697. "Fetus Used for Experimentation, A Responsum," *CCAR Yearbook* 95, pp. 250ff.

698. "Children of 'Messianic Jews,' A Responsum," *CCAR Yearbook* 95, pp. 259ff.

699. "Sequence of Lighting Hannukah Candles, A Responsum," *CCAR Yearbook* 95, p. 249.

700. "Convert with A Christian Family, A Responsum," *CCAR Yearbook* 95, pp. 248ff.

701. *A Selection of Sermons, 1985–1986, 5746*, Rodef Shalom Pulpit—Second Series 18: 1–7, 46 pp: "Dedication of the Spear Windows"; "Rededication of the Great Synagogue in Augsburg"; "Einweihung Der Synagoge in Augsburg"; "Spokojony and Breuer"; "Homecoming"; "The American Sukkah"; "Hope and Despair."

702. "'Revealing Questions from the Holocaust,' A Review of Robert Kirschner's *Rabbinic Responsa of the Holocaust Era," The Jewish Chronicle of Pittsburgh*, September 4, p. 19.

703. "The Statue of Liberty," (SP) *RSTB*, September 10: p. 3.

704. "Introduction to Solomon B. Freehof," (SP) *RSTB*, September 17: p. 3.

705. "Balaam and Bishops," (SP) *RSTB*, October 1: p. 3.

706. "Workers of Our World," (SP) *RSTB*, October 29: p. 3.

707. "Benefits of Chaos," (SP) *RSTB*, November 5: p. 3.

708. "The Great Communicator," (SP) *RSTB*, November 26: p. 3.

709. "Rebuilding," (SP) *RSTB*, December 10: p. 3.

710. "Flyspecks?" (SP) *RSTB*, December 24: p. 3.

711. "Congratulations!" (SP) *RSTB*, December 31: p. 3.

1987

712. "Gifts to Organizations Inimical to Reform Judaism," *Journal of Reform Judaism* 34: 1 (Winter), pp. 45–46.

713. "Genealogies," (SP) *RSTB*, January 7: p. 3.

714. "Problem Children," (SP) *RSTB*, January 21: p. 3.

715. "Menorah and Magen David," (SP) *RSTB*, February 4: p. 3.
716. "Leo Baeck Rabbinic College of London," (SP) *RSTB*, February 18: p. 3.
717. "The Pollard Affair," (SP) *RSTB*, April 15: p. 3.
718. "The Modern Synagogue," (SP) *RSTB*, April 22: p. 3.
719. "Our Changing Seder," (SP) *RSTB*, May 6: p. 3.
720. "Words and Melodies," (SP), *RSTB*, May 13: p. 3.
721. "Portion of the Week," *The Jewish Chronicle of Pittsburgh*, April 12, p. 4.
722. "Portion of the Week," *The Jewish Chronicle of Pittsburgh*, April 30, p. 11.
723. "Report of the Committee on Responsa," *CCAR Year book* 96, pp. 229f.
724. "Alzheimer's Disease, A Responsum," *CCAR Yearbook* 96, pp. 230ff.
725. "A Ban on Smoking, A Responsum," *CCAR Yearbook* 96, pp. 323ff.
726. "Banks for Human Organs, A Responsum," *CCAR Year book* 96, pp. 233ff.
727. "Burial in a Christian Cemetery, A Responsum," *CCAR Yearbook* 96, pp. 235f.
728. "Burial of 'Messianic Jews,' A Responsum," *CCAR Year book* 96, p. 237.
729. "Concealing Jewish Identity, A Responsum," *CCAR Year book* 96, pp. 237ff.
730. "A Dangerous Experiment," *CCAR Yearbook* 96, pp. 240f.
731. "Jewish Reaction to Epidemics, A Responsum," *CCAR Year book* 96, pp. 241f.
732. "Responsibility for Cemeteries, A Responsum," *CCAR Year book* 96, p. 243.

733. "Selling a Human Kidney, A Responsum," *CCAR Yearbook* 96, pp. 244f.

734. *A Selection of Sermons and Lectures, 1986-1987, 5747,* Rodef Shalom Pulpit, Second Series 19: 1–6: "Liberal Judaism"; "To Learn, To Teach, To Fight, To Help"; "Creating and Resting"; "Dedication of the Biblical Garden"; "Dedication of the Banners of the Decalogue"; "Hear, O Israel."

735. "Portion of the Week," *The Jewish Chronicle of Pittsburgh,* November 26, p. 27.

736. "The Lord's Prayer, A Responsum," *Journal of Reform Judaism* 34: 2 (Spring), p. 79.

737. "Tickets for Admission to the *Yamim Noraim* Services, A Reform Responsum," *Journal of Reform Judaism* 34: 3 (Summer), pp. 73–75.

738. "Selling Human Blood for Medical Purposes, A Reform Re sponsum," *Journal of Reform Judaism* 34: 4 (Fall), pp. 73 ff.

739. "A Gentile as a *Kvater* at a *Brit Milah*," *CCAR Yearbook* 97, pp. 184ff.

740. "Synagogue Honors," *CCAR Yearbook* 97, pp. 185f.

741. "Ben Zakhar," *CCAR Yearbook* 97, pp. 186f.

742. "Reunion Class of 1922," (SP) *RSTB,* September 9: p. 3.

743. "Tribute to Solomon B. Freehof on his Ninety-fifth Birthday," (SP) *RSTB,* September 16: p. 3.

744. "Consolation," (SP) *RSTB,* October 7: p. 3.

745. "From Generation to Generation," (SP) *RSTB,* October 21: p. 3.

746. "Judges," (SP) *RSTB,* October 28: p. 3.

747. "The Pope and the Jews," (SP) *RSTB:* November 4, p. 3.

748. "The Constitution," (SP) *RSTB,* November 18: p. 3.

749. "Renewal," (SP), *RSTB,* November 25: p. 3.

750. "Cruise Supreme," (SP) *RSTB,* December 2: p. 3.
751. "Our Tests," (SP) *RSTB,* December 16: p. 3.
752. "Where Are We Going?" (SP) *RSTB,* December 30: p. 3.

1988

753. "Ideals," (SP) *RSTB,* January 20: p. 3.
754. "Making Sense of the Past," (SP) *RSTB,* January 27: p. 3.
755. "A Sense of Balance," (SP), *RSTB,* February 10: p. 3.
756. "Two New Years," (SP) *RSTB,* February 17: p. 3.
757. "The National Sisterhood's Seventy-fifth Anniversary, (SP) *RSTB,* March 2: p. 3.
758. "Reform Judaism in Israel—New Power," (SP) *RSTB,* April 20: p. 3.
759. "Matza, Beyond Affliction," (SP) *RSTB,* April 27: p. 3.
760. "Where Shall We Go?" (SP) *RSTB,* May 4: p. 3.
761. "Influence for Change," (SP), *RSTB,* May 11: p. 3.
762. "The Responsibility of an AIDS Carrier, A Reform Responsum," *Journal of Reform Judaism* 35: 2 (Spring), pp. 81–83.
763. "Tombstone with Christian Markings, A Reform Responsum," *Journal of Reform Judaism* 35: 1 (Winter), pp. 67ff.
764. "As We Age, Portion of the Week," *The Jewish Chronicle of Pittsburgh,* April 28, p. 14.
765. "Exploring Jewish Views on Adoption and Fertility, A Review of *And Hannah Wept; Infertility, Adoption, and the Jewish Couple* by Michael Gold," *The Jewish Chronicle of Pittsburgh,* July 14, p. 10.
766. With Irene Jacob, "Forgotten Immigrants: Plant Immigrants to Israel through Three Thousand Years," 23 pp.
767. "A Blessing for Pets, A Reform Responsum," *Journal of Reform Judaism* 35: 3 (Summer) pp. 79f.

768. "Portion of the Week," *The Jewish Chronicle of Pittsburgh*, August 4, p. 7.

769. "The Reform Stake in Jewish Law," *Reform Judaism* 17: 1 (Fall), pp. 9ff.

770. With Irene Jacob, "A Garden Celebration of Israel's Fortieth Anniversary," *The Jewish Spectator* 53: 2 (Summer), pp. 36–37.

771. Portion of the Week," *Jewish Chronicle of Pittsburgh*, September 1, p. 10.

772. "Portion of the Week," *Jewish Chronicle of Pittsburgh*, September 22, p. 4.

773. "Changing the Name of an Adopted Child after the *B'rit*, A Reform Responsum," *Journal of Reform Judaism* 35: 4 (Fall), pp. 71ff.

774. *A Selection of Sermons, 1987–1988, 5747–5748* 20: 1–5: "Vision Meets Vision"; "The Decalogue"; "My Visit of Poland"; "The Occupied Territories"; "Looking For ward." 33 pp.

775. *Liberal Judaism and Halakhah* (editor), Rodef Shalom Press, Pittsburgh, Pa., 155 pp.

776. "The First Violent Step toward the Holocaust," *Aufbau Sonderbeilage zum 50 Jahrestag des November Pogroms*, November (4), p. 29.

777. "The German Jew in America—The Last Wave of Immi grants," *American Jewish Archives—The German-Jewish Legacy in America 1938–1988*, A Symposium (November) No. 2, pp. 351–53.

778. "The Greatest American Jewish Leaders." A Symposium, *American Jewish History* 78: 2 (December), pp. 178–80. 779. "Celebrating Solomon B. Freehof on the Occasion of His 96th Birthday," (SP), *RSTB*, September 21: p. 2.

780. "Have We Used Our Freedom Wisely?" (SP) *RSTB,* September 28: p. 3.
781. "What Did Moses Omit?" (SP) *RSTB,* October 5: p. 3.
782. "Prepare, Prepare," (SP) *RSTB,* October 12: p. 3.
783. "From One Sukkah to Another," (SP) *RSTB,* November 2: p. 3.
784. "A Bar Mitzvah and Wedding Blessing," (SP) *RSTB,* November 9: p. 3.
785. "Lekh Lekha" (SP) *RSTB,* November 30: p. 3.
786. "Who Is a Jew? A Letter," (SP) *RSTB,* December 14: p. 3.
787. "Righteousness," (SP) *RSTB,* December 21: p. 3.

1989

788. *"Pidyon Haben,"* A Reform Responsum, *Journal of Reform Judaism,* 36: 1 (Winter) pp. 87f.
789. "The American Reform Jewish Dream—An Appraisal," *CCAR Yearbook,* New York, pp. 30–33.
790. "Responsibility of an AIDS Carrier, A Responsum," *CCAR Yearbook,* New York, pp. 153—55.
791. "Changing the Name of an Adopted Child after the B'rit, A Responsum," *CCAR Yearbook,* New York, pp. 155ff.
792. "Preferential Treatment of Children in Estates, A Responsum," *CCAR Yearbook,* New York, pp. 156–58.
793. "B'rit for 'Messianic Jews' or 'Jewish Christians,' A Responsum," *CCAR Yearbook,* New York, p. 158f.
794. "Portrait in a Synagogue, A Responsum," *CCAR Yearbook,* New York, pp. 159–60.
795. "Transporting the Torah, A Responsum," *CCAR Yearbook,* New York, p. 160f.
796. "Jewish Cemetery in a General Cemetery, A Responsum," *CCAR Yearbook,* New York, pp. 161f.

797. "Congregation and Talit, A Responsum," *CCAR Yearbook,* New York, pp. 162f.

798. "Portion of the Week," *The Jewish Chronicle of Pittsburgh,* May 11, p. 17.

799. "Symbols and Holocaust," (SP) *RSTB,* January 11: p. 3.

800. "The Law of Return," (SP) *RSTB,* January 18: p. 3.

801. "Diaspora Past and Present," (SP) *RSTB,* February 1: p. 3.

802. "Our Favorite Book," (SP) *RSTB,* February 8: p. 3.

803. "Jewish Influence," (SP) *RSTB,* February 15: p. 3.

804. "Desert in Our Life," (SP) *RSTB,* March 8: p. 3.

805. "Forgotten Decalogue," (SP) *RSTB,* March 15: p. 3.

806. "The Roots of the Synagogue," (SP) *RSTB,* March 9: p. 3.

807. "Profane to Sacred," (SP) *RSTB,* April 5: p. 3.

808. "Portion of the Week, Naso," *The Jewish Chronicle of Pittsburgh,* June 15, p. 16.

809. "Our Medical Heritage," (SP) *RSTB,* May 10: p. 3.

810. "Some Medical Plants of Ancient Israel," *PapyruS* 1: 1, (Summer), 4pp.

811. "Assyrian Medical Plants," *PapyruS* 1: 3 (Summer), 4pp.

812. "Scattering Ashes of the Dead, A Reform Responsum," *Journal of Reform Judaism* 36: 2 (Spring), pp. 69f.

813. *A Selection of Sermons and Lectures, 1988–1989, 5748–5749* 49 pp.: "Our Temple"; "A Report from Germany on *Kristallnacht"; "Reichskristallnacht Gedenkfeier"; "Zakhor al Tishkah*—Remember and Do Not Forget"; "Harvest for the Young"; "Sacrifices"; "Who Is Holy?" 22: 49 pp.

814. "The German Jew in America—The Last Wave of Immigrants," in Peck.

815. "Prayer for the Day," *Pittsburgh Book of Daily Prayer 1990,* St. Thomas Publishing House, Wexford, May 29.

816. "Hearing More than Seeing," (SP) *RSTB,* September 13: p. 3.

817. "Introduction to Solomon B. Freehof on the 84th Anniversary of His Bar Mitzvah," (SP) *RSTB*, September 20: p. 3.
818. "When We Are Older," (SP) *RSTB*, October 4: p. 3.
819. "Auschwitz," (SP) *RSTB*, October 18: p. 3.
820. "The Schofar," (SP) *RSTB*, October 25: p. 3.
821. "Abraham's Way and Ours," (SP) *RSTB*, November 1: p. 3.
822. "Knowledge," (SP) *RSTB*, November 22: p. 3.
823. "Garden of Eden," (SP) *RSTB*, November 29: p. 3.
824. "East Germany Now," (SP) *RSTB*, December 13: p. 3.
825. "Beyond Gratitude," (SP) *RSTB*, December 20: p. 3.

1990

826. "Their Struggle, Our Struggle," (SP) *RSTB*, January 3: p. 3.
827. "The East/West Struggle—A Different Approach," (SP) *RSTB*, January 10: p. 3.
828. "Hannukah Themes, Hannukah Tensions," (SP) *RSTB*, January 17: p. 3.
829. "The Uneasy World," (SP) *RSTB*, February 28: p. 3.
830. "Sweet Victory," (SP) *RSTB*, March 7: p. 3.
831. "What Is the Law," (SP) *RSTB*, March 14: p. 3.
832. "Installation of Officers," (SP) *RSTB*, March 28: p. 3.
833. "Their Concerns," (SP) *RSTB*, April 17: p. 3.
834. "Hope," (SP) *RSTB*, April 25: p. 3.
835. *"L'Shanah Habah,"* (SP) *RSTB*, May 2: p. 3.
836. "Our Problem—A Wish Fulfilled," (SP) *RSTB*, May 9: p. 3.
837. "Minimal Standards," (SP) *RSTB*, May 16: p. 3.

838. *"Taharah* and AIDS—A Reform Responsum," *The Jewish Funeral Director* 59: 2 (Summer), pp. 18ff.

839. "The Pressured Mohel, A Reform Responsum," *Journal of Reform Judaism* 37: 1 (Winter), p. 85.

840. "The Never Ending Debate," *Reform Judaism* 18: 3 (Spring), pp. 23–25.

841. "Introduction," Solomon B. Freehof, *Today's Reform Responsa,* Hebrew Union College Press, Cincinnati.

842. *"Taharah* and Aids," A Reform Responsum, *Journal of Reform Judaism* 37: 2 (Spring), pp. 65ff.

843. "Review of George L. Berlin, *Defending the Faith,"* *American Jewish History* 79: 2 (Winter), pp. 294ff.

844. "Report of the Committee on Responsa," *CCAR Yearbook* 99, pp 229f.

845. "A Reform *Get," CCAR Yearbook* 99, pp. 231ff.

846. "Financial Responsibility toward Jewish Homes for the Aged," *CCAR Yearbook* 99, p. 234f.

847. "Living Will," *CCAR Yearbook* 99, pp. 235ff.

848. "Adult Bar/Bat Mitzvah and Adultery," *CCAR Yearbook* 99, p. 239.

849. "Marriage with a Unitarian Universalist," *CCAR Yearbook* 99, pp 239f.

850. "Reform Support for Orthodox Institutions," *CCAR Year book* 99, pp. 241ff.

851. "An Elderly Patient Who Refuses Dialysis," *CCAR Yearbook* 99, pp. 242f.

852. "Circumcision without Parental Consent," *CCAR Yearbook* 99, pp. 243f.

853. "Rabbi as Educator," *Harper's Dictionary of Religious Education* (San Francisco: Harper Row).

854. "Rabbi Akiba," *Harper's Dictionary of Religious Education,* (San Francisco: Harper Row).

855. "Community Fellowship and Care (Jewish)," *Dictionary of Pastoral Care and Counseling* (Nashville: Abington Press).

856. "Flavius Josephus," *PapyruS* 2: 1, p. 3.

857. *A Selection of Sermons and Lectures, 1989–1990, 5749–5750,* Rodef Shalom Pulpit—Second Series 22: 1–6: "A Tribute to Solomon B. Freehof"; "Restoration"; "Fifty Years in America"; "Paths for Leaders and Followers"; "Our Three Rabbinic Wives"; "Facing Death."

858. "Writing the Rules," *Manna* 29 (Autumn), London, pp. 8ff.

859. "Partnership," *The Jewish Chronicle of Pittsburgh,* November 1, p. 45.

860. "Shavuot Confirmation," (SP) *RSTB,* September 12: p. 3.

861. "Facing Death," (SP) *RSTB,* September 26: p. 3.

862. "The Jewish Work Ethic," (SP) *RSTB,* October 10: p. 3.

863. "Toward a Better Future," (SP) *RSTB,* October 31: p. 3.

864. "Germany," (SP) *RSTB,* November 7: p. 3.

865. "Evil," (SP) *RSTB,* November 21: p. 3.

866. "Good Potential," (SP) *RSTB,* November 28: p. 3.

867. "Evil," (SP) *RSTB,* December 5: p. 3.

868. "A Broader Vision," (SP) *RSTB,* December 26: p. 3.

1991

869. "A New Age," (SP) *RSTB,* January 30: p. 3.

870. "War or Peace," (SP) *RSTB,* February 13: p. 3.

871. "From War to Peace," (SP) *RSTB,* February 20: p. 3.

872. "Bad Deeds, Dirty Thoughts," (SP) *RSTB,* March 6: p. 3.

873. "Down from the Mountain Top," (SP) *RSTB*, March 13: p. 3.

874. "Judaism on Warfare," (SP) *RSTB*, March 20: p. 2.

875. "Toward a New Peace," (SP) *RSTB*, April 3: p. 2.

876. "Concessions to Weakness," (SP) *RSTB*, April 10: p. 2.

877. "Ghetto or Integration," (SP) *RSTB*, April 17: p. 2.

878. "Kosher for Pesah," (SP) *RSTB*, April 24: p. 2.

879. "First Day of Pesah," (SP) *RSTB*, May 1: p. 2.

880. "Honoring Our Religious School and the Goldmans'," (SP) *RSTB*, May 22: p. 2.

881. "Solomon B. Freehof Plaque Dedication," (SP) *RSTB*, May 29: p. 3.

882. "Shavuot Confirmation," (SP) *RSTB*, June 26: p. 3.

883. "Judaism on Revolution," (SP) *RSTB*, July 31: p. 5.

884. "The Market Economy and Other Moral Quagmires: Ethics After the Cold War," *Drury Magazine* 1: 1 (January), pp. 20f.

885. "Organ Transplants—A Reform Jewish Perspective," in Don Keyes, *Transplant Ethics* (Clifton, N.J., Humana Press), p. 196f.

886. "Sex and Disease," *The Jewish Chronicle of Pittsburgh*, April 18, p. 15.

887. "Message from the President," *CCAR Newsletter* 37: 11 (July), p. 1.

888. "Some Historical Antecedents," *PapyruS* 3: 3, pp. 3 and 4.

889. "Solomon B. Freehof—In Memoriam," *CCAR Yearbook* 100, pp. 190f.

890. *A Selection of Sermons and Lectures, 1990–1991, 5750–5751* 23: 1–7: "The Rededication of the Temple"; "Acceptance Address as President of the Central Conference of American Rabbis"; "The Eternal Light"; "Toward the

Future"; "War or Peace"; "Leaders and Our Questions"; "The Solomon B. Freehof Plaque Dedication"; 38 pp.

891. "What Matters," (SP) *RSTB,* September 4: p. 3.
892. "America's Contribution," (SP) *RSTB,* September 18: p. 5.
893. "A New Look at the Shema," (SP) *RSTB,* October 2: p. 3.
894. "The Call of the Shofar," (SP) *RSTB,* November 6: p. 3.
895. "First Day of Sukkot," (SP) *RSTB,* December 4: p. 3.
896. "The Struggle between Pessimism and Optimism," (SP) *RSTB,* December 18: p. 3.
897. "Migration as Pilgrimage," *The Jewish Chronicle of Pittsburgh,* October 17, p. 33.
898. "The Judeo-Christian Dialogue in the Twentieth Century: The Jewish Response," *Toward a Theological Encounter,* L. Klenicki, (ed.) (New York: Paulist Press).

1992

899. "Initial Thanks," *CCAR Newsletter* 37: 11 (July), p. 1.
900. "Some Thoughts for the New Year," *CCAR Newsletter* 37: 12 (August), p. 1.
901. "Sukkot and Beyond," *CCAR Newsletter* 38: 1 (September October), p. 1.
902. "Beyond Thanksgiving," *CCAR Newsletter* 38: 2 (November), p. 1.
903. "On Responsa," *CCAR Newletter* 38: 3 (December), p. 1.
904. "Rabbinic Finances," *CCAR Newsletter* 38: 4 (January), p. 1.
905. "Liturgy Projects," *CCAR Newsletter* 38: 5 (February), p.2.
906. "A Visit to Israel," *CCAR Newsletter* 38: 6 (March), p. 1.
907. "We Wish Joe Glaser Well," *CCAR Newsletter* 38: 7 (April), p. 1.

908. "Reform Halakhah," *CCAR Newsletter* 38: 8 (May/June), p. 1.

909. "People of the Book, but Not of the Cookbook," *CCAR Newsletter* 38: 9 (July), p. 1.

910. "New Year's Message," *CCAR Newsletter* 38: 10 (August/September), p. 1.

911. "Rabbinic Study," *CCAR Newsletter* 39: 1 (October), p. 1.

912. "The Inter-Religious Dialogue Revisited," *CCAR Newsletter* 39: 2 (November), p. 1.

913. "The New or Old Germany," *CCAR Newsletter* 39: 3 (December), p. 1.

914. "Prayers," (SP) *RSTB*, February 5: p. 3.

915. "How to Survive," (SP) *RSTB*, March 4: 13, p. 3.

916. "Beyond Purim," (SP) *RSTB*, April 15: p. 3.

917. "A Good Jew—A Better Jew," (SP) *RSTB*, August 5: p. 3.

918. With Irene Jacob, "Flora," *Anchor Bible Dictionary*, Vol. 2, (New York: Doubleday), pp. 803–17.

919. "Standards Now," *Reform Judaism* 21: 1 (Fall), p. 64.

920. "Theology," Portion of the Week, *The Jewish Chronicle of Pittsburgh*, October 29, p. 45.

921. "President's Message," *CCAR Newsletter* 39: 1 (October), p. 1.

922. "The Tallit," (SP) *RSTB*, September 16: p. 2.

923. "Shoftim," (SP) *RSTB*, November 4: p. 2.

924. "Saints and Sinners," (SP) *RSTB*, December 30: p. 2.

925. *A Selection of Sermons and Lectures, 1991–1992 (5752)* 24: 1–7, 40 pp.: "Standards Now—Presidential Address"; "An Enigmatic Tale"; "Choices We Must Make"; "What Is Prayer?"; "Survival Then and Now"; "From Generation to Generation"; "The Tallit."

926. "A Gift to the Generations," Review of *Rabies Is Jewish Priests and Other Zeydeh Myses,* by Leonard Winograd, *The Jewish Chronicle of Pittsburgh,* May 28, p. 34.

1993

927. "Darkness and Light," (SP) *RSTB,* March 24: p. 2.
928. "Women's Rights," (SP) *RSTB,* July 7: p. 2.
929. "Director of Rabbinic Services," *CCAR Newsletter* 39: 4 (January), p. 1.
930. "New Proposals," *CCAR Newsletter* 39: 5 (February), p. 1.
931. "Are They Serious, Are We?" *CCAR Newsletter* 39: 7 (April), p. 1.
932. "Holocaust Museum Dedication," *CCAR Newsletter* 39: 8 (May), p. 1.
933. "Thanks and Farewell," *CCAR Newsletter* 39: 9 (June) p. 1.
934. "Standards Now," *Wexner Heritage Review,* No. 7, p. 20. 935. "Response and Acceptance," Installation as President of the CCAR, *CCAR Yearbook* 101, pp. 70ff.
936. "President's Message," *CCAR Yearbook* 102, pp. 19ff.
937. "Report of the President," *CCAR Yearbook* 102, pp. 826f.
938. "Michael N. Farhi," Memorial Tribute, *CCAR Yearbook* 102, pp. 221f.
939. "Frankincense and Myrrh," *PapyruS,* Rodef Shalom Biblical Botanical Garden 5: 1 (June), p. 2.
940. "Incense in the Ancient Near East" (Guest Editor), *PapyruS,* Rodef Shalom Biblical Botanical Garden 5: 2 (July), 4 pp.
941. "What Did Moses Omit," Portion of the Week, *The Jewish Chronicle of Pittsburgh,* July 22, p. 29.
942. "Serious Religious Commitment," Portion of the Week, *The Jewish Chronicle of Pittsburgh,* May 27, p. 33.

943. "Medical Plants of the Bible—Another View," in Walter and Irene Jacob, *The Healing Past—Pharmaceuticals in the Biblical and Rabbinic World* (Leiden: Brill Publishers), pp. 27–46.

944. *A Selection of Sermons and Lectures, 1992–1993 (5753)* 25: 1–5, 37 pp.: "Once in a Lifetime"; "Presidential Address"; "Our Relationships"; "The Holocaust Museum Dedication"; "Women's Rights—What Is the Future?"

945. "Forced Cesaerean Section, A Responsum," *HalakhaH* 1: 1 (September) p. 6.

946. "Judaism and Cults, A Responsum," *HalakhaH* 1: 2, p. 3.

947. *HalakhaH* (ed.) 1: 1 (September), 4 pp.

948. *HalakhaH* (ed.) 1: 2 (December) 6 pp.

949. "Judaism and Cults, A Responsum," *HalakhaH* 1: 2 (December), p. 3.

950. "Two New Years," *The Jewish Chronicle of Pittsburgh*, December 30, p. 23.

951. "Where Are We Going," (SP) *RSTB*, September 1: p. 2.

952. "Sounds and Seasons," (SP) *RSTB*, September 15: p. 2.

953. "Neglected Opportunities," (SP) *RSTB*, November 3: p. 2.

954. "The First Day of Sukkot," (SP) *RSTB*, November 17: p. 2.

955. "Our Creation Story," (SP) *RSTB*, December 22: p. 2.

1994

956. "Schindler's List," (SP) *RSTB*, March 2: p. 2.

957. "Two Joseph Stories," (SP) *RSTB*, March 16: p. 2.

958. "The Desert Sanctuary Seen Again," (SP) *RSTB*, April 27, p. 2.

959. "What We Are and Wish to Be," (SP) *RSTB*, May 11: p. 2.

960. "What Do We Confirm?" (SP) *RSTB*, June 29: p. 2.

961. "Reminiscences or Hopes—Our Dilemma," (SP) *RSTB*, August 31: p. 2.
962. *HalakhaH* (ed.) 1: 3 (April) 8 pp.
963. "Organ Allocation—Who Shall Live, A Responsum," *Hala khaH* 1: 3 (April), pp. 3ff.
964. "The Next Generation," Portion of the Week, *The Jewish Chronicle of Pittsburgh*, May 12, p. 37.
965. "Hearing More Than Seeing," *The Jewish Chronicle of Pittsburgh*, July 28, p. 29.
966. "Color in Ancient Israel," *PapyruS* 6: 1 (June), p. 2.
967. "Egyptian Dye Technology," *PapyruS* 6: 2 (July), p. 3.
968. "Pictures of Dyed Objects," *PapyruS* 6: 2 (July), p. 3f.
969. *HalakhaH* (ed.) 1: 4 (August), 6 pp.
970. "Pre-Nuptial Agreement and the Ketubah," A Reform Responsum, *HalakhaH* 1: 4 (August), pp. 4ff.
971. "*PapyruS* (Guest ed.) 6: 3 (August), 4 pp.
972. "Conversion and the Developing Reform Halakhah," *Conversion to Judaism in Jewish Law—Essays and Responsa*, Pittsburgh and Tel Aviv, pp. 115ff.
973. "Courage for the New Year," *The Jewish Chronicle of Pittsburgh*, August 18, p. 33.
974. *A Selection of Sermons—1993–1994 (5754):* "Risk Takers"; "No Gifts Please"; "Two Josephs in Egypt"; "A Toast to the Past and the Future," Pittsburgh 26: 1–4, 24 pp.
975. "Building a Biblical Garden," *The Herb Quarterly* (with Irene Jacob) 63 (Fall), pp. 26–31.
976. *HalakhaH* (ed.) 2: 1 (November), 8 pp.
977. "A Destroyed Jewish Cemetery," A Reform Responsum, *HalakhaH* 2: 1 (November), pp. 3–4.
978. "Moses' Advice to Us," (SP) *RSTB*, September 28: p. 2.
979. "Volunteer Shabbat," (SP) *RSTB*, October 26: p. 2.

980. "Sixty Years of Book Reviews—An Intellectual Harvest," (SP) *RSTB*, November 9: p. 2.

981. "Hearing More Than Seeing," Portion of the Week, *The Jewish Chronicle of Pittsburgh*, July 28: p. 29.

982. "Courage for the New Year," Portion of the Week, *The Jewish Chronicle of Pittsburgh*, August 18, p. 34.

983. "President's Message," *CCAR Yearbook* 103, pp. 3ff.

984. "Report of the President," *CCAR Yearbook* 103, pp. 9ff.

985. "Installation of the New Officers," *CCAR Yearbook* 103, p. 103.

986. "Installation of the New President," *CCAR Yearbook* 103, p. 104.

1995

987. *HalakhaH* (ed.) 2: 2 (February), 6 pp.

988. "Changing the Torah Portion, A Reform Responsum," *HalakhaH* 2: 2 (February), pp. 3, 4.

989. "Judaism for Sophisticates," *The Jewish Chronicle of Pittsburgh*, January 12, p. 31.

990. *HalakhaH* (ed.) 2: 2 (February), 6 pp.

991. "Views of Diaspora," (SP) *RSTB*, January 18: p. 2.

992. "The Temporary and the Permanent," (SP) *RSTB*, February 1: p. 2.

993. "Changing Our Mood," (SP) *RSTB*, March 1: p. 2.

994. "The Poet within Us," (SP) *RSTB*, March 15: p. 2.

995. "Our New Gallery," (SP) *RSTB*, April 12: p. 2.

996. "The Real Elijah," (SP) *RSTB*, April 26: p. 2.

997. "Diverse Roads," (SP) *RSTB*, May 31: p. 2.

998. "Beyond the Budget," Portion of the Week, *The Jewish Chronicle of Pittsburgh*, June 15, p. 33.

999. "Balaam and Bishops," Portion of the Week, *The Jewish Chronicle of Pittsburgh*, July 13, p. 29.

1000. "What is Learning?" Portion of the Week, *The Jewish Chronicle of Pittsburgh*, November 30, p. 29.

1001. "A Rebirth in Central Europe," *The Jewish Chronicle of Pittsburgh*, December 7, p. 9.

1002. "Wheat in Ancient Israel," *PapyruS* 7: 1, p. 2.

1003. "Problems in Ancient Agriculture," *PapyruS* 7: 1, p. 6.

1004. "Barley in Ancient Israel," *PapyruS* 7: 2, p. 2.

1005. "Grain for the Poor—The Corners of the Field," *PapyruS* 7: 2, p. 2.

1006. "Millet," *PapyruS* 7: 3, p. 2.

1007. "Ancient Flour," *PapyruS* 7: 3, pp. 2–3.

1008. "Roasted Grain," *PapyruS* 7: 3, p. 5.

1009. "Bread and Salt," *PapyruS* 7: 3, p. 5.

1010. "Long Range Transportation," *PapyruS* 7: 3, p. 6.

1011. *HalakhaH* (ed.) 2: 3 (June).

1012. "Jewish Priorities in Communal Service, A Reform Responsum," *HalakhaH* 2: 3, pp. 3–7.

1013. *HalakhaH* (ed.) 3: 1 (Fall/Winter).

1014. "The Jewishness of Jewish Agencies, A Reform Responsum," *HalakhaH* 3: 1, pp. 3–7.

1015. *Gallery* (ed.) 1: 1 (Autumn).

1016. "Von der Duldung zum aktiven Entgegenkommen—Übertritt in den Vereinigten Staaten," *Nicht durch Gerburt allein*, (ed. W. Homolka, E. Seidel) (Munich: Knesebeck), pp. 168ff.

1017. "Introduction of the Executive Vice-President," *CCAR Year book* 104, p. 104.

1018. "Azkara," *CCAR Yearbook* 104, pp. 169f.

1019. "Revolutions," (SP) *RSTB*, September 13: p. 2.

1020. "The Numbers Game," (SP) *RSTB*, November 8: p. 2.

1021. "Tolerance and Confidence," (SP) *RSTB*, December 6: p. 2.

1022. "Republicans or Democrats," (SP) *RSTB*, December 20: p. 2.

1023. "Revolutions," (SP), *RSTB*, September 13: p. 2.

1024. "Fourth World Conference on Women in Beijing, (SP) *RSTB*, October 25: p. 2.

1025. "The Numbers Game," (SP) *RSTB*, November 8: p. 2.

1026. "Tolerance and Confidence," (SP) *RSTB*, December 6: p. 2.

1027. "Republicans and Democrats," (SP) *RSTB*, December 20: p. 2.

1996

1028. "Varieties of Renewal," (SP) *RSTB*, January 3: p. 2.

1029. "Paths toward Peace," (SP) *RSTB*, February 14: p. 2.

1030. *HalakhaH* (ed.) 3: 2 (Winter/Spring), 8 pp.

1031. "Annual Report," Law Institute, *HalakhaH* 3: 2 (Winter/ Spring).

1032. "A Mohel and Malpractice, A Reform Responsum," *Hala khaH* 3: 2 (Winter/Spring) 8 pp.

1033. *Gallery* (ed.) 1: 2 (Winter), 4 pp.

1034. *Gallery* (ed.) 1: 3 (Spring), 4 pp.

1035. *HalakhaH* (ed.) 3: 3 (Spring/Summer), 8 pp.

1036. "Non-Jew and the Talit, A Reform Responsum," *HalakhaH* 3: 3, (Spring/Summer), pp. 6f.

1037. "Minutes, Annual Meeting of the Institute of Progressive *Halakhah*," *HalakhaH* 3: 3 (Spring/Summer), pp. 7f.

1038. "A Torah Permanently in a Museum Case," *Gallery* 1: 3 (Spring), pp. 2f.

1039. "Proefdieren en halacha" (Experimental Animals and the *Halakhah), Leven Joods Geloof,* Jubileummeditie rabbijn David Lilienthal 25 jaar in rabbinaat, 42: 9 (July) pp. 34–37.

1040. "Advice from Moses, Portion of the Week, *The Jewish Chronicle of Pittsburgh,* August 29, p. 29.

1041. "Contents of the Ebers Papyrus," *PapyruS* 8: 1, p. 2f.

1042. "Assyrian Medicinal Plants," *PapyruS* 8: 1, pp. 3f.

1043. "Some Medicinal Plants of Ancient Israel," *PapyruS* 8: 1, pp 4ff.

1044. "Incense in Ancient Israel," *PapyruS* 8: 2, pp. 3f.

1045. "Wheat in Ancient Israel," *PapyruS* 8: 3, p. 2.

1046. "Barley in Ancient Israel," *PapyruS* 8: 3, pp. 2f.

1047. "Millet," *PapyruS* 8: 3, p. 3.

1048. "Roasted Grain," *PapyruS* 8: 3, p. 4.

1049. "Portion of the Week," *The Jewish Chronicle of Pittsburgh,* October 17, p. 37.

1050. "What Are We Studying?" *CCAR Newsletter* 44: 2 (October), p. 4.

1051. *Gallery* 2:1 (Autumn) 4 pp.

1052. *HalakhaH* 4: 1 (Autumn/Winter), 8 pp.

1053. "German Speaking Jews," (SP) *RSTB,* January 31: p. 2.

1054. "Paths toward Peace," (SP) *RSTB,* February 14: p. 2.

1055. "Learning from an Outsider," (SP) *RSTB,* April 10: p. 2.

1056. "Step by Step," (SP) *RSTB,* May 29: p. 2.

1057. "King for a Day," (SP) *RSTB,* June 26: p. 2.

1058. "Who Shall We Confirm?" (SP) *RSTB,* July 31: p. 2.

1059. "The Interreligious Dialogue: A Personal View," *It Takes a Congregation—Festschrift for Boardman Wright Kathan,* Phladelphia.

1060. *A Selection of Sermons and Lectures* (with Irene Jacob),
Rodef Shalom Pulpit—New Series 25: 1–5, 1995–1996,
47 pp: "A Tribute to My Brother"; "One Hundred and
Forty Years, A Blessing or a Burden"; "Building the
Rodef Shalom Biblical Botanical Garden, Our Tenth
Anniversary" (Irene Jacob); "Celebrating Lillian Freehof
at Ninety"; "Synagogues around the World, An Inaugu
ral Lecture."

1997

1061. "The Roots of the Synagogue," Portion of the Week,
The Jewish Chronicle of Pittsburgh, February 13, p. 29.
1062. "Women's Rights," Portion of the Week, *The Jewish
Chronicle of Pittsburgh,* May 29, p. 29.
1063. *Gallery,* A Publication of the Associated American Jewish
Museums 2: 2, 4 pp.
1064. *Gallery,* A Publication of the Associated American Jewish
Museums 2: 3, 8 pp.
1065. *HalakhaH,* A Publication of the Solomon B. Freehof
Institute of Progressive Halakhah 4: 2, 6 pp.
1066. "The Last Stages of Lavons Syndrome," *HalakhaH* 4: 3
(Spring/Summer), pp. 6, 7.
1067. *HalakhaH,* A Publication of the Solomon B. Freehof
Institute of Progressive Halakhah 4: 3, 8 pp.
1068. "Private Ordination—Need We Be Concerned?" *CCAR
Journal,* A Reform Jewish Quarterly 44: 1 (Winter),
pp. 3–8.
1069. Review of *Reform Jewish Ethics and the Halakhah: An
Experiment in Decision Making,* edited by Eugene B.
Borowitz, *CCAR Journal,* A Reform Jewish Quarterly
44: 1 (Winter), pp. 83–85.

1070. "Tribute to Moshe Zemer," *CCAR Yearbook* 105, p. 112.

1071. "Jewish Paper," *PapyruS,* A Publication of the Rodef Shalom Biblical Botanical Garden 9: 3 (August), p. 3.

1072. "Early Jewish Printing," *PapyruS* 9: 3 (August), p. 4.

1073. "Mass Produced Jewish Books," *PapyruS* 9: 3 (August) p. 4.

1074. *Gallery* (ed.), A Publication of the Associated American Jewish Museums 3: 1 (Summer/Autumn), 6 pp.

1075. "Prenuptial Agreement and the Ketubah," *HalakhaH,* A Publication of the Solomon B. Freehof Institute of Progressive Halakhah 5: 1 (Autumn), pp. 4f.

1076. *HalakhaH* (ed.) 5: 1 (Autumn).

1077. "The Primacy of the Diaspora," *Israel and the Diaspora in Jewish Law—Essays and Responsa,* Pittsburgh, pp. 149–63.

1078. "Conversion and Outreach in the United States," *Not by Birth Alone* (London: Cassel), pp. 74–82.

1079. "Vorwort," Theodor Moch, *Das Judentum—Wie Es Wirklich Ist* (Vienna).

1080. "A Soft Answer," Portion of the Week, *The Jewish Chronicle of Pittsburgh,* October 2, p. 37.

1081. "Leo Baeck und Claude Montefiore—Die Evangelien aus jüdischer Sicht," *Leo Baeck—Zwischen Geheimnis und Gebot* (Karlsruhe: Bertelsmann Buch AG), pp. 185–92.

1998

1082. "Introduction," Marga L. Randall, *How Beautiful We Once Were,* Cathedral Publishing, Pittsburgh.

1083. *HalakhaH* (ed.) 5: 2 (Winter/Spring).

1084. "Beyond Methusela—Who Is Old?", *Aging and the Aged in Jewish Law—Essays and Responsa* (ed. with Moshe Zemer), Pittsburgh, pp. 1–14.

1085. "The *Eruv* and Community Opposition," A Reform Responsum, *HalakhaH* 5: 2 (Winter\Spring), pp. 5–7.

1086. *Gallery* (ed.) 3: 2 (Winter/Spring).

1087. *HaklakhaH* (ed.) 5: 3 (Spring/Summer).

1088. "The Blessing *Al Akhilat Matzah* after the Seder," A Reform Responsum, *HalakhaH* (Spring/Summer) 5: 3, p. 7.

1089. *Gallery* (ed.) 3: 3 (Spring/Summer).

1090. "Beer in the Mishnah and Talmud," *PapyruS* 10: 1 (June), p. 2.

1091. "Beer among the Greeks and Romans," *PapyruS* 10: 1 (June), p. 5.

1092. "The Techniques of Ancient Brewing," *PapyruS* 10: 1 (June), pp. 5f.

1093. "Beer in the Jewish Middle Ages," *PapyruS* 10: 2 (July), p. 3.

1094. "Monasteries and Beer," *PapyruS* 10: 3 (July), p. 4.

1095. "Worte zum Gedenktag", *Rundbrief Liberale Jüdische Gemeinde München* (Juli/August), p. 1.

1096. *HalakhaH* (ed.) 6: 1 (Autumn/Winter).

1097. "Liquor in the Social Facilities of the Synagogue, A Reform Responsum," *HalakhaH* 6: 1 (Autumn/Winter), pp. 3 ff.

1098. *Gallery* (ed.), 4: 1 (Autumn/Winter).

1099. "Sich Erinnern und New Bauen," *Freundesbrief* (Sommer), Verein zuzr Forderung des Christlich-jüdischen Gespräch in der Evangelische-Luth. Kirche Bayern, p. 9.

1100. "Benno Jacob," *Dictionary of Biblical Interpretation,* Abingdon Press, Nashville.

1999

1101. *HalakhaH* (ed.) 6: 2 (Winter/Spring).
1102. "Torah and Kiddush," *HalakhaH* 6: 2 (Winter/Spring), pp. 4ff.
1103. Review, "John D. Rayner, Jewish Religious Law, A Progressive Perspective," *HalakhaH* 6: 2 (Winter Spring), pp. 5ff.
1104. "2000 Years of Jewish Costumes," *Gallery* 5: 1 (Summer/Fall), pp. 1–4.
1105. *Gallery* (ed.), 5: 1 (Summer/Fall), 6 pp.
1106. *HalakhaH* (ed.), 6: 3 (Summer), 10 pp.
1107. "The Pittsburgh Platform on Halakhah," *HalakhaH* 6: 3 (Summer), pp. 1-8.
1108. *PapyruS* (guest ed.), 11: 2 (July), 6 pp.
1109. "Nachwort," *Die Lehren des Judentums Nach den Quellen,* Walter Homolka, Ed., Vol. 2, Berlin.
1110. Synagogues around the World—A Guide," *Gallery,* n.d., 6 pp.
1111. "Off the Beaten Path—Neglected Museums of Israel: An Exhibit Guide," *Gallery,* n.d., 4 pp.
1112. "Courage Renewed," Portion of the Week, *The Pittsburgh Jewish Chronicle,* August 26, p. 33.
1113. *HalakhaH* (ed.) 7: 1 (Autumn/Winter), 10 pp.
1114. "Review, John D. Rayner, *Principles of Jewish Ethics,*" *HalakhaH* 7: 1, p. 9.
1115. "Flora in the Dead Sea Scrolls" (with Irene Jacob), *Encyclopedia of the Dead Sea Scrolls,* Oxford and New York, Oxford University Press.

2000

1116. "Synagogues Around the World - A Guide through the Exhibit," *Gallery*, (February), 6 pp.
1117. "Springtime for Liberal Judaism," *Aufbau*, Vol. 66, No. 8, (April 20, 2000), pp. 1-2.
1118. *HalakhaH*, (ed.), 7:2, (Winter/Spring).
1119. *HalakhaH* (ed.), 7,:3 Summer.
1120. "The Obligation to Say Qaddish," *HalakhaH*, 7:3, (Summer), pp. 6-7.
1121. "Three-Storey Garden," *PapyruS*, 12:1, (June), p. 3.
1122. "Plowing," *PapyruS*, 12:2, (July), p. 3.
1123. "Draft Animals," *PapyruS*, 12:2, (July), pp. 3- 4.
1124. "Bee Keeping," *PapyruS*, 12:2, (July), p. 4.
1125. "Dry Land Farming," *PapyruS*, 12:3, (August)), p. 3.
1126. "Transportation," *PapyruS*, 12:3, (August), p. 3.
1127. "The Ancient Kitchen," *PapyruS*, 12:3, (August), pp. 4-5.
1128. *Gallery* (ed.), 6:1, (Summer/Autumn), 6 pp.
1129. "Survivors: Eastern European Synagogues Today - A Guide through the Exhibit," *Gallery*, (August), 6 pp.
1130. "Rabbi Alexander Schindler - In Memoriam," *Aufbau*, (September), p. 14.

2001

1131. *HalakhaH*, (ed.), 8:1, (Winter/Spring), 8 pp.
1132. "Kaddish," A Reform Responsum, *HalakhaH*, 8:1, p.7.
1133. "Rabbi Alexander Schindler," *Keschet*, 6:4, (January-March), p.17.

1134. "Halachische Traditionen," *Handbuch der Juden in Europa*, (J. Schoeps, ed.), II, Wissenschaftliche Buchgesellschaft, Darmstadt.

1135. "Women in Reform Judaism - Facing or Avoiding the Issue,"Gender Issues in Jewish Law - Essays and Responsa, Berghahn Books, New York, London.

1136. *HalakhaH*, (ed.) 8:2 (Spring/Summer) 6 pp.

1137. "Modern Applications of Jewish Law" by Nahum Rakover, A Review, *HalakhaH*, 8:2 (Spring/Summer), pp. 4f.

Books and essays accepted, but not yet published:

Benno Jacob Auslegung als Wissenschaft. (Ed. and au. with Almuth Jurgensen), CalwerVerlag, Stuttgart, 2001, 245 pp.

"Samuel H. Goldenson," *Reform Judaism in America, A Biographical Dictionary and Source Book 1824-1980,* Greenwood Press, Westport.

"Renewing Reform Judaism—From Pittsburgh to Pittsburgh," *Reform Judaism Reexamined,* Indiana UniversityPress, Bloomington.

"The Law of the Lord is Perfect—Halakhah and Antinomianism in Reform Judaism," *Festschrift for Stanley Dreyfus.*

"Dina Demalkhuta Dina—An Expanding Principle," *Foundations of Reform Halakhah,* Berghahn Books, New ɔrk and London.

BIOGRAPHICAL DATA

DEGREES:

Drury College (BA) (with honors) - 1950
Hebrew Union College - Jewish Institute of Religion,
Cincinnati, Ohio (MHL) (with honors) - 1955
Hebrew Union College - Jewish Institute of Religion,
Cincinnati, Ohio (DHL) - 1961
Hebrew Union College - Jewish Institute of Religion
(DD) (Honorary) - 1975
Drury College - DLit (Honorary) - 1990

POSITIONS:

President - Abraham Geiger College - 1999 -
Rabbi - Rodef Shalom Congregation - 1955, 1957 - 1997
Rabbi Emeritus, Senior Scholar - 1997 -
Chaplain - United States Air Force - 1955-1957

CURRENT NATIONAL OFFICES AND BOARDS:
President - American Friends of the Union of Progressive Jews in Germany, Austria, and Switzerland 1998 -
President - Solomon B. Freehof Institute for Progressive Halakhah, an International Association, 1989 -
President - Associated American Jewish Museums, 1974 -
Oberrabbiner - Munich, Germany - 1996 -
Editorial Advisory Board, *European Judaism*, 1997 -
Advisory Board: American Forum for Jewish-Christian Cooperation, Inc., 1988 -
Avodah National Dance Company, 1981 -
International Responsa Committee: World Union for Progressive Judaism, 1981 -
Rabbinic Cabinet: World Union for Progressive Judaism, 1981 -

PAST NATIONAL AND STATE OFFICES AND BOARDS:
President - Central Conference of American Rabbis, 1992 - 1994
President: Religious Education Association of America, 1981 - 1985
Vice President: World Union of Progressive Judaism, 1990 - 1994
World Union for Progressive Judaism, North American Board 1990 -
Chair, Standards Committee, Central Conference of American Rabbis, 1993-1999
Chairman - Responsa Committee, Central Conference of American Rabbis, 1976 - 1990
Chairman - Publications Committee, Hebrew Union College Press, 1976 - 1999
Synagogue Council of America, Executive Board, 1989 - 1994
Union of American Hebrew Congregations, Executive Board, 1989 - 1993
Overseer - Hebrew Union College-Jewish Institute of Religion, Cincinnati, New York, Jerusalem, 1966 - 1997.
Interfaith Committee: National Zionist Association of America, 1976 - 1990
Board of Directors: *Jewish Spectator*, 1982 - 1989
National Commission on Conversion: Union of American Hebrew Congregations, 1979 - 1991
Union of American Hebrew Congregations Task Force on Outreach, 1979 - 1989

BIOGRAPHICAL DATA

Editorial Board: *Religious Education Journal*, 1977 - 1996
Editorial Board: *Journal of Reform Judaism*, 1976 - 1981
Executive Board: Central Conference of American Rabbis, 1975 - 1977; 1989 - 1995
Board of Governors: Hebrew Union College - Jewish Institute of Religion, 1974 - 1979; 1989 - 1994
Health and Welfare Association Citizens Assembly, 1972 - 1976
Board of Trustees: Biafra International Foundation of Rehabilitation, 1971 - 1973
Chaplain: PA Association for Retarded Children: State, 1969 - 1971
Board of Directors: Jewish Statistical Bureau, New York, 1969 - 1978
Honorary Chairman: PA Equal Rights Council, 1968 - 1978
National Committee on College Youth & Faculty, 1968 - 1970
Council of Jewish Federations & Welfare Funds, Inc., New York, 1967 - 1985
Religious Advisory Council: Pittsburgh Area Religion in American Life Board, 1967 -

PAST LOCAL OFFICES AND BOARDS:
President: Horizon Homes, Inc., 1967 - 1975
President: Greater Pittsburgh Rabbinic Fellowship, 1970 - 1972
President: Project Equality of Western PA, 1968 - 1970
Vice President: Friends of Phipps Conservatory, 1986 - 1990
Vice President: Pittsburgh Pastoral Institute, 1981 - 1988
Co-Convener: Pittsburgh Area Race & Religion Council, 1966 - 1995
Co-Convener: United Farm Workers Inter-religious Council, 1972 - 1976
Mental Health/Mental Retardation Board of Allegheny County, 1981 - 1991
Chairman: Evaluation of Health, Strike Force: Health & Welfare Association, 1973 - 1974
Chaplain: Variety Club of Pittsburgh, Tent #1, 1969 - 1979
Board of Directors: American Red Cross, 1968 - 1974
Board of Directors: Craig House Technoma Workshop, 1962 - 1968
Board of Directors: Jewish National Fund, 1989 - 1991
Organ Artists Series, 1982 - 1986
Board of Directors: Pittsburgh Jewish Chronicle, 1988 - 1994
Advisory Board: Abortion Justice Association, 1967 - 1972
Advisory Board: The Historical Society of Western PA -
 Pittsburgh Jewish Archives, 1987 - 1998
Advisory Board: International Poetry Forum, 1967 - 1973
Advisory Board: Metropolitan ADL 1966 - 1976
Advisory Board: Residential Care Committee: Allegheny County Chapter of PA Association for
    Retarded Children, 1978-1984
Metropolitan ADL, 1966-1976
Honorary Board: PA Guild for Infant Survival, Inc., 1965 - 1970
Greater Pittsburgh Literacy Council Advisory Board, 1997-
Friends of Phipps Conservatory, 1985 - 1991
Task Force for Excellence, Pittsburgh Board of Education, 1983 - 1986

322

BIOGRAPHICAL DATA

United Jewish Federation, 1983 - 1987
American Jewish Committee, 1977 - 1980
Religious Coalition for Abortion Rights: Western PA Committee, 1973 - 1977
Jewish Community Day School, 1976 - 1986
Health & Welfare Association Citizens Assembly, 1972 - 1975
Pittsburgh Chamber Music Society, 1970 - 1975
Israel Task Force: Community Relations Committee of the United Jewish Federation, 1969
WQED Communications, 1968 - 1994
Horizon Homes, Inc., 1967 - 1984
United Cerebral Palsy Association of Pittsburgh District, 1966 - 1974
National Cystic Fibrosis Research, 1965 - 1968
Advisory Council of Consumer Credit Counseling Services, 1965 - 1975
Israel Room: University of Pittsburgh, 1964 - 1970
Project Equality of Western PA, 1963 - 1973
Community Advisor: Office of Cultural Affairs, City of Pittsburgh, Mayor's Office, 1962 -1968
William & Mildred Orr Compassionate Care Center, Board of Directors, 1993 - 1998
Allegheny Board of Volunteers, 1989 -1997
Forbes Health System: Advisory Board, 1977 - 1997
Chaplain: Dr. Eli Goldstein Lodge, B'nai B'rith, 1976 - 2000
Epilepsy Foundation of America (Honorary) 1973 - 1984
Honorary Board of Directors: Pittsburgh Zionist District, 1967 - 2000

TEACHING:
Chatham College, Pittsburgh, 1999
Potsdam University, Potsdam, Germany, 1998
Pittsburgh Theological Seminary, Pittsburgh, 1968 - 1974
Guest Lecturer - Duquesne University, University of Pittsburgh; Bethany College, Hebrew
Union College, New York,

HONORS:
Bnai Zion, Humanitarian Award - 2000
Knight Commander of the Federal Republic of Germany - 1999
Q Award WQED Educational Television - 1994
Israel Bond National Leadership Award - 1993
Union of American Hebrew Congregations - Citation of Leadership Award - 1993
American Jewish Committee, Human Relations Award - 1992
Alleghenians Ltd., Inc. The J. A. Williams Award, 1991
Jewish National Fund, 1991
Drury College - DLit (Honorary) - 1990
Israel Bond Heritage Award - 1984
Anti-Defamation League: B'nai B'rith: Distinguished Service Award, 1981
Man of the Year in Religion, Vectors/Pittsburgh, 1981

BIOGRAPHICAL DATA

Hebrew Union College: D. D. (Honorary), 1980
Drury College: Distinguished Alumni Award, 1975
Pittsburgh Association for Retarded Citizens: Distinguished Service, 1971
Zionist Organization of America: Interfaith Understanding Award, 1967
Jewish Welfare Board: Distinguished Chaplaincy Service, 1964

Born Augsburg, Germany, March 13, 1930. Parents: Rabbi Ernest I. Jacob and Annette Loewenberg Jacob. Brother: Dr. Herbert Jacob. Married to Irene Loewenthal (1958); children: Claire Helen (1959-1974); Kenneth Gabriel (1962-1999); Daniel Benjamin, 1966; grandchildren: Bari 1985; Zachary , 1995; Madeliene 1997.